THE SOUL

of the

BRETHREN IN CHRIST

Essays on Church Identity

D. Ray Hostetter

THE SOUL
of the
BRETHREN
IN CHRIST

Essays on Church Identity

D. Ray Hostetter

Evangel
Publishing House
Nappanee, Indiana 46550

The Soul of the Brethren in Christ: Essays on Church Identity

Copyright 2009 by D. Ray Hostetter

Unless otherwise noted, Scripture quotations are from the Holy Bible, King James Version, or the New International Version (North American Edition). Copyright © 1973, 1978, 1984 by International Bible Society. Used by permission of Zondervan Publishing House.

Cover design by Larry Stuart.

Requests for information should be addressed to:

Evangel Publishing House
2000 Evangel Way
P.O. Box 189
Nappanee, Indiana 46550
Phone: (800) 253-9315

Website: www.evangelpublishing.com

ISBN: 978-1-934233-07-8

Library of Congress Control Number: 2009925279

09 10 11 12 13 EP 6 5 4 3 2.

To Audrey

Beloved wife, valued counselor,
true companion, and constant encourager.

The author's father, C. N. Hostetter, Jr., was a bishop in the Brethren in Christ church and served as the fourth president of Messiah College. The author's grandfather, C. N. Hostetter, Sr., also served as a bishop and was the second president of Messiah College. His great-grandfather, Jacob Hostetter, born in 1799 and died in 1888, also served as a bishop. Jacob's burial was in the Cross Roads Brethren in Christ cemetery. His obituary, as cited in the local Mt. Joy, Pa., paper, stated: "He was the oldest bishop of the Brethren in Christ in the United States; he was bishop over 45 years."

Contents

Introduction

This book's essays seek to unfold fuller insight regarding the Brethren in Christ. The identity of a denomination is affected by the doctrines it emphasizes, the traditions it embraces, and the patterns of life it follows. Variations of these ingredients provide a profile that distinguishes one denomination from another. Consequently, these studies consist of analyzing doctrinal trends, reviewing key events, considering thematic tendencies, and examining priorities of the denomination. Existing identity theories and presentations regarding the denomination are also analyzed.

This study presents an overriding thesis that the Brethren in Christ denomination, although relatively small in numbers, over the course of more than two centuries has demonstrated a unique and valued *raison d'être*. There are rich and unusual elements that provide strong justification for being a distinct body. Also, there are some distinguishing marks that have heretofore failed to be sorted out of the complexity that can accompany a group that embraces a multi-theological tradition.

It is generally recognized that the birth of the Brethren in Christ in the late eighteenth century was due to the intersection of beliefs and values from two theological traditions, namely Pietism and Anabaptism. [1] The group of founding believers, of German descent, who lived by the Susquehanna River in Lancaster County, Pennsylvania, was not alone in experiencing a dialectic between these two theological streams. A neighboring group to the Brethren in Christ sometimes referred to as "River Brethren," the German Baptist Brethren stood within these same two traditions, and had done so for nearly a century prior to the founding of the Brethren in Christ. This is not the place to examine why the early Brethren in Christ failed to join the German Baptist Brethren ranks, and instead started a new church body.

Society itself is ever changing and denominations need to recognize such change.

The values of a religious group, even if enduring in nature, need to be continually expressed in new ways; therefore it is insufficient to portray a denomination's identity by simply citing the theological streams that shaped the denomination at its origin. It is utterly inadequate to then add theological forces that subsequently affected the denomination without serious attempts to qualify and elaborate on their relative impact. Such a shortcut approach to identity leads to a conglomerate description that conveys little meaning and even less understanding. More importantly, to state without qualification that three or more theological traditions have been decisive to the church's present identity, infers a sense of rootlessness and creates the illusion of an unfettered eclectic spirit, both of which have not been normative to the brotherhood. Furthermore, to simply recite multi-theological streams, unqualifiedly, as identity markers not only fails to fully describe the Brethren in Christ in historical terms, it can be even less accurate in representing who they are at present.

The process of examining the two founding theological streams of the Brethren in Christ has led this writer, along with other recent historians and theologians, to take exception to what appears to be faulty definitions of historic Pietism and historic Anabaptism. Particular exception is taken to presenting the two traditions as polarities. Examples of misplaced stereotypes include viewing Pietism as being less than highly attentive to biblical obedience and light in portraying a social conscience. On the other hand, the historic identity of Anabaptism becomes misconstrued when it is viewed as placing less than high priority on spiritual change and the Christian's inner life. Key elements of Brethren in Christ uniqueness can be hidden when meanings are distorted by caricaturing and stereotyping aspects of the faith.

Essays in this volume examine the influences of varied theological traditions on Brethren in Christ by assessing several factors: 1) their degree of theological impact, 2) the ways they altered denominational life, and 3) how they impacted distinctive elements and priorities of the denomination throughout its history.

Within the initial chapters of this book the writer makes some judgments about where the denomination's identity is today. He then raises questions about that identity. Chapter 1 considers benefits that the reader may gain as one examines Brethren in Christ identity. Chapter 2 is devoted to defining theological traditions that have been linked to the denomination, and several concepts used to categorize the denomination are examined.

In an attempt to give a composite picture of the denomination's identity, an overall thesis and five sub-theses are offered in chapter 3, and a newly aligned description is given regarding the theological sources that have influenced the denomination. In chapters 4, 5, 6, and 7 identity variations in the denomination's history from its beginning to the present are traced, and shifts of the identity toward or away from its root-heritage traditions are analyzed. Chapter 8 reviews several distinct qualities of the denomination. Chapter 9 is devoted to ordering four cardinal priorities of the Christian faith to priorities of the Brethren in Christ. Chapter 10 offers suggestions as to how the denomination can authentically describe itself today. There is also an attempt to avoid future misunderstandings that may accompany the denomination's present name, and the question of reviewing the name is raised. Chapter 11, entitled "Beyond the Present," looks at the question of how well the denomination is prepared to serve in today's postmodern times by analyzing and comparing Brethren in Christ with key emergent church principles (the emergent church professes to be fitted for ministry in postmodern times). Chapter 12 is a short essay that interprets the essence of the Brethren in Christ. It contends a denomination's true identity cannot be contrived because it springs from the very soul of a people.

---

[1] The Brethren in Christ are firmly grounded in two root heritages, Pietism and Anabaptism. They later supplemented their original vision by making two major modifications. After the turn of the twentieth century the church's General Conference added a provision to its doctrine on sanctification, "entire" sanctification, and at the middle of the twentieth century the church shifted, albeit gradually, to a more integrated and holistic worldview, in contrast to a categorically dualistic view, thus amending their interpretation of separation from the world. Theological implications of the denomination's change in worldview are analyzed in chapters 4 through 7 of this work.

Chapter I

Why Study the Identity of a Denomination?

After the ascension of Jesus and the revelation of the Holy Spirit at Pentecost, the mission of the early church was first led by Christ's disciples and His apostles—those summoned by Him to preach the Gospel. These pioneer missionaries carried the Christian message to varied countries and lands. Over time there were bishops in numerous places during the early centuries—Jerusalem, Alexandria, and so on. The church was perceived to be universal in scope and at oneness on essential truths (This is not to say that the church was without apostasy).

By the fourth century the jurisdictional activity of the church became centered in Rome where the Bishop of Rome (successor to the line of St. Peter) began exercising papal authority over bishops located in other areas of the church. (It was the emperor Constantine who helped make the church imperial over bishops throughout the Roman empire.)

From the fifth century onward, however, the church began to experience tensions and discord between two segments—the east and the west, which culminated in a division. The split was finalized by the mutual excommunication of Michael Cerularius, the patriarch of Constantinople, and Pope Leo X (Rome) in 1054. This divide continued in the form of independent spheres—the Roman Catholic Church in the West[1] and the Eastern Orthodox Catholic church in the East.

In the sixteenth century the church centered in Rome came into division with a third major branch called Protestants, who specifically protested the corruption in the church and its lack of biblical centeredness. These protest groups established church bodies called territorial churches (in varied regions), some of which later became referenced as denominations.

Since the Reformation and territorial churches denominationalism has dominated the structure of Protestant Christianity. It seems assured that varied interpretations of the faith will continue in the future whether in the form of denominations, independent churches, or other alignments. Individual Christian perceptions differ widely regarding the value of religious denominations. Views range from cherished dependence on a denomination to seeing denominations as unnecessary, outmoded, or factional.

The break-up of the universal church into denominations began when Martin Luther disputed the church by posting his "Ninety-Five Theses" on the church door at Wittenburg. His protest ignited the Protestant Reformation as he, and other "justification by faith" believers formed the Lutheran Church in Germany. Further divisions followed as the Protestant movement expanded to other territories and new established (government sanctioned) churches were formed. Additional partitioning ensued as dissenting groups arose in opposition to the varied established churches. Since religious freedom was often curtailed by the territorial churches, many dissenters sought refuge in the new world. As a result, the early colonies in America included settlers seeking religious liberty. These outposts of free worship became seedbeds for further splintering of Protestant groups after the new nation was formed.

A new explosion of denominational beginnings and separations occurred in North America in the wake of the Great Awakenings (broad-sweeping religious revivals) in the eighteenth and nineteenth centuries. While, in time, many of the new denominations moderated their sectarian tendencies, religious distinctions endured, and theological partitioning was often abetted by ethnic, cultural, and class differences. Some denominational bodies, especially non-conformist types, gave emphasis to their differences and maintained them through separatist lifestyles.[2]

However, in spite of continuing group religious divisions, it appears that Christians today may view denominationalism as of declining importance. Abetted by a more mobile society, persons in the pew seem less compelled about fidelity to a single group, less committed to nuanced ecclesiastical views, and less fascinated by unique heritage topics than at any time since the Reformation in the sixteenth century. A weakening regard for denominational imperatives is borne out in the growing strength of independent and local mega-church movements, the marked decline in membership of many mainline denominations,[3] and the less-visible but growing number of denominations often needing to reduce church-wide development because of diminishing financial support.

This study is about a denomination that was formed in America in the late eighteenth century—the Brethren in Christ. From their beginning to the present, this body has been relatively small in number, yet as an historic group with a distinct identity, it should not be overlooked. It was conceived at the time the new nation was founded. The Brethren in Christ first called themselves "Brethren" but soon accepted the term *River Brethren*. They were the first indigenous church group to be formed in North America that continues today.[4]

While the Brethren in Christ would theologically surely identify with John the Revelator who speaks of "the churches" (Revelation 1:4 in the plural), they, as well, would not argue with Lon Allison, director of the Billy Graham Center, who affirms the notion of "church" as opposed to "churches." Allison says, "the term 'Christian churches' is as much an oxymoron as 'independent church,'" and continues, "there is one church and it is Christ's church (Col. 1:18; Mt. 16:18)." When particular denominations neglect understandings that foster inter-church connection they become victims of a restricted Christianity, portraying meager regard for the biblical ideal—the oneness of Christ's church. While it seems acceptable to create a church identity that assists its members in knowing why they believe and act the way they do, any devotion to particularities that smack of subtleties or high detail may undermine Christian community, and create a sense of exclusive possession of the faith.

Since a denominational identity study must be strongly introspective, a valid question arises: In view of growing uncertainty about a substantial place for religious denominations, how much effort and time should be devoted to analyzing a denomination's identity? A number of reasons are offered as to why attention to corporate identity is appropriate and timely for the Brethren in Christ. The study is justified under a seven-point rationale. Several of the points allude to a second argument, as well—that denominations can provide cross-spiritual benefits that independent or free-standing congregations, limited as to the breadth of their outreach and the diversity of their composition, may fail to give.

An awareness of the past and current identity of the Brethren in Christ is important because:

1. There are a number of unanswered questions about Brethren in Christ identity, and there appears to be a need for greater precision in recognizing who the Brethren in Christ are.
2. As the first indigenous denomination to be formed in colonial America that continues in ministry today, for general historic and comparative analysis reasons alone, the identity of the Brethren in Christ would seem to merit careful attention.[5]
3. For the Brethren in Christ denomination to project a future vision in accord with its historic vision, an up-to-date knowledge of the church's identity is needed so as to acquire points of reference.
4. The question as to whether a denomination continues to have a distinct "reason for being" can only be answered as its identity is acknowledged (such clarification is especially needed when merging with another denominational group is considered).[6]

5. An identity review is useful for helping to assure there is integrity of mission within the denomination, and to educate potential leadership regarding its true identity.
6. A clear knowledge of denominational identity is critical so as to communicate with diverse cultures.[7] To gain an understanding of particular denominational perspectives can be of assistance in serving communities that are increasingly pluralistic.
7. An awareness of one's denominational identity can assist individual Christians and their local church body in understanding more fully the broad implications of the Christian faith.

Several of the above reasons for seeking understanding of one's particular church identity merit additional elaboration. Reason 4, regarding the question of whether the particular denomination has "a distinct reason for being," is examined because most major denominations can point to distinct differences between them and other denominations at their time of origin. But through time vivid contrasts among groups often become less significant. As a result their variances tend to reside largely in historic tradition and form, rather than in deeply held beliefs or distinct life patterns. It then follows that self-images of church bodies, at an earlier time quite clear in the minds and hearts of its members, give way to blurred self-understandings. The question that invariably follows such a condition is whether there are good reasons to continue being a unique denomination.

A diminished sense of denominational uniqueness has been a major reason for church unions. Unfortunately, when a denomination concludes there is little justification for (independent) existence, it often has a declining sense of mission, which in turn contributes to sharp losses in membership. Apparently, this is the case with some of the mainline denominations in recent years.

There will be times when groups, perhaps even the Brethren in Christ, will decide to merge with another group. They can only recognize that day, assuredly, if they have thought clearly about the past, the present, and the future of the denomination.

As to reason 5, an identity review is useful for helping assure there is integrity of mission within the denomination, and to educate potential leadership regarding its true identity. The Brethren in Christ have historically been a close-knit group. However, since the mid-twentieth century when the church turned away from a position of pronounced "separation" to more active engagement with the world, the denomination's composition and leadership have become increasingly diverse. This trend toward heterogeneity has been augmented by a rising geographical and professional mobility in the general society. When one adds to these factors the readiness of the denomination's Board for World Missions to institute new efforts in varied international settings,[8] and the churches of Canada and the United States giving special attention to extending their ministries to areas that are predominately cross-cultural and quite different from the rural roots of the group, it seems important to ascertain and communicate the identity of the denomination.

Integrity of mission for a religious denomination is of special importance since a particular faith and the religious values that accompany it have long had an integrating and binding effect on society (the word *religion* comes from the Latin *religiare* meaning "to bind together"). Religions, at their very best, are expected to convey time-tested beliefs and understandings that are highly beneficial to the general society.

Also, a clear understanding of the Brethren in Christ identity is required because of a growing diversity among its leadership ranks—particularly with respect to its pastoral recruits. This diversity may partially be due to the denomination not having its own seminary. Rod White in the September, 1997, issue of *Evangelical Visitor* reported that a majority of the Brethren in Christ pastors (53%) came to the church as adults—not having been raised in Brethren in Christ families and not having attended a denominational church or school. A 2003 study by Dorothy Gish which gave no consideration to whether the current pastors had studied in a Brethren in Christ institution, found that just 37.5 per cent of the pastors had come out of a Brethren in Christ background. These demographic facts alone are sufficient signal for the denomination to devote serious care to church identity issues.[9] The church's pastoral leadership needs to have a clear understanding of who the Brethren in Christ are in order to proclaim with integrity the essential truths and historic vision of the church to which they have been called.

As to reason 6, a clear knowledge of denominational identity is critical so as to communicate with diverse cultures. The gaining of a lucid understanding regarding denominational perspectives assists in serving communities that are becoming increasingly pluralistic. A recent estimate from the U.S. Census Bureau projected that the four hundred million population milestone of the United States will be reached around 2043, and that "between the last official census in 2000 and the one of 2050, non-Hispanic whites will have dwindled from 69 percent to a bare majority of 50.1 percent. Those who are Hispanic will have doubled to 24 percent. Asians will have doubled to 8 percent of the population. African-Americans will have edged up to 14 percent. In other words, the United States will be on the verge of becoming a "majority of minorities."[10]

We live in a new kind of world. At the very time world cultures and peoples are becoming more interdependent, and commerce, transportation, and communications more connecting, churches—especially at the local level— often remain comparatively separated. They, in contrast to the general economy, have made far less significant advances in reaching across plural lines of culture and race. Mark Noll, in observing that the cross-cultural richness of the early church is becoming increasingly evident, contends that "translating the gospel message from one culture to another turns out to define the Christian faith itself."[11]

A clear understanding of a denomination's historic and current identity can be helpful in activating a broader cross-cultural vision. In regard to serving and ministering to a pluralistic society, denominations that show a vitality of outreach need broad and encompassing strategies to serve in a connected but fragmented world. Such strategies can best be formulated in a body with a global perspective—one that is cross-cultural in composition and trans-national in scope. An awareness of one's denominational connections and identity can help congregations and individuals gain a more informed vision of the diverse composition of the church and its many needs and opportunities for service.

As to item 7, an awareness of one's denominational identity can assist individual Christians and their local church body in understanding more fully the broad implications of the Christian faith. The biblical way to interpret authentic Christianity is in concert with fellow believers. David Schroeder, at a Council of International Ministries gathering stated:

> We need to recognize the power of God at work in cultures
> other than our own. Churches with different backgrounds will
> also have different insights into the faith.[12]

The receiving of cross-cultural insights is facilitated by being part of a denominational body. As one examines the historic and current identity of a particular denomination, one can experience a breadth of fellowship, can affect broadened understandings, and can be informed by widened "leadings" regarding priorities and direction for the church. Through denominational identity study, one can encounter fuller implications of the faith.[13]

In sum, the above seven points detail benefits that can be derived when a denomination and its people study its ongoing identity.

---

[1] The Roman Church came to have discrete classifications such as differing monastic orders (Franciscans and Jesuits for example) but all were amenable to the Roman Church jurisdiction.

[2] The *Yearbook of American and Canadian* Churches, 2004 edition (Abingdon Press, Nashville), cites the National Council of the Churches of Christ as consisting of 36 member communions representing over 50 million members, and the National Association of Evangelicals as serving 50 denominations, and 43,000 congregations nationwide. While representing a broad range of theological traditions, all National Association of Evangelical member denominations subscribe to the distinctly evangelical statement of faith of the Association. The Evangelical Fellowship of Canada serves 31 denominations and the Canadian Council of Churches serves 19 member groups.

[3] Between 1965 and 1990 many mainline denominations experienced severe declines in their membership rolls. The greatest loss came to the Disciples of Christ also known as the Christian Church. The Disciples lost 45.8 percent of its membership (this sharp decline included a schism). But other denominations didn't do much better. The Presbyterian Church (USA) lost 33.1 percent; the Episcopal Church dropped 28.7 percent; the United Church of Christ lost 22.8 percent; the United Methodist had 19.5 percent drop out. Others did a little better. The Reformed Church in America had 15 percent walk away or die; the Evangelical Lutheran Church in America dropped 7.8 percent; and the American Baptists lost only 1.5 percent. During the same period some conservative Christian churches grew at phenomenal rates. The Assemblies of God grew 281 percent; the Church of God (Cleveland, Tennessee) added 202 percent to its

rolls and the Seventh Day Adventists grew by 97 percent. (Reported by Bruce Forbes, professor of American Religion, at Morningside College, Sioux City, Iowa, and cited in the Fort Myers News Press, Dec. 5, 1998, E1.) An additional 1998 source reported that during the last ten years the combined membership of all Protestant denominations declined by 9.5 percent while the general population increased by 11.5 percent, and every year 3500 churches closed their doors for good, and that only 1200 new churches were planted. (From a Church Smart Resources report as cited in the *Evangelical Visitor*, October, 1998, p. 29.)

A more recent source: *Yearbook of American and Canadian Churches*, 1997 and 2006 editions, indicates declines in the mainline denominations (by million members) as follows: United Methodist Church from 8.5 to 8.2; Evangelical Lutheran Church in America from 5.2 to 4.9; Presbyterian Church (USA) from 3.7 to 3.2; Episcopal Church from 2.5 to 2.3; Disciples of Christ from .93 to .74; American Baptist from 1.5 to 1.4; United Church of Christ from 1.5 to 1.3. But membership in four other major denominations grew during this same time (in millions): Roman Catholic from 60.6 to 67.8; Southern Baptist from 5.7 to 16.3; Mormons from 4.7 to 6; Assemblies of God from 2.4 to 2.8

[4] Further elaboration about this fact is given in chapter 4.

[5] It is a fact that can potentially contribute to general, social, or religious history in American analyses.

[6] During the late twentieth century the long-term tendency within Protestantism toward division, by the starting of new denominations, turned in the direction of denominations uniting by way of formal mergers. This trend toward consolidation continues, but at a reduced rate.

[7] Minority Americans who composed 20 percent of the population in 1990 and became approximately 30 percent in 2000, and will move toward majority levels early in the next century (Russell Edgerton, American Association for Higher Education Bulletin 43, no. 8, April 1994, p. 4). For an additional authoritative projection on minority population growth in America into the twenty-first century, see note in chapter 2 regarding the projection made by the U.S. Census Bureau.

[8] During recent decades the Brethren in Christ extended their mission and ministry beyond North America and other nations where they had standing churches (including Zimbabwe, Zambia, India, Japan, Cuba, and Nicaragua), to these additional nations: Venezuela (1982), Colombia (1984), Thailand (1987), Malawi (1987), South Africa (1988), Spain (1990), Honduras (1990), Nepal (1992), England (1992), Mexico (1994), Mozambique (1997), Tibet (1997), Botswana (1998), and the Dominican Republic (1998).

[9] E. Morris Sider, who participates in instructing groups of new Brethren in Christ pastors in a course on the history and life of the denomination, described the diversity of Brethren in Christ pastoral recruits as ranging widely (theologically)—in a letter dated December 24, 1997.

[10] From the Christian Science Monitor News Service as cited in the Oct. 16, 2006, issue of the *Mennonite Weekly Review*, p. 3

[11] Mark Noll, *Books and Culture*, November/December 1996, p. 37.

[12] David Schroeder, *Evangelical Visitor*, March/April 1991, p. 27.

[13] In a relatively recent release from the Brethren in Christ church offices stress was placed on the importance of cross-communal conversation and decision as follows: "We can usually trust mutual discernment (as to biblical "way") within a community of congregations . . . . Together they weigh and test their sense of emerging vision to determine whether it truly comes from God. Even good understanding should be submitted to the larger community of faith. Through the process of talking and listening, we can receive guidance, encouragement, and even correction from the group." (From pages 2 and 3 of *BIC @ 2000: Moving Toward a New Millennium.*)

Chapter II

Traditions, Movements, and Concepts Linked to the Brethren in Christ

Papers read at the study conference on "Exploring the Brethren in Christ Identity," published in the April 1996 issue of *Brethren in Christ History and Life,* stirred new interest for me about who the Brethren in Christ are. It is obvious that the conference presenters took their assignments seriously. They raised key identity issues. The papers were thoughtful. They portrayed awareness that the Brethren in Christ were conditioned by forces and factors that go beyond the typically cited theological streams of Pietism, Anabaptism, and Wesleyanism. Moderator Harvey K. Sider in his opening address wisely acknowledged that "both secular and sacred forces leave an indelible imprint on individuals and groups. Like most others the Brethren in Christ have been affected."[1]

Some very good understanding came out of the conference on church identity. The new mindset theory presented by David Weaver-Zercher[2] and insights from Luke Keefer, Jr. about origins of the denomination's sanctification doctrine are of particular note.[3] To clarify the aspects of identity means we can better explore the issues involved. But in spite of the fine historical and analytical work that transpired at the conference, there seemed to be an awareness that more needs to be done in clarifying identity issues. Further, a degree of rivalry between traditions surfaced when the traditions were critiqued and hastily described in a reactive fashion.[4] Perhaps some of the conflicting overtones could have been avoided by giving more attention to definition.

The identity of a religious denomination is determined, to a significant degree, by the theological forces that shaped it, and their impact on the denomination. But a clear portrayal of identity also requires defining the meaning of the given forces (theological traditions or thought systems), and their characterizations. It is only as terms and concepts are clarified and understood that we can clearly focus on identity. Yet a precise defining of the Brethren in Christ vision by describing the traditions and concepts that had been of significant impact on the vision has not always been done well. Therefore, in this search for greater clarity regarding identity, we start by defining terms.

For the past two generations (since the mid-20ᵗʰ century), three theological traditions have been acknowledged by scholars as contributing to a Brethren in Christ theological synthesis—Pietism, Anabaptism, and Wesleyanism. Beyond these three, however, additional theological streams are described because of being judged by certain scholars or thought leaders as being of influence on Brethren in Christ theological understandings. Questions have been raised about whether or not Evangelicalism should be classified as significantly influencing the denomination in new directions.[5] Also, in an attempt to sort out whether the Brethren in Christ have veered toward a "mild Calvinism," as one scholar put it,[6] the Reformed tradition is examined.

In the process of examining the meaning of these respective theological movements or traditions a prior assumption is made that a given theological stream is defined most fairly (1) by citing its key beliefs or practices at the time of its origin, (2) by referencing its initial theological center, and (3) by discerning whether these have been maintained over the course of time.[7] It is further thought that such a review is particularly needed to accurately set forth the claims of denominations, such as the Brethren in Christ, which professes to being shaped by more than one given understanding of the faith.

Since denominations, both single-tradition and multi-tradition, tend to alter their theological understandings over time, the process used for determining the validity of such influence was first to seek to project a normative stance regarding what composed the given tradition(s) in question. And again, the position here is that a particular denomination is most accurately judged by comparing it with the theological essence of its shaping tradition(s) at founding—and then seeking to determine whether those emphases were maintained across the years.

Pietism Is Defined

Pietism entered the theological scene of Western Europe following the Protestant Reformation. Its intent was to regenerate the church from what was interpreted as a drift toward "dead orthodoxy." While the movement initially was directed toward revival of the German churches (Lutheranism), in time it affected other European territorial churches, and in turn reached well beyond the "old world." It influenced and stirred numerous theological and denominational entities in America and was the antecedent to Evangelicalism. But Pietism in its finest sense was and is more than spirit and spirituality. The Pietist understanding of conversion-regeneration appears to have been the critical factor shaping the Brethren in Christ church at the time of its origin. But a number of additional characteristics of the movement are consonant with the early vision and life of the church.

Pietism originated in Germany during the seventeenth century. The leaders of the movement were Johann Arendt (1555-1621), Philipp Jakob Spener (1635-1705), and Augustus Hermann Francke (1663-1727). The central theological motifs of the early movement were the reformation of the church (conventicles),[8] an emphasis on the Bible (anti-traditionalism), the reformation of life (orthopraxy), the theology of experience (conversion-regeneration), and hope for the world (social responsibility and involvement).[9]

Pietism has often been stereotyped as turning inward and concerned almost exclusively with devotional exercises and private moral scruples. Two core beliefs of Pietism, orthopraxy (living out the faith), and social involvement and responsibility, are frequently overlooked in this stereotype. There is a tendency to misconstrue Pietism as piety. But Pietists stood for much more than piety alone. Originating as a reform movement, Pietists sought to correct the churches which had become infatuated with "justification by faith" and had rejected deeds. In their reaction against the Catholic church most Protestants of the time had abandoned works altogether. The new movement of Pietism was concerned about "right living" and grounded in the belief that conversion-regeneration brings a "saving grace" change to the sinner, with provision of Divine assistance so that those "reborn" may live rightly. Historian, F. Ernest Stoeffler, describes the advent of Pietism and its breadth of contribution to the church and society as follows: "There was a new vision of a Christian's responsibility toward community and nation, a new sensitivity to the needs of the disadvantaged, the sick, and the dying, and a new awareness of the dire necessity of adequate educational institutions."[10]

Pietists were doers of the Word. Their key doctrine of conversion incorporated the concept of action into the "new life" of the Christian. They did not see conversion and conduct as separate entities. The early movement was quite socially conscious, and they appeared to have a greater "works" impact on the world about them than the Anabaptists who were more socially withdrawn.[11]

One might wonder why many scholars fail to give a full picture of Pietism. They miss the point that "obedience to God" was intrinsic to Pietism, and that faith and deeds were inseparable for the true Pietist. It may be that many of the scholars who studied Pietism were European and heavily focused their attention on Germany where Pietism was born; and on later manifestations when it lost both the spirit and message of its historic beliefs.

But there is another positive aspect to historic Pietism that at times is overlooked—the theology of spiritual experience[12]—wherein conversion-regeneration to the believer not only opened the door to a direct relationship with God, but beyond that gave access to Divine assistance and enablement for the believer to live above sin. In the finest Pietist tradition, the early Brethren in Christ were exposed to and experienced "a living faith"[14] that provided divine enablement for believers.

Yet, in spite of the breadth of ministry of early Pietism, a truncated definition of Pietism persists. Even some Brethren in Christ historical writing seems to fall short in recognizing the broad dimensions of early Pietism. Perhaps this is the reason some of the church's identity writings approach the traditions of Anabaptism and Pietism as polarities rather than emphasizing their commonalties.[14] To the contrary, Pietism was concerned with both a spiritual relationship and personal obedience to God. And also, historic Pietism was concerned with more than conversion and regeneration of the believer; it was interested in Divine enablement and empowerment for the believer to live a transformed life.

Anabaptism Is Defined

The Brethren in Christ church started in Lancaster County, Pennsylvania, where the general culture was significantly shaped by groups of settlers representing both Anabaptist and Pietist religious views. Since many of the newly formed denominations came out of groups within the Anabaptist tradition it seems predictable they would adopt Anabaptist values and forms they considered to be highly biblical.

Studies of the origins of Anabaptism point out that the early movement had diverse beginnings. It started with varied theological emphases under different leaders in distinct territories of Europe. The original defining doctrine from which the movement received its name was an emphasis on a new-believer's baptism. This meant newly converted believers sensed a need to be re-baptized—the meaning of Anabaptism (from the Greek).

As one seeks to define Anabaptism at its origin we look primarily at the theology of the early Anabaptist leader, Menno Simons, since he was the founder of the Mennonites who were the primary Anabaptist body transplanted to Pennsylvania. The Mennonites were also the chief Anabaptist group in the vicinity of Lancaster County, where the Brethren in Christ were born.[15]

More than a century after Anabaptism started, when the Brethren in Christ began, they were deeply affected by Anabaptism as one of their primary shaping streams—but it was a different Anabaptism from the original version. It differed in ways that perhaps the Brethren in Christ would have found a church home with their Mennonite neighbors had they been more closely aligned to their early European forebear's views at that given time.

The most visible and renowned scholar on Anabaptism was Harold S. Bender, who after diligent study of the movement, and close interchange with Robert Friedmann,[16] produced his work entitled "The Anabaptist Vision." In it he offered a three-part set of essential truths as follows: (1) they viewed the church as a voluntary fellowship rooted in the local gathering of believers; (2) they insisted that true faith must find tangible expression in daily discipleship; and (3) they held to an ethic of love and forgiveness, modeled on the life of Christ, which extended even to the enemy. These views, dated December 1943, when Bender presented the presidential address to the American Society of Church History, began a new era in the study of Anabaptism.

For more than half a century Bender's interpretation of the "Anabaptist Vi-sion" held rather full sway among scholars. However, more recently questions have been raised as to whether Bender's appraisal of the original vision is suf-ficiently complete without citing a principle that might include missions, grace or spirituality. There is a seeming oversight of the importance of the "new birth" as a fourth expression of the historic Anabaptist faith. Therefore, in order to most accurately define Anabaptism a key question is: How well does Bender's "Anabaptist Vision" interpretation match the historic Menno Simons (one of the founders of the tradition and namesake of the Mennonites, the most visible An-abaptist body today) brand of the tradition?

John C. Wenger who edited the writings of Simons, *The Complete Writ-ings of Menno Simons*,[17] states in the book's introduction, "It will be immedi-ately evident to every reader that Menno was a sound evangelical, a true saint of God united to Christ by faith, born again, and sanctified by the Holy Spirit."[18] Clearly Wenger's introductory description of Simons as a person, which was based on his analysis of Menno's overall writings, do not fully correlate with the essential truths as outlined in Bender's "Anabaptist Vision." Simons, who is frequently cited as being the most influential of the early Anabaptists, pos-sessed spiritual qualities and views that were either overlooked or discounted as Bender reviewed the broader movement.

After making a personal review of Simons writings I accede to Wenger's analysis that the "new birth" was central to his Christian life and ministry. I further affirm there appears to be a spiritual element, and an undeniable testi-mony to a relationship to Christ through the Holy Spirit that is not manifested in Bender's three summary points describing Anabaptism. It seems surprising that Simons extensive writings on the "new birth" (some sixteen pages of the compilation), his clear personal testimony about conversion, his calls for true repentance, his (Simons) repeated references to "evangelical truth" and other allusions of a definitive spiritual nature, failed to translate into sufficient strength to be recognized as part of the life-changing legacy that he and others left to the church.

Since Menno's emphasis on the "new birth" led directly to instituting "be-liever's baptism" wherein new Christians of the Simons variety felt the need to be baptized again, and since rebaptism essentially moved these newly born

Christians out from under the domain of the territorial churches, the "new birth" for the Anabaptists unlocked other historical developments. The "new birth" conjoined with "two-kingdoms" (due to territorial Church assumptions), became the critical acknowledgement that led to many Anabaptist Christians losing their lives as martyrs for the faith. Therefore, it appears essential that that the "new birth" or some other way of recognizing inner spiritual conversion in the believer be clearly acknowledged as being a basic part of who the historic Anabaptists were.[19]

In regard to other Anabaptist leaders it needs to be recognized that Menno Simons was not alone in emphasizing the importance of a personal life-changing spiritual experience for the Christian believer. For example, Michael Sattler, who is believed to be the writer of an early Anabaptist confession, *The Schleitheim Confession* (*Bruderliche Vereinigung*), in recounting essentials (from the *Confession*) stated in the first article:

> Baptism shall be given to all those who have learned repentance . . . and who believe truly that their sins are taken away by Christ, and to all those who walk in the resurrection of Jesus Christ and wish to be buried with him in death.

Additional writings of Sattler emphasized the personal forgiveness of sins and an inner reality. He observed in a letter to Bucer and Capito, "Faith in Christ reconciles us with the Father," that Christ came to save those who believe on him, and that "the action is inward and heavenward." In a letter to the congregation at Horb he wrote, "Pray that reapers may be driven out into the harvest, for the time of threshing has come near."[20]

Again, assuming that a theological tradition is best defined according to its original manifestations, and referencing its center, the views of Menno Simons and Michael Sattler lead this writer to join in classifying early Anabaptism as honoring the necessity of inner spiritual change for the Christian. This fact has recently been more emphasized by Mennonite scholars.

It was initially cited by Steve Dintiman in an article entitled "The Spiritual Poverty of the Anabaptist Vision" that appeared in the February 23, 1993 issue of the *Gospel Herald*. Soon thereafter historian John Roth fully acknowledged the modern acceptance of Bender's thesis in this way: "for more than fifty years (since 1944) the 'Anabaptist Vision' . . . has served as a symbolic theological anchor within the Mennonite Church." However, in his work *Refocusing a Vision*, Roth further opens the revision door to the long-held "Anabaptist Vision."[21] Karl Koop followed Roth with an additional study entitled *Confessions of Faith in the Anabaptist Tradition, 1527-1660*,[22] wherein he collects 14 English translations of early Anabaptist confessions of faith, some of which had never been translated before. In the work, Koop contends that the respective confessions indicate that Anabaptism can't be reduced to certain ethical principles. He likened the confessions to a way of life expressed through prayer, worship, spirituality, and deeply held beliefs.

As has been the case in many religious streams, the values that were normative at their founding, were not always extant in other periods of their history. Anabaptists became cool spiritually at different times and in different places—which assists in explaining why early Brethren in Christ chose to start a new church body.[23]

Wesleyan Theology Is Described

John Wesley (1703-1791), a clergyman in the Church of England, founded a church he never intended[24] (the Methodists), endorsed a doctrine he never claimed to possess (entire sanctification),[25] and perpetuated a theology that corresponded closely with Pietism. He protested to his dying day that he was a loyal member and minister of the established church. His loyalty to the Church of England was to its essence rather than its outer form. There seems to be little doubt that in a remarkable ministry of sixty-five years, he brought about both the formation of a new denomination, and a desired reformation of his native church. And while he never experienced "entire sanctification," he professed seeing it demonstrated in others he thought were freed from the root of sin.

Wesley's theology was affected by his exposure to a Pietist group, the Moravian Brethren, whom he encountered while on a church service stint to the colony of Georgia. He was impressed by their spiritual certainty of being children of God. Some years later at the age of thirty-five, when Moravian Peter Bohler visited him in England, Wesley was led to a personal assurance of salvation. The similarity of Wesley's theology to that of early Pietism shows in numerous ways. In his "Rules" he insisted that church members should avoid evil, do good, and seek holiness. These were core values of the Pietists. Also, the deep concerns of Pietists for the inner testimony of the Holy Spirit, and for the centrality of the sanctification concept, became basic truths that Wesley communicated as part of the gospel message. In fact the late Brethren in Christ historian and theologian, Martin H. Schrag, wrote that "it is one of my theories that the reason the Brethren in Christ accepted (what was later to be termed) Wesleyan holiness, was due to the fact that they had a Pietistic orientation."[26] He continued, "many historians see Wesleyan (theology) as a form of Pietism."

The major doctrinal emphases of Wesley were salvation by faith, confirmed and exemplified by good works, and a witness of the Holy Spirit to the believer. Wesley had a conviction about the Christian having a personal experience of faith. The Brethren in Christ connection to Wesleyan theology is in the area of *entire* sanctification. Even though the Brethren in Christ holiness terminology corresponds most closely with American camp-meeting language, the Church's ultimate quest for Christian perfection, traditionwise, has kinship with that of Wesleyanism—and ultimately with Pietism. And since the Brethren in Christ body and its scholars have for two generations termed "life in the Spirit" as being Wesleyan in nature, it is treated here as being a related theological stream—one worthy of careful study and interpretation.

Evangelicalism Is Defined

Although Evangelicalism has not previously been designated as a historic shaper or a primary source of Brethren in Christ theology, it is defined here because several leadership voices have suggested that it be considered a significant shaper of who they are theologically. While it is reasoned in later chapters that in terms of contributing any new or distinct theological doctrines to the Brethren in Christ synthesis Evangelicalism should not be considered a primary shaper of doctrines of the Brethren in Christ—thus differing from Pietism and Anabaptism in that respect—but rather that the evangelical movement is the current theological expression most representative of the basic doctrinal values of early Pietism.[27] The chief theological emphasis points of classical Pietism are analogous to those of "neo-evangelicalism."[28] The term Pietism is not used in today's general theological discourse to describe the primary doctrinal commitments that are both Pietist and Evangelical in nature (the term "Evangelical" is generally used). Since the term Evangelical is viewed by Brethren in Christ members as the best one-word descriptor of the denomination today,[29] it therefore seems important that Evangelicalism be defined for clarification purposes.

The evangelical faith has deep roots in the history of the Christian church. It did not merely rise from eighteenth- and nineteenth-century revivals. As one seeks to define and fully understand Evangelicalism, it should be noted that numerous historians perceive Pietism to be the direct antecedent to the Evangelical movement.[30]

The Reformers called themselves "Evangelicals" because they believed that the doctrine of "justification by faith" is central to the Gospel (the Good News). Since the biblical word to depict action regarding the Gospel is evangel, to be an evangelical in this historic sense was to be a gospeller, or an advocate of "justification by faith."[31]

The word *evangelical* has been defined in numerous ways to describe a variety of aspects of conservative Christianity. Donald Dayton and Robert Johnson called evangelicalism a movement whose multiple centers are more easily identified than its shifting and overlapping boundaries. They identified the three centers as being Protestant Orthodoxy, personal commitment to Christ, and evangelism.[32] John Stott states that "evangelical Christianity is theological in its character, biblical in its substance, original in its history, and fundamental in its emphasis."[33] Evangelicalism may be most straight-forwardly defined today as a trans-denominational movement consisting of those who believe in the Gospel and seek to promote it throughout the world. Evangelicals are recognized for emphasizing a high view of Scripture, and conversion and regeneration through Christ.[34]

The beliefs that can readily be tied to the term evangelical comprise what C. S. Lewis labeled "Mere Christianity." Alister McGrath identifies evangelicals as holding six controlling convictions that are grounded in Scripture. They are: (1) the supreme authority of Scripture as a source of knowledge of God and a guide to Christians; (2) the majesty of Jesus Christ both as incarnate God and Lord and as the Savior of sinful humanity, (3) the lordship of the Holy Spirit; (4) the need for personal conversion; (5) the priority of evangelism for both individual Christians and the church as a whole; (6) the importance of Christian community for spiritual nourishment, fellowship, and growth.[35]

In essence, these varied theological definitions of what it means to be evangelical, as cited by scholars, have remained quite consistent. Regrettably, however, these true meanings have often been distorted and misunderstood. The term evangelical has been preempted for ulterior ends, as has the term Christian. It receives its greatest misuse when it is applied to political purposes. Beyond this political misappropriation, fundamentalist-type Christian leaders who are known for their pugnacious spirit and fine distinctions, claim the name or are assigned it by the press, pollsters or pundits.[36] But the word evangelical is not a political concept and it technically should not be claimed by either the political left or right. Today's American varieties of evangelicals run the gamut from the left's Jim Wallis of "Sojourners" (social justice matters), to include Richard Cizik who is known for representing "green" concerns (caring for God's creation), to Ron Sider of Evangelicals for Social Action (a pacifist who is also committed to broader social action), and on to Jim Dobson of Focus on the Family—who tends to lean toward political issues that are further to the right. These rather vocal leaders, all who rally under the banner of being evangelical, are known to be somewhat directive in their respective social views. However, alongside them are many other evangelical leaders, as well as rank and file evangelicals, who represent a full spectrum of positions ranging from the left to the far right on varied social and political matters. Evangelicals would also claim within their ranks those who refrain from voicing or even participating in making political decisions.

Yet Evangelicalism is the recipient of much misinformation and it seems that many define it the way they wish. But the essence of Evangelicalism is the Gospel (good news) and its supporting doctrines. It is not a political movement of any sort. The true center of evangelical fellowship is spiritual and theological in nature.

Reformed Theology Is Described

The Reformed branch of Protestantism, a significant part of the differentiation made at the time of the Protestant Reformation, was started by Ulrich Zwingli. But he died an early death. It was the multi-talented John Calvin (1509-1564) who continued the work started by Zwingli. Reformed theology spread throughout Europe and became the most prolific Reformation branch—even exceeding Lutheranism. Reformed theology is often referred to as Calvinism with the principle source of Calvin's thought being *The Institutes*—a book best understood as a work on Christian doctrine and social duty.

The theology of John Calvin, along with the other Reformers, emphasized the centrality of Christ and was deeply committed to the work of the Holy Spirit. Its basic motif is the sovereignty of God from which man's eternal destiny—predestination to salvation or damnation—is reasoned. While Calvin always wished to emphasize God's majesty as the overarching theme of biblical religion, the concept of predestination emerged as the best known feature of Calvin's thought.[37] Calvin's concerns also included the notion that societal implications of the Christian faith needed to be implemented. He went so far as to rely on control of the political arm to supervise the morals and religious faith of general citizens.[38]

A careful examination of the Reformed tradition will grant that in seventeenth and eighteenth century Europe the influence of the Pietist movement reached well beyond German-seated Lutheranism and penetrated Calvinist-oriented religious groupings (along with Arminian bodies) in Europe. These Pietist spiritual gleanings were in turn carried to the Colonies where the first Great Awakening in America started in New England, evidenced by a spiritual revival that began under the Calvinist preaching of Jonathon Edwards (1703-1759). The first Great Awakening in time became extended to the other Colonies as well.

There is, in addition, a sub-area from the framework of Reformed thought that a significant segment of Brethren in Christ, especially academics, have been highly attentive to and even grasped—a unified view of truth, and the Christian worldview.[39] The origin's concepts that might be termed the "Christian worldview," are seated in the Middle Ages—particularly with writings of Thomas Aquinas (1255-1274).[40] It is a view that runs counter to the dualism projected by Anabaptists in the Two Kingdom Theory (as it relates to both truth and a highly separated life), which until the 1950s was a dominant view of Brethren in Christ. These new understandings that came to the foreground are cited as being Reformed because this Protestant group was most noted for advancing the unity of God's truth idea.[41] The contribution of Reformed scholars, gifted in articulating this concept, has been particularly helpful in more recent times as many denominationally founded Colleges and universities lost sight of their Christian moorings (presuppositions). Their contributions have also been of great help in assisting educational efforts to integrate truths of revelation with truths of creation.[42] To be more specific, the Christian worldview represents all truth as centering in Jesus Christ, and recognizes all truth as being God's truth,[43] but additionally, it perceives that Christian faith needs to be integrated into all sectors of a Christian's life.

However, since there are many possible Christian vocations (callings), the Christian worldview and its integration into one's life carries with it strong academic overtones. Therefore, if the church is to be correctly engaged in pursuit of the unity of truth, it needs to have assistance from Christian academia.[44] It is particularly in the academic-groundings area that Brethren in Christ, and especially its Colleges, are judged to have intersected with Reformed thought or theology, even if only tangentially so.

After having implied movement by Brethren in Christ toward Reformed and Thomas Aquinas' interpretations regarding a Christian world and life view, and away from dualism of truth understandings, there are differing ways in which such life views can be expressed. For example, in the political realm—while Brethren in Christ do not rule out political participation for Christians, they clearly do not accept the extreme Reformed idea of seeking to use the political arm (as in Calvin's Geneva, or in Kuyper's Holland, or being immersed today in efforts of "Christian" political rightists or leftists). Nor do they approve of a Christian realism that identifies the kingdom of God with any political ideology. Yet this holistic and integrative concept is real in varied areas of potential Christian participation. It entered the denomination as its colleges examined the Scriptures and sought to determine the most beneficial kind of education for Christians. As a result the philosophical and theological views of the colleges were broadened and they became Christian colleges of the arts and sciences.

Since these later views are manifested in Christian acts toward extending the kingdom of God and improving society, they are not inconsistent with the denomination's Pietist and Wesleyan values, or with the service values of Anabaptism, but still they are best ascribed to the Reformed tradition because their grounding is in holistic concepts emphasized by that tradition. It also appears that a significant portion of the Brethren in Christ church as well as its college,

Messiah, have essentially moved away from a categorical "Two Kingdom Theory" as it applies to the truths of God, and service to Him.[45] There appears to be no longer a dualism regarding truth. All truth is considered God's—natural revelation and special revelation alike.

Concepts Employed, at Times, to Categorize or Critique Theological Positions of the Brethren in Christ

Turning from defining theological traditions or movements that range on a spectrum from being vitally to tangentially linked to the denomination, we review several concepts that have sometimes been used to categorize the Brethren in Christ. Since surface generalizations that stand alone without informed analysis can distort the picture of a movement or a denomination, to determine true identity one needs to deal occasionally with generalizations and broad characterizations to describe theological traditions. Unfortunately the trans-denominational movements of early Pietism and contemporary Evangelicalism are recipients of considerable misinformation. It is not just the media or laymen that dispense generalizations of unfair labels and stereotypes. Preachers and scholars have also succumbed to such lapses.

George Steiner speaks of one problem in communications today as being one of misinformation. He says: "misinformation does not mean false information. It means misleading information—misplaced, irrelevant, fragmented, or superficial information—information that creates the illusion of knowing something, but which in fact leads one away from knowing."[46] Generalizations that stand alone are devoid of a context that transmits true understanding and insight. Three most frequently used misleading generalizations that have influenced the Brethren in Christ are individualism, subjectivism, and acculturation. These characterizations are examined in greater detail.

Individualism

Are Brethren in Christ a group that is somewhat individualistic, or are they a unified body composed of converted individuals subject to the group's understanding of biblical truth?

The theological traditions that emphasize Christian experience (professing conversion) Pietism, Wesleyanism, and Evangelicalism, are occasionally accused of fostering individualistic Christianity. An additional charge in the same vein, but more specific and sweeping, is that experiential Christians are preoccupied with personal morality and overlook collective sins. But these criticisms seem to be misplaced. Conversion, "the new birth," is a biblical teaching that sinful people need the personal and divine work of God's grace to change their lives.

Within each and every Christian tradition there are many who fail to meet the high ideals of Christianity. The lapses can involve nominal Christians as well as those who profess a "new birth" experience. Zealous commitment can, at times, degenerate into manipulation—for example, where evangelism efforts succumb to maneuvering or undue control. Yet it is a misconception to levy charges of promoting individualism on Christian groups that can rightfully bear witness to individual life-changing conversion experiences. The self-reproach and individual repentance associated with one's "new birth" relationship to God, and the spiritual attainment of sanctification wherein one's values and will become surrendered to God, are antithetical to individualism. It is an error to conclude that those who profess "an infilling" of the Holy Spirit in their lives become more rugged in their individualism. The two are mutually exclusive. Also, in the Arminian tradition an individual relationship to God is maintained as one stands in obedience to God.

Another factor that counters strident individualism within the two primary traditions of the Brethren in Christ is the view that Christianity is a communal thing. It involves covenantal commitments to the church which supersede self interests. The pursuit of Christian perfection is both an individual and a group matter.[47] The small Bible study group and the congregation serve as obedience check-points to give individual and group counsel about service to God and others.

While intemperate individualism seems to be less than Christian, individuality is highly Christian. There is no essential virtue to uniformity. Each person is unique in the eyes of God and is prized to an extent that "the very hairs on one's head are numbered." A personal decision to become a Christian is intrinsic to conversion regeneration, and the Scriptures give much attention to personal development. God's placement of a prominent place for the individual is manifested as He anoints persons with power, bestows varied gifts on individuals, and conveys a singular calling on distinct persons. Individuality should not be construed as the cult of individualism.

At the other pole, the individual should not be viewed as being part of a machine. The 1982 *Time* magazine's person of the year was designated as a machine—the personal computer. A mere twenty-four years later, after being empowered by the computer, the individual chosen by *Time* to be the 2006 person of the year was named—"you." The final cover of *Time*, in 2006, sports a small mirror so individuals can contemplate themselves—as controllers of the information age—the point being that we humans are empowered to share our daily activities and innermost thoughts with thousands of our closest friends and associates through blogs, pages on MySpace or Facebook, and videos on

YouTube. To the contrary, for the Brethren in Christ, rather than "you" or "me" being in control—the ideal is that each one of us should be under God's direction.

Subjectivism

Are the Brethren in Christ a group that is highly subjective, or are they a transformed group characterized by communion with God and by Holy Spirit enablement?

Human beings are spiritual and emotional as well as physical. Their relationship to God is a subjective thing. It cannot be objectively measured nor can it be totally verified. At the deepest level of man is his soul. Religion, prayer, meditations, and worship are all personal in character. Each of these elements involve some degree of human subjectivity. While modernism has been hesitant to recognize a personal religion, one's religion has to be personal or it becomes a set of empty ideals. All religions by their very nature deal with the subjective.

There is wide divergence within Christianity between the varied denominations regarding the degree of subjectivity they show. It is sometimes said that the most subjective Christian group is the Society of Friends because of their "inner light" interpretation. The "inner light," however, is similar to the Pietist movement's "illumination" concept. Pietism is distinctly subjective among the Christian traditions. The emphasis it places on the anointing by the Holy Spirit is highly subjective in nature. And the accompanying efforts to "extend the kingdom of God" by winning others to a saving knowledge of Christ, is personal and very subjective. Add to this that when a Christian talks about the presence of God being real and she or he professes she or he "is not alone," subjectivity comes into play. Cell groups, testimony meetings, conventicles, camp meetings, revivals, and worship services are spiritual in nature, and therefore are quite subjective.

Since Pietism is highly subjective one needs to wonder about the boundaries of true spirituality. For Christians there is presumably too much subjectivity in play if it turns to subjectivism. At the point Christian experience becomes the supreme good and is measured by the experience alone or solely by favorable feelings about the experience, then a state of subjectivism occurs as reason is undermined and experience is deemed to be where religion resides.

While Pietism is quite subjective it also has a strong objective dimension. The Christian life is more than an experience. It is, as termed in an early confession of the Brethren in Christ, "a living faith." It goes beyond thought or feeling about one's own condition. Being a Christian makes a difference in the way one lives. A newborn Christian will seek to live according to biblical norms and will follow the example of Christ. The feeling that one is indeed a true child of God is brought to the touchstone of Scripture. A "living faith" is veri-fiable by other Christians through the good works and right attitudes that flow from one's love for Christ.

Therefore, a person professing a "new birth" relationship to a personal Lord is not necessarily subjective. The experience of the "new birth" does not put Christians on a track whereby decisions are made for them, and by them, and in them by some outside force. To the contrary, while the decision to accept Christ is personal, it entails changes in attitude, a turning from sin, and a sense of mutuality with other Christians. As these factors come into play, the Chris-tian is prevented from moving into deluding subjectivism. Also, if there is re-peated failure to live a life of obedience, the Christian is subjected to the ultimate in objectivity, a broken relationship with the Divine.

Acculturation

Are the Brethren in Christ a group that has "sold out" to the general cul-ture, or are they a group that is discriminatingly engaged in the world?

Acculturation is a process of intercultural borrowing whereby new and blended patterns of life are adopted by individuals or groups. As such the process appears to be neutral. But acculturation becomes injurious when core values are lost or diluted. As a consequence of such loss a sense of blame or guilt can be assessed. The strong inference of the term, when used in connec-tion with the church, seems to be that change consists of an aimless drift toward "the world" and secular values.

Undoubtedly, there are Christians who, at times, too easily conform to the general culture. On the other hand, many Christians carefully deliberate and alter their ways only when assured that changes are consistent with biblical principles. But many changes in Brethren in Christ life during the past half cen-tury appear to have been tied to new understandings about the world and cul-ture itself. These changes included an increasing awareness that culture is not totally secular and that every person is in some degree a product of the general culture—also, that there are many cultures and God shows no predilection to any given culture.[48] In the life of the Brethren in Christ, over the past two gen-erations, there has come to be an increasing recognition that accommodation is necessary to effectively engage in Christian witness and ministry to people in other cultures.

Lamin Sanneh, a Yale University historian of Gambian background (who witnessed first-hand the dynamism of that nation's developing church) points out that when translating the Scriptures into local languages for differing cul-tures a number of unexpected results can be produced. He found that at mini-mum they encouraged local revitalization, and often stabilized shaky local cultures—stimulating a form of Christianity that surprises the missionary trans-lators.[49] Sanneh argues that Christianity preserves indigenous life and culture, whereas cultures converted to Islam soon lose the ability to think religiously in their mother tongues.

Matthew Kustenbauder, a graduate of Messiah College and Yale Divinity School, affirms Sanneh when he says, "The worldwide church helps us to see the image of Christ through the lens of other cultures." Kustenbauder calls for cross-cultural Christians to address issues that plague the world and says: "Communities of faith are at their best when they address areas of critical human need."[50]

Paul's admonitions in Galatians 3:28-29 and Colossians 3:11 clarify that the Gospel moves from culture to culture without changing. It would appear that those who evaluate faithfulness to the church largely by a separation from the general culture yardstick are, according to H. Richard Niebuhr's analysis, part of the "Christ against culture" model. Carried to its logical end, "Christ against culture" can turn into subculture Christianity.[51] But even more negating, when Christians fully turn their backs on the culture, it is a betrayal of the biblical mandate that calls for God's sovereignty over all of life. Indeed, without being swallowed up by the culture, Christians have a responsibility to discerningly as-sist in reforming it. Although not controlled by the general culture, since the lat-ter half of the twentieth century the Brethren in Christ seem to increasingly represent the view that they should help to impact the general culture for good, and that the gospel is open to cultural pluralism. Christians need to respond to the culture, but they should not necessarily expect the culture to be Christian.

A rebuking use of the term *acculturation*, which at times comes into use when it is perceived that individual Christians or the church are unduly ac-commodating to the general culture (typically expressed as "drifting toward the world") can imply that there is a distinct Christian culture that the church should commit itself to. However, while there will be much in every culture a Christian needs to oppose, and a Christian dare not become fully acculturated,[52] there is no Christian culture *per se*.[53] Therefore, instead of making sweeping ac-culturation judgments or charges, the Christian needs to be both judicious and specific as to values, standards, or attitudes the church should abide by, in order that it "be in the world but not of the world."

In summary, linking the concept of individualism to Christian conversion is a stereotypical error. It is recognized that Christians who witness to a "new birth" and more nominal types of Christians can become individualistic and fail at times to demonstrate the faith in their day-to-day lives. However, there is evidence that those involved in services to others, and those who liberally share of their resources, are often those who profess a more vital relationship with God.[54]

The tying of the concept of subjectivism to experiential Christian faith also needs to be critiqued. There are forms of objectivity that can be used in assessing authentic Christianity. These include the Christian's accountability to his/her local congregation, or to a cell group within the church. Also there is a clear measure of objectivity in that the Brethren in Christ, as Arminians, recognize that Christians who continue in a track of disobedience to God can fall from "the faith."

As to the charge of acculturation, there is probably no ideal Christian culture today or even from the biblical past. The Gospel transcends culture. It can at the same time challenge or approve cultural norms. The early church reached beyond culture as it lived out the faith in many diverse settings. Christianity and culture do not converge into one set of customs, one body, or the characteristics of one period of time, just as the church is not embodied in one racial or ethnic culture.[55]

Turning now to the task of identity clarification, the meaning of a denomination is more than the sum of the traditions that have influenced it. Also, denominations should not be married to their tradition or traditions *per se*. Traditions, at best, merely help to define who one is, and a true identity extends beyond the beliefs and actions of a religious body. A denomination's identity involves mindsets, dispositions, and other characteristics that may be uncovered. Therefore, the search for and determination of a denomination's identity is a dynamic process which due to changing conditions and the natural succession of people is never fully completed.

Having defined key traditions and prescribed limits to several concepts as related to the Brethren in Christ, our identity-clarification task begins by examining the denomination's early vision. The initial views of the group are best set forth in the contents of the first *Confession* of the Brethren in Christ.[56] The early *Confession*, which was written around 1780, is reviewed in the next chapter.[57]

[1] Harvey R. Sider, *Brethren in Christ History and Life*, Vol. XIX, No. 1. p. 5.

[2] For further analysis of the Weaver-Zercher theory see the section of chapter 7, under the heading of "Mindsets."

[3] The Brethren in Christ doctrine of "entire" sanctification, while referred to as Wesleyan, came out of the American holiness movement rather than from Wesley's writings, or as a testimony to his own spiritual experience.

[4] Dan Chamberlain, who was designated to conclude the presentations with a review of the Conference, responded by offering nearly five pages of observations to clarify potential misconceptions about Wesleyanism. It was apparent he felt that both Wesleyanism and Evangelicalism had been somewhat caricatured in the proceedings. For further consideration about the church's theological synthesis showing signs of conflict, see section on "Traces of Division Regarding the Vision" in chapter 4.

[5] A question elicited by Luke Keefer Jr. and moderator Harvey Sider at the Church Identity Study Conference held at Grantham, Pennsylvania, in 1996.

[6] A question raised by Luke Keefer Jr. at the Identity Study Conference.

[7] The item (3) cited, of course, for analysis purposes, needs to be compared with item (1) as a reference point. This in no way should be construed as the writer making negative value judgments when such changes or modifications are cited, because it is expected that denominational interpretations become adjusted in changing times. However, in this chapter the writer takes great pains to not only define Anabaptism at its time of origin, but to cover some transitions, since more than a century after Anabaptism began, when the Brethren in Christ started, it appears they were affected by Anabaptism as one of their primary shaping streams—yet it appeared to be a different Anabaptism from the original version. It differed in ways that perhaps some of the initial Brethren in Christ would have found a church-home with the Mennonites if they had been more closely aligned to their early theological positions at that given time.

[8] Conventicles were small assembly groups that met for religious worship and devotion—in the interest of reforming the Lutheran church and other established churches from what was perceived to be spiritual coldness or lukewarmness.

[9] Dale Brown, *Understanding Pietism,* William B. Eerdman's Publishing Company, pp. 27, 28.

[10] *Continental Pietism and Early American Christianity*, Eerdmans, 1976, p. 10.

[11] The Anabaptists were especially withdrawn at this time because people were trying to kill them. The Pietist concept of obedience was emphasized often in their literature and was expressed by Spener, Francke, and Arndt as *Nachfolge Christi*. Their social concerns were not limited to the quality of life within the gathered group of believers. Spener counseled the use of economic means for the welfare of neighbor and Francke's interest in the destitute was

widely known. Page 131 of Brown's *Understanding Pietism* reads: "There is probably nothing in which historians have been more unfair to Pietism than in defining the mission of the church to society. A frequent stereotype of Pietistic Christianity portrays it as almost preoccupied with inward devotion and private moral scruples. On the contrary, the Pietist milieu resulted in the desire to transform the living conditions of the poor and the oppressed, reform the prison system, abolish slavery, break down rigid class distinctions, establish a more democratic polity, initiate educational reforms, establish philanthropic institutions, increase missionary activity, obtain religious liberty, and propose programs for social justice. For example, at Halle (a University founded by Spener), the treatment of the poor and orphans as educable was in itself socially transforming."

[12] While it appears that both Arendt and Francke were deeply committed to a theology of experiencing God through conversion, Morris Sider found, as a Young Fellow in 2000, that Spener's writings failed to confirm the conversion-regeneration aspect generally associated with Pietism—which may be the reason that as a Pietist-related group the Church of the Brethren have leaned more toward "baptismal regeneration." Having said this, the writer clearly recalls that during the 1960s and early 1970s Rev. Jacob Miller, a Church of the Brethren minister from the York, Pennsylvania area, who then served on the Messiah College Board of Trustees (and contributed Miller Residence for men, in honor of his late son who had been a student) spoke of their particular congregation continuing to hold what he termed, "revival meetings." However, it is not known how their brand of "revival meetings" may have differed from other brands that stressed experiencing God.

[13] "A living faith" is excerpted from the initial *Confession of Faith* written around 1780, and is set forth in the final chapter of this work as epitomizing "the Soul of the Brethren in Christ." Perhaps there was less urgency for parts of the Church to accept a "second definite work of grace" (the sanctified life) because Pietist literature frequently cited sanctification as part and parcel of the "initial work of grace" for the new believer.

[14] C. O. Wittlinger, *Quest for Piety and Obedience*, Evangel Publishing House, Nappanee, Ind., 1978, pp. ix, 21. In his history of the Brethren in Christ, Wittlinger perhaps played too strongly to his book title as he gave undeserved contrast between Pietism and Anabaptism (particularly because of his limited definitions of the two, at origin, on the cited pages). In what seems otherwise to be a complete and scrupulously accurate work, Wittlinger defined Pietism as piety and identified obedience exclusively on the Anabaptist side of the equation. While the word "and" within the title does not suggest contrast, the rather simplistic definitions of "piety" and "obedience" that were offered, and then connecting them rather exclusively to the given religious traditions—which can be unduly polarizing to both concepts.

[15] Today there are upwards to approximately two score of Anabaptist-related church bodies in the United States.

[16] Robert Friedmann, a Jewish-Christian refugee from the Nazi regime, who left Austria in 1939, influenced Bender's classic, "The Anabaptist Vision." According to historian, Albert N. Keim, "Friedmann helped shift Bender's attention from the fundamentalist-modernist focus on correct belief to a new concern with how belief and life could be knit together. The Protestant temptation and habit of separating salvation and ethics now became a central concern of Bender." (from *Mennonite Weekly Review*, 11/30/2000, p. 13.) Keim further analyzed that Bender learned from Friedmann, "that Pietism and Anabaptism were antithetical. . . , that the effect of Pietism was to blunt the prophetic voice of faith. (from *MWR* 12/28/2000, p. 9.). Currently among Brethren and Mennonite scholars, Friedmann is seen as unduly prejudicial against Pietism.

[17] Bender collaborated with Wenger by writing the biography of Simons that was included in this writing's compilation.

[18] John C. Wenger, editor, *The Complete Writings of Menno Simons*, Herald Press, Scottdale, Pa., 1956, p. vii.

[19] While it appears that the "new birth" was at the spiritual crux of many Anabaptists losing their lives, it is argued that from an economic and political standpoint the princes of the land supported the church in persecuting Anabaptists because the recording of baptisms was the basis on which taxes were assessed. There was, it appears, a mix of spiritual motivations on the one hand, and practical and political intent on the other.

[20] C. Arnold Snyder, *The Life and Thought of Michael Sattler*, Herald Press, Scottsdale, Pa., 1984, pp. 111-134.

[21] Additional serious scholarly scrutiny as to matters of spiritual vitality in early Anabaptism appear to be gathering, as evidenced in the work edited by Roth entitled, *Refocusing a Vision*. This publication has a chapter by Levi Miller under the subject, "A Reconstruction of Evangelical Anabaptism," which indicates the need to resurrect evangelical emphases among Anabaptists. Positive support for spiritual type concerns also show in other scholarly contributions to this work. Roth, himself, in an article entitled "Do Denominations Matter?" published in Brethren in Christ History and Life, (Aug.'99, p. 229) stated "Like most evangelical Christians the Anabaptists believed in the necessity of conversion. They consistently and tirelessly taught that sinful humans come to salvation in Christ through the gifts of God's grace and through our response in faith and gratitude."

Returning to the views of Harold Bender, while the "Anabaptist Vision" was the encompassing interpretation for which he is noted, Bender does acknowledge a spiritual dimension within Mennonites due to the effects of Pietism. This view appears in an introduction to Friedmann's, "Mennonite Piety," p. viii.). The impact of Pietism on Mennonites is also affirmed in Richard K. MacMaster in *Land, Piety, Peoplehood: The Establishment of Mennonite Communities in America, 1683-1790*, pp. 164, 165.

[22] Pandora Press, 2006.

[23] At the time of birth of the Brethren in Christ, it appears that Lancaster County Mennonites emphasized nurture of the home and the church as the means for entry into the church. During this period, Martin Boehm, a Mennonite minister (later Bishop) testified that he dreaded his preaching appointments because he felt he lacked a vital message, and later became converted, in a plowed field, as he prayed to God asking how to teach others the way of salvation. He was led by God to his own need for salvation, later described as follows: "Midway in the field I could go no further, but sank in the field, crying Lord save me, I am lost . . . in a moment a stream of joy flowed over me." Quoted in Henry G. Spayth's, *History of the Church of the United Brethren in Christ* (Circleville, Ohio: United Brethren in Christ, 1851), pp. 29-30. The fact that the Mennonites of that time in Lancaster County were hesitant to accept the teaching of the "new Birth" is attested by Christian Newcomer, a onetime Mennonite and associate of Boehm (in Newcomer Journal, p. 13), and by the fact that Boehm was eventually banned from the bishopric of the Mennonite Church, for mixing with worldly elements.

[24] As a matter of interest, it appears that John Wesley prior to his death in 1791 was part of the beginnings of the Methodist Church (England), a body he never intended to found, at a time conterminous to the starting of the "River Brethren"—which was the first indigenous church body founded in the Colonies.

[25] Entire sanctification is defined as being saved from the power of sin. Wesley gave witness to the "glorification," emphasis of the sanctification component wherein one justified from the guilt of sin is saved from the judgment of sin.

[26] Quoted from a letter to D. Ray Hostetter dated March 7, 1974.

[27] In 1949 the Brethren in Christ became part of the Evangelical movement as they joined the recently organized National Association of Evangelicals (1943). The term "neo-evangelicals"

was used to describe the revamped movement. Several crucial changes in conservative theological thinking made the "neo" prefix applicable to the name. One difference (especially compared to Fundamentalists) was an acknowledgement of the importance of social action. Another difference was a new openness regarding diversity, including the recognition that "evangelicals" from all denominations were welcome to be part of the Association—they were members of His church. Both of these factors closely paralleled early Pietism. And their mutual emphases on conversion, biblicism, and evangelism demonstrated strong similarities between new-evangelicals and classical Pietists.

28 Roger E. Olson sets forth the characteristics of evangelical theology, which are clearly kindred to the theological characteristics of early Pietism, and therefore it is contended that Evangelicalism is the current theological expression that is most representative of early Pietism (see chapter entitled "Descriptive Designations to Identify Who the Brethren in Christ Are"). Olson's characteristics of evangelicalism are: 1) It looks to the Bible as the supreme norm of truth for Christian belief and practice: 2) It holds a supernatural worldview that is centered in a transcendent, personal God who interacts with, and intervenes in creation; 3) It focuses on the forgiving and transforming grace of God through Jesus Christ in an experience called conversion as the center of authentic Christian experience; 4) It believes that the primary task of Christian theology is to serve the church's mission of bringing God's grace to the whole world through proclamation and service. (From the article, "Christ the Controversialist," London, Tyndale Press, 1970, p. 46.)

Thus Pietism and Evangelicalism, in one sense might be considered a sort of generic conservative Protestant Christianity in that Evangelicalism is "new birth" Christianity just as conservative Christianity is "new birth" Christianity.

29 John R. Yeatts, and Ronald J. Burwell, "Brethren in Christ History and Life," Vol. XIX, No.1, p. 112.

30 A recent major work setting forth this view is that of W.R. Ward, emeritus professor of Modern History at the University of Durham, who in his book, *Early Evangelicalism: A Global Intellectual History, 1670-1789*, offers a genealogy of evangelicalism that transforms our understandings of its intellectual roots. He begins his story with the Pietist scholars who shared with what he called a common "thought world" that stood in opposition to the scholastic, Aristotelian character of Lutheran and Reformed Orthodoxy.

31 This earlier use of the term "evangelicals" initially referenced all Protestants in Europe, and in some parts of Europe this interpretation of Evangelical continues today. Current religious descriptions in South America also often refer to any non-Roman Catholic Christian group as being Evangelical. For additional consideration of twentieth and twenty-first century Evangelicalism see chapter 10.

32 *The Variety of American Evangelicalism*, University of Tennessee Press, 1991.

33 John R. W. Stott, *The Encyclopedia of Religion*, Mircea Eliade, Editor, Simon and Shuster, New York, Vol. 5, p. 91, refers to a movement that emphasizes (1) the Bible as authoritative and reliable; (2) eternal salvation as possible only by regeneration (being "born again"), involving personal trust in Christ and His atoning work; and (3) a spiritually transformed life marked by moral conduct, personal devotion, such as Bible reading and prayer, and zeal for evangelism and missions.

34 Evangelical Christianity as defined in "The Future of Evangelical Theology," *Christianity Today*, Feb. 9, 1998, p. 40.

35 McGrath, *A Passion for Truth: the Intellectual Coherence of Evangelicalism*, Intervarsity Press, Downers Grove, Ill., 1996.

36 The press in particular is to blame for many of the misunderstandings. They tend to attach evangelicals to conservative politics. Peggy Wehmeyer, a reporter with ABC News, who is

knowledgeable about religion, states that "what amazes me is the level of ignorance in most newsrooms about the affect of religion on people's lives." She contends that the press in general does not understand those individuals who put their faith above everything else. *USA Weekend*, Dec. 4-6, 1998, pp. 4-6.

[37] In Calvin's sermons he points out that he talked about predestination because it was a biblical term and to encourage those weaker in the faith.

[38] Calvin's leadership could be characterized as magisterial. He believed that political power should be used to bring about ecclesiastical reforms to the people within a given territory.

[39] The biblical ingredients of these views from the New Testament books of Colossians and John's Gospel were deemed by the Brethren in Christ to be simply guidance from the Bible, rather than Reformed insights. This understanding will be expanded in the next chapter.

[40] Centuries preceding the Reformed movement came into being, St. Thomas Aquinas, the noted theologian of the thirteenth century made an important contribution to Christian thought through his teaching on God's revelation. During the thirteenth century, Islam was spreading rapidly and Islamic philosophers became famous both inside and outside of the Islamic world. These philosophers were particularly known for teaching what was called "Double Truth Theory of Knowledge." This theory states that something can be true according to special revelation but false according to natural knowledge (and vice versa). Aquinas taught that we know some things from the Bible, such as the Trinity, we know other things by studying God's revelation in nature. An example of the latter would be our understanding of the complexity of the human body. Finally, he said there are some things we can know both from special revelation and from natural revelation. An example of this is our knowledge that God exists. Aquinas further contended that when both natural revelation and special revelation are rightly understood the truth learned from one will never contradict the truth learned from the other. The Christian worldview emphatically holds that all of reality centers around the existence of a personal, holy, and transcendent creator.

[41] While early Pietists demonstrated an increasingly holistic worldview in the sense that they were concerned about reforming society and providing social services to those around them, Pietism itself fell short of the reformed tradition in areas of discerning and perpetuating the philosophical and broad academic foundations needed for Christians to be of fullest impact on the general culture around them.

[42] The presuppositions are that Christianity is not merely a religion defined narrowly as personal piety, corporate worship, and being obedient to God, it is also an objective perspective on all of reality—a complete worldview—wherein all culture, all science, and all knowledge should be brought into subjection to the sovereignty of God, and be understood in the light of God. Key biblical sources for this view include Colossians 1:18 (cited by Messiah College trustees in the mid-twentieth century) and John 1:1-14, which can be considered the creation story as rendered in the New Testament. (This subject will be considered in more detail in chapter 3.)

[43] Both the Christian world view, and education with a Christian perspective are built firmly on the premise that revealed truth and discursive truth (the truths of nature) are God's.

[44] Most Christian colleges of arts and sciences (regardless of their theological background) that are serious about integrating the faith with all of life, including with all the academic disciplines (God's created truths—natural revelation—are joined with His revealed truths—special revelation) essentially follow these views that have been integral to the Reformed thought system. While Bible colleges, which began out of the revivals of the nineteenth century, recognized the importance of a strong service emphasis, their vision of translating Christian calling and service was primarily to church ministries or to missionary service. They did not fully internalize the concept that those preparing for other vocations are also called by God to His service for

the benefit of both society and the church. Nor did they sufficiently internalize the full importance of acknowledging that the truths of the varied academic disciplines are God's truths, as are His revealed truths.

[45] The "Two Kingdom Theory," as applied to the truths of God, is not cited as such in either the Denomination's Manual or the Messiah College Catalog.

[46] George Steiner, *Extraterritorial*, Harmondsworth: Penguin, 1969, p. 168.

[47] Pietist-oriented groups are often presumed to be more individualistic than those professing stronger communal commitments (faith is considered a personal or individual matter). It is interesting to note that in the Kauffman-Harder Study of 1975, two Pietist-Anabaptist groups, the Brethren in Christ and the Mennonite Brethren, scored considerably higher in their "faith under the communal canopy" rankings, than did Mennonite groups considered to be more exclusively Anabaptist, and generally thought to be more communally oriented. J. Howard Kauffman and Leland Harder, *Anabaptists Four Centuries Later: A Profile of Five Mennonite and Brethren in Christ Denominations*, Herald Press, 1975, pp. 96, 97.

[48] The Brethren in Christ church represents many nations (at least 16) and manifold cultures. If God should tarry—the United States Census Bureau projects that between 2050 and 2100 the United States won't have any racial or ethnic majority (A prediction of this sort is not available for Canada).

[49] *Translating the Message: the Missionary Impact on Culture*, Marynoll, NY: Orbiz, 1989.

[50] Quoted from the *Messiah College Bridge*, Fall 2006, p. 30.

[51] The Brethren in Christ view on culture in the twenty-first century would probably fit Niebuhr's "Christ Above Culture" classification whereby one confesses a Lord who is both of this world and the other world. H. Richard Niebuhr, *Christ and Culture*, Harper and Row, New York, 1951, p, 120.

[52] Culture, by definition, is the sum total of the ways of living built up by a group of human beings, and since individuals, as Brethren in Christ believe, are not above evil ways (they are born in sin), any diverse group that constitutes a given culture is also prone to error. The individual Christian should refrain from divergent cultural traits or patterns that are unchristian in nature.

[53] Christianity appears in different cultural forms in different centuries in different places. This is part of the argument Tertullian used to suggest that Christians are good citizens of Rome.

[54] For documentation see footnote clarification in chapter 9.

[55] Culture is a structure rather than content. Christianity has a conflict with the culture when it demands (as examples) non-Christian content such as abortion and tolerance for war.

[56] The *Confession* was signed by eight members of the first congregation, including the leader Jacob Engle. A copy of the translation *Confession* (Circa 1780) is in the Appendix of this work.

Chapter III

Theses Concerning Essential Truths of the Brethren in Christ

In recent times leaders of the Brethren in Christ church have become increasingly active in exploring issues related to denominational identity. A significant step in identity clarification was a denominational identity study conference, made up of church-wide participants, in November 1995 at Grantham, Pennsylvania. This was followed by a study conference on the subject of "the Brethren in Christ church and Culture" in October 1997 at the same location. In 1999 *Reflections on a Heritage: Defining the Brethren in Christ,* E. Morris Sider, editor, with an introduction by Moderator Warren L. Hoffman, was published by the Brethren in Christ Historical Society and Evangel Publishing House. Another contribution clarifying who the Brethren in Christ are followed in the year 2000 when ten core values of the denomination were examined in a work entitled *Focusing Our Faith*, edited by Terry Brensinger. These developments contribute much to understanding the identity of the denomination.

Outcomes of the above study conferences were positive in that excellent papers were delivered, new insights were shared, and a clearer understanding of the denomination emerged. But total clarity was not the result of all of the proceedings. Participants in the 1995 conference raised repeated questions, directly or by inference, as to whether the church is being faithful to principles of its origin. For example, concern was especially noted that adherence to Anabaptist principles is in decline, but at the same time studies were reported indicating that the Brethren in Christ are in the mainstream of Anabaptist denominations as to values and identity.[1]

The above discrepancy between scholarly studies and individual perceptions is only one indication of the need for continued study, precision, and care when dealing with identity issues. Varied partisan theological voices along with the suggestion from conference participants that action should be taken to affirm the church's identity[2] join with other factors to make it necessary to establish reliable interpretations to facilitate making identity-related decisions. On issues of importance where exactness cannot be obtained, depth of analysis and strong consensus regarding interpretations are needed to make prudent judgments.

There are two areas of uncertainty that call for more study and to which general accord is basic to resolving identity questions. Feelings of uncertainty regarding Brethren in Christ identity center on the following:

One: There is vacillation between accounts of primary theological sources forming who the Brethren in Christ are today. Are there two (Pietism and Anabaptism) or are there three (including Wesleyanism)? At the study conference on church identity a proposal was made that a fourth significant theological stream of major influence on the denomination should be considered (Evangelicalism).[3]

Two: The denomination's position on "separation from the world," one of three major distinctions of the denomination at its founding and the basic doctrine that seems to have undergone the most pronounced theological change, has drawn comparatively minor analysis and speculation as to whether an additional theological source influenced, informed, or comprehended the conceptual understandings for such change.

In order to improve confidence in the denomination's true identity and pursue future identity issues, it is necessary to seek reasonable consensus in at least two areas. They are to:

1. Ascertain the theological heritages that significantly contributed to the vision of the denomination at its founding and evaluate the extent of impact each gave to the vision.
2. Ascertain the theological streams or views that have modified the original vision, and evaluate the extent of impact of each on the vision.

Theological Heritages and the Founding Vision

There is strong agreement among Brethren in Christ historians that two essential traditions, Anabaptist and Pietist, contributed to the founding vision of the Brethren in Christ. Various authors have named denominational groups, rather than broader theological streams as being of primary influence on the fledgling body. Invariably those attributed as affecting the founding views of the Brethren in Christ, whether German Baptist Brethren,[4] Mennonites, Moravian Brethren, or revivalists such as the United Brethren in Christ,[5] all fit neatly into either the Pietist or Anabaptist traditions or both. The German Baptist Brethren stood within two traditions. The Mennonites, at the time of Brethren in Christ founding, were largely Anabaptist in their orientation. The remaining groups, the Moravian Brethren and the emerging United Brethren in Christ were more singularly Pietistic.

The comparative impact the two component traditions had on the newly formed body and its founding vision has received minor attention by historians of the church. Asa W. Climenhaga, the first to write a general history of the denomination, did observe that the German Baptist Brethren, later to be known as the Church of the Brethren, exhibited greater influence than any other denomination on the young church group. However, he offered only minor analysis to support his finding. His conclusion centered on the fact that the newly formed denomination adopted most of their practices and ordinances from the German Baptist Brethren (of special importance was the mode of baptism).[6]

Historian, C. O. Wittlinger, acknowledged that a strong tendency of the new body was to follow the German Baptist Brethren in form and practice when such differed from Mennonite patterns, but did not attempt to explain why this was the case.[7] However, it does seem important to note that preference for forms, practices, and ordinances were directed toward the more Pietistic denomination in both background and orientation. While the German Baptist Brethren had lost much of the evangelical spirit of their early roots, they continued to use the language of Pietists.[8]

Both Climenhaga and Wittlinger offered some analysis regarding the *Confession* document of the young group but refrained from evaluating it from the standpoint of denominational or theological influences. Therefore, because of this seeming void, an evaluation that attempts to assess the extent and intensity of the most prominent theological views of the body at its founding (Pietism and Anabaptism), as well as throughout different periods of its history, seems to be long overdue.

The earliest confession of faith, believed to be written around 1780,[9] gives penetrating insight into the aims and purposes held by the new group. The *Confession* may be divided into three theological parts—salvation and the conversion experience, the nature of the church, and the believer in relationship to the world.[10] These areas are examined further.

The Conversion Experience

Early members of the Brethren in Christ valued most highly their individually held but common experience of the "new birth." Conversion was to them the very essence of being a Christian and its most valid expression. Asa W. Climenhaga termed conversion-regeneration the most prominent teaching of the infant group.[11] Owen H. Alderfer called the provision and experience of salvation "central" to the confession of the body.[12]

The new group affirmed that "new birth" was more important than mere church membership since, following conversion; they could presumably have entered fellowships that held similar religious views (except for the emphasis on conversion).[13] But the new birth was the critical doctrine that hindered affiliation with the standing groups and it was apparently not to be compromised. According to C. O. Wittlinger, the Mennonites did not accept the heart-felt, life-changing conversion teachings of the new birth, and the German Baptist Brethren did not regard a personal, spiritual experience as normative for beginning the Christian life.[14]

The Brethren in Christ, as thorough Pietists, emphasized the sinfulness of humankind. Numerous times in the church's early *Confession* the typical Pietist ascription regarding the condition of humanity, "poor sinners," was used.[15] In addition, the early *Confession* of the "River Brethren" offers strong and clear statements regarding the fallen nature of humanity,[16] and the need for repentance.[17] It indicates a belief in the pervasive reality of sin. The Brethren in Christ, as did Pietists, believed strongly in the depravity of human beings.

However, when one looks at the religious and social context of early Brethren in Christ and reflects on the lives of Menno Simons, the sixteenth century Anabaptist after whom Mennonites were named, as well as Alexander Mack Sr., the early eighteenth century Pietistic German Baptist Brethren founder, the need for a new fellowship on the basis of the experience of the "new birth" seems somewhat incongruous. Both testified to encountering personal conversion experiences prior to leaving the "established" church. An obvious question arises—How is it that these pivotal leaders' distinctive conversion experience was lost or disregarded?

One response is that any declining sense of regard by some Mennonites in colonial America for the evangelical-type experience of Menno Simons centuries earlier needs to be seen in the light that Anabaptists in Europe had become quite diverse in their religious views.[18] Furthermore, Martin H. Schrag, an Anabaptist-oriented Brethren in Christ historian cited a source which characterized Mennonite spiritual ardor and mission as waning in colonial Pennsylvania and described the loss as being "associated with their sojourn to the new world and getting settled into the wilderness."[19] A seeming confirmation to this Schrag-reported condition was the fact that Martin Boehm, a leading late-eighteenth century preacher-evangelist (one who greatly affected the initial body that became River Brethren), was eventually banished by his Mennonite church co-leaders. This banishment seems to be confirmation that manifesting a warm spiritual intensity regarding the "new birth," at this particular time in history could be interpreted as being undesirable. Boehm, the banned evangelist, continued to preach. A decade or so later, he was named, along with William Otterbein, to be the first overseers of the newly formed United Brethren in Christ denomination.

Donald F. Durnbaugh, a Church of the Brethren historian, described that denomination's change from pronounced evangelical-type perceptions as simply a shift of the denomination from a position of "radical Pietism" in thought and practice, to the adoption of Anabaptist patterns of brotherhood. The "disciplined brotherhood," for the German Baptist Brethren in the latter part of the eighteenth century, called for obedience as the prerequisite to salvation.[20]

Also, it appears that the Mennonites, although acknowledging original sin, were less concerned about the guilt of original sin. As Luke Keefer, Jr., points out, "the Anabaptists never considered humankind merely as sinners apart from God's grace."[21] And as John Zercher observed, the Mennonites were more optimistic in their view of man and the human condition, and pessimistic in their view of the society.[22] To the Mennonites original sin was not counted as sin to a person until they willfully chose evil.[23] To deeply ingrained Pietists who believed in original sin, as did Brethren in Christ, this view might have been seen as tantamount to "birthright religion." The Anabaptist interpretation of salvation is that the "new birth" breaks the power of sin and dethrones it. With a lesser emphasis on the depraved nature of man, some Pietists may at times have perceived Mennonites as attaching more emphasis to socialization than to conversion and transformation.

In theological comparison with the German Baptist Brethren, it seems apparent that the early River Brethren believed the German Baptists to be insufficient to fully satisfy their perceived ministry needs.[24] The two groups stood firmly within the same traditions. The River Brethren adopted the German Baptist Brethren's ordinances and forms. Even though they chose a similar name (Brethren),[25] it appears that there may have been a doctrinal interpretation that stood in the way of joining the German Baptist Brethren. The River Brethren initially went to a German Baptist Brethren elder to ask him to baptize them in their mode. They took his counsel to do it as Alexander Mack had done when starting the German Baptist Brethren church (the first members baptized each other). However, River Brethren seemed to be at odds with German Baptist Brethren doctrine in one particular area,[26] "water-baptism regeneration." Their doctrine appeared to join discipleship with salvation (which was likely viewed as tending toward "works righteousness" instead of "free grace").

A "lack of full fit" between the two groups' doctrines shows in the *Confession* where it states that the believer is "reconciled . . . unto the Father. This, however, is all of grace and not of works."[27] Each group would probably have agreed that both a "new birth" (salvation) and a "new life" (obedience) were expected of the believer. The German Baptist Brethren foresaw the need for the potential believer to portray a "new life" (works and deeds) prior to regeneration, with the experience of regeneration accompanying water-baptism (a baptismal regeneration similar to the Lutheran belief—except that it applied only to adult believers). On the other hand, the River Brethren understood that the believer needed to have an assurance of salvation through grace (not by works) prior to water baptism, and that the "new birth" needed to transpire prior to baptism. It is presumed by this writer the "not of works"[28] reference was inserted into the *Confession* to clarify a difference with other church bodies (including the German Baptist Brethren) who viewed regeneration as transpiring at baptism. It seems that in using this confessional inference regarding "salvation by faith," and "through grace" instead of works, they did not have the Catholics in mind as did Martin Luther.[29]

The *Confession* affirms that water baptism is to follow the example of Jesus, but stresses that it is "an outward bond token" (a symbol) for the previously "newborn" in Christ.[30] It further emphasizes another difference with the German Baptist Brethren, "where there is a lacking (of the spirit) there always will remain a lack, and water cannot give or make good that which is wanting."[31]

In spite of these differences, River Brethren in the first century of their history seemed to have more in common with German Baptist Brethren than with other denominations.[32] It appears some of the German Baptist Brethren leaders were held in high regard by the Brethren in Christ. In comparison, ties with Mennonites, when judged by submissions and references in the church periodical, the *Evangelical Visitor*, were less frequent. This was likely because Mennonites, on the whole, were less Pietist disposed.[33]

The section on conversion and regeneration in the early *Confession* offers these lines: "We also acknowledge a growth in grace according to the Holy Scriptures, cleansed, sanctified, and saved by the washing of regeneration and renewing of the Holy Ghost."[34] These words and concepts are all classically Pietistic in character. In fact, it is generally recognized that this entire section of the original confession is thoroughly Pietistic and its placement at the beginning of the statement seems to add to the significance of this particular premise. Clearly, the conversion of the believer was central to the faith.

The Nature of the Church

The Brethren in Christ concept of the church from its founding has invariably been characterized as Anabaptist in form. There is much to be said for this view. It is affirmed in the early *Confession* by phrases such as "the body of Christ," "ask (for) brotherly advice," "submission to the church," "separation of disorderly members," and "the household of God according to Matthew 18."[35] The beginning church was intent on being a covenant community that testifies to the presence of the kingdom of God on earth. As community, the church sought to practice mutual accountability among its members. It also dealt with the sin of erring members in order to maintain the integrity and purity of the church. The Brethren sought to be God's visible church.

The notion of the church being visible is first and foremost a human condition wherein the church is viewed as the gathered community of believers handling certain missional and cultural challenges. But there is another dimension of the early Brethren in Christ understanding of the church that too frequently is overlooked. The church is invisible as well. It is a mystical body joined in Christ, born through the animating power of the Holy Spirit, it consists of all the true followers of Jesus around the world. Those who contend for the invisible church (as Brethren in Christ do) believe the expression "the body of Christ" is more than a metaphor for some social dynamic between Christ and His church. It is an ontological reality—just as Christ is ontologically real in the hearts of regenerated believers, He is present in His church through His Word and sacrament—the church in its essence is nothing other than the presence of Christ.

The early Brethren in Christ acknowledged Christ's promise, "Where two or three are gathered together in my name, there am I with them." They believed that Jesus was in their midst. Beyond their own spiritual gatherings, the denomination from its beginning, in line with Pietistic tendencies, portrayed a belief in God's invisible church[36] consisting of all the redeemed—those who trust Jesus as Savior and follow Him as Lord regardless of church affiliation.[37]

While the Brethren in Christ church from its inception to the 1950s practiced closed communion (an Anabaptist characteristic), and its members surely expected high standards of professing Christians (adherence to biblical precepts, including witnessing to a personal conversion), they acknowledged members from heart- and life-change groups as being true Christians (a Pietist characteristic). Indications of this include their initial seeking to have baptism administered to them from at least one "outside" believer[38] and the use of hymns written by German Baptist Brethren, Moravian Brethren, and later many other Christians.[39] Also, early issues of the *Evangelical Visitor* freely reported information about Christian leaders from other groups and frequently referred to members of such groups as "brother" and "sister." The *Visitor* also included articles about other Christians who represented diverse churches and even gave coverage about German Baptist Brethren colleges.[40]

The primary indication of a Pietistic understanding of the church, however, resides in the text of the confession of faith. It states that in order to accomplish "growth in grace" it is necessary to have "private gatherings . . . where the penitent souls can confess and relate their experience" so that "God in their heart will increase their faith and their confidence be strengthened."[41] This generalized description, however, should not be interpreted to mean that nearby Anabaptist church bodies at the River Brethren beginnings totally failed to care for spiritual aspects of the faith. The Mennonite churches of the area, when compared to the Pietist revivalists, it appears, were somewhat tepid or lukewarm in spiritual matters during this era. On the other hand, the early Brethren in Christ in their "private gatherings for spiritual strengthening" (as described in the Brethren in Christ *Confession of Faith)* corresponded well with the early Pietist meetings called conventicles, which is surely how the mother congregation of the River Brethren began. These were likely the pattern for other newly planted congregations that followed. Furthermore, it was not merely the small size of the groups that corresponded with early Pietism—it was their commitment to devotional sharing that placed them closely in line with the early Pietists.

Another churchly function that is Pietistic in character is that of mission and outreach. The early *Confession* admonished that there be "public gatherings where the Word is preached and the people are exhorted to repent."[42] The cited objective for the public meetings was to have people "saved by the washing of regeneration and renewing of the Holy Ghost." Even though the holding of "revival meetings" was not formally approved by the denomination until 1872, it is apparent that some form of public evangelism and preaching was intended from the time of inception of the brotherhood, and indeed, the church's growth indicates that it was carried out.[43]

The final sentence of the *Confession* seems to affirm the "public gatherings" method of outreach when it says "We wish from God the all highest, that He may build and plant and keep His church in healthy growth (underline added), and that we also may be green branches on the true vine, and remain so in all the length of eternity, through Jesus Christ. Amen."[44] The words "and plant" indicates that their evangelism was to go beyond their own families. This church-growth-oriented closing to the *Confession* is highly Pietistic and was borne out in the early Brethren in Christ as they "colonized" to new areas[45] and then sent visiting ministers from the established districts to help maintain and build the new church.

The Brethren in Christ from their outset were inwardly focused toward purity of the church. They were a gathered and disciplined community. But they were also outwardly focused toward calling others to repentance so as to build the church wherein the Holy Spirit enters every individual soul as a cell in the mystical body of Christ. They did not emphasize differences between the visible and the invisible church. They seemed to realize that both dimensions were necessary. In true Pietist fashion it was recognized that being mindful only of the visible church can lead to the trap of thinking all that is necessary for salvation is to be in good standing with the church. While this dimension was important to them, they also recognized that the true church was composed of those who were renewed by the power of the Spirit.

This leads to **sub-thesis 1**: *Contrary to some prior interpretations or assumptions that the nature of the early Brethren in Christ church was Anabaptist in character, it is affirmed that the understanding of the church, according to the early* Confession, *was both Anabaptist and Pietist at one and the same time.*

Separation from the World

The third theological part of the *Confession* dealt with members and their relationship to the world. It gives specific direction regarding marriage by stating an expectation that both partners be from within the church, prohibits service "in worldly government offices," and forbids the "taking of oaths." The "sword," "revenge," and "self-defense" were also forbidden.[46]

The "unspiritual" items forbidden as being worldly, in this initial document, seem rather few in number for a group that took seriously the idea of separation. It is interesting that in light of the church's later stands on plain dress no connection was made in the early *Confession* between apparel and the concept of separation from the world. The lines of the *Confession* that point out, "Where the teachings of our Lord Jesus and that of the Apostles are silent, there we will be silent also," likely were the reason for lack of specifics at this time. Also, the flood of newer devices for general living, but later were declared "inconsistent" (worldly), were yet to be developed in the industrial revolution.

Both Anabaptism and Pietism in certain respects were founded as "world negating" Christian movements. They were counter to culture and, even though early leaders of these movements were virtually all learned individuals, they critiqued reason as being secondary to illumination, and frequently devalued parts of learning.[47] For Pietism there was an anti-worldly separation of the church as they moved apart into conventicles. But the Pietists' "break" from the world was not as complete as it was for Anabaptists.[48] Pietists, with help from God, sought to transform the world. They held to a discriminating separation from anti-spiritual worldliness, rather than near total severance from society and culture, as was the case for most Anabaptists.

The early Brethren in Christ position on separation from the world appears to have been rather complete (even though the forbidden items in the initial *Confession* overlooked attire, and other specifics were added at a later time). Because of the near-total break with the world, it seems most valid to connect the third part of the *Confession* rather closely to Anabaptism. Add to this a review of the items forbidden in the section: the sword, revenge, taking oaths, and government office, and we see a strong Anabaptist influence prevailed on attitudes toward the world.

This analysis and assessment leads to the conclusion that the first part of the early *Confession* about new birth is highly Pietistic; the next section on the church is both Anabaptist and Pietist in function and form; and the last theological part, separation from the world, is primarily Anabaptist. The doctrinal views seem to be rather evenly divided between the two traditions.

But, in fairness to history, there is an additional factor that should be considered when weighing the theological "beliefs" that constituted the initial vision. It seems proper to assign extra consideration to the theological view(s) which caused the new denomination to be created. The church itself was begun in a Pietist revival. Simply stated, if they had been solely or dominantly committed to Anabaptism, they would have likely joined the Mennonites. They were not. In a more divided way, if they desired to be Pietist and partly Anabaptist, they likely would have become part of the German Baptist Brethren. They did not. It appears they were more Pietist-inclined than were the German Baptist Brethren.

If one analyzes the above Pietist-Anabaptist conclusion doctrinally, the Pietist characteristics seem to mount. Consider the following: First, a "new birth" experience, which the early Brethren in Christ commonly held, was the causal factor for their coming together as a spiritual fellowship. Second, the Pietist interpretation that all are "poor sinners" needing redemption and regeneration was the controlling doctrine which likely precluded union with normative Anabaptist communions. (At this time Mennonites tended to display a lesser consciousness regarding an inherent sin factor.) Third, the prominent place that spiritual conversion received in the early *Confession* (cited first, which denotes its critical importance). Fourth, add the fact that the name of the group was Pietistic in character (Brethren).[49] From their start, they were evaluated by their contemporaries. "Outsider" appraisals of them were strongly Pietist—according to varied monikers tagged to the group including: Brethren, New Brethren, and River Brethren. In addition, E. Morris Sider, a careful scholar, and clearly the most productive writer on Brethren in Christ history, concluded that "Pietism was the most decisive factor in the formation of the Brethren in Christ."[50]

In summary, if one adds to the above that the early Brethren in Christ showed a distinct preference for copying ordinances and modes of the German Baptist Brethren, who were born in Pietism and continued to perpetuate its theological language, the influence center of gravity seems clearly in the direction of Pietism as being more determinative as they started a new body.

This evaluation leads to the expression of **sub-thesis 2**: *Although devoted to both traditions, Pietism and Anabaptism, their initial founding as a new body appeared to be driven and motivated by their deep Pietist inclinations.* While this conclusion could be considered duplicating Morris Sider's judgment cited above, I choose to word it more strongly. In light of the arguments offered, I believe the Pietist tradition was most determinative of who the Brethren in Christ were at their time of initial founding.[51]

This thesis raises a question as to the meaning of the word *determinative*. It is interpreted as involving two points: (1) It was Pietism and a local sense of spiritual revivalism that provided the impetus for founding the River Brethren, and (2) Pietism emphasized the *sine qua non* of the Christian faith for the denomination—in that, integral to the Christian faith is salvation from sin and regeneration of the believer. These are concerns that are considered prior and are consistently emphasized as being essential to the concept of not only Pietism, but also of being a genuine Christian.

A Wesleyan Supplement to the Founding Vision

A denomination's initial vision can become modified as time passes. For the sake of integrity, it is important that one look beyond the starting theological emphases of a body to examine if there has been an ensuing shift from the originally subscribed beliefs. It follows that any substantive changes in vision of a given denomination should be traced from the founding times to current times. Several questions might be kept in mind: How have the doctrinal commitments of the original vision changed? What are the theological or philosophical rationales that lie behind these changes in doctrine or practice?

Unquestionably, the two root heritages, Anabaptism and Pietism, were of determinative influence in shaping the Brethren in Christ. But, it appears none of the scholars who have done major historical writing about the denomination have established, or even attempted to offer, a rationale that a third primary theological stream significantly shaped the denomination. However, the assumption that there is a third major heritage persists. The theological tradition of Wesleyanism is often added to the mix of formative streams, when the denomination's identity is addressed.

There are many similarities between the core character of the Brethren in Christ and Wesleyanism. The community accountability and mutuality along with spiritual edification of the early "private gatherings" for the Brethren in Christ correspond to the early Methodist "class meetings." The Wesleyan concern to meet social needs and the developing social conscience of the Brethren in Christ parallel each other. Resemblances are especially strong in interpretations of the conversion experience and the ministry of the Holy Spirit in the life of the believer. But these similarities have their roots in Pietism, which surely affected both John Wesley and the initial group of Brethren in Christ believers during the same era.

The one doctrine of the Brethren in Christ typically classified as Wesleyan in character is "entire" sanctification, also referred to as "a second work of grace." This doctrine emphasizes the "cleansing of the believer" from sin and the attainment of "Christian perfection." But each of these concepts: sanctification, cleansing from sin, and perfectionism were not new to the spiritual beliefs and vocabulary of classical Pietists. Johann Arndt, the earliest of the Pietists, was quoted in the Brethren in Christ church periodical, dated October 1894 as follows:

> For truth and saving faith reneweth the whole man, purifieth the spirit, sanctifieth the soul and maketh clean the heart. It knitteth this when cleansed, and uniteth it fast to God; and the heart when it is thus purged and set free from earthly desires, then soareth easily heavenward.[52]

This quote from Arndt was appropriately published during a time when the process of heart purification, cleansing, and sanctification was being debated in the denomination. It indicates that the promise of holy living was imbedded in Pietist theology. The holiness messages in the writings of the first Pietist, Johann Arndt, in the seventeenth century, resemble the themes of a modern-day, holiness preacher.[53]

The doctrine of sanctification was Brethren in Christ belief from their inception. The church's *Confession* stated: "We also acknowledge a growth in grace, according to the Scriptures, cleansed, sanctified, and saved by the washing of regeneration and renewing of the Holy Ghost."[54] But a new sanctification dimension was added in the 1890s when "entire" sanctification was introduced to parts of the Brotherhood. The fresh aspect was the attainment of complete sanctification, God imparting holiness to the believer, through a second "work" of grace.

From 1890 to 1910, sanctification as a second experience of grace, and sin eradication for the believer became the objects of considerable debate at sessions of the annual General Conferences.[55] The doctrine of "entire" sanctification was eventually approved by the denomination at the General Conference of 1910. There is no record of discussions at General Conference floor surrounding the question of holiness during this two-decade period. It could be that one reason the brotherhood experienced difficulty accepting the "second definite work of grace" was because they sensed that the church body from its origin was committed to a "living faith"—a deep spiritual life—interpreted to be a direct relationship with the living God, and to divine enablement.[56] The church's position on sanctification was amended. According to Luke Keefer, Jr., the denomination used American-holiness-camp-meeting language—it has similarities with Wesleyan theology, but it is not identical to Wesley's own formulation.[57]

The denomination describes sanctification today as "a full surrender and commitment of the will to Christ, (which) results in freedom from the control of sin and empowerment to the holy life." Alongside this statement, and in some contrast to it, the denomination continues to state a belief that sanctification is an "ongoing journey of yielding to God and growing in grace."[58] This latter interpretation is consistent with the explanation of "sanctification" given in the early *Confession* of the Brethren in Christ. In addition to using the word "sanctified," the original *Confession* contained expressions like: the "renewing of the Holy Spirit," the Christian being "cleansed," and "a growth in grace." These expressions affirm that the doctrine of sanctification was part of the church's belief system from its beginnings. The new understanding, an experience of "entire" sanctification, came as a fresh insight a century after the denomination started. Therefore, it is a supplement enriching the doctrine of sanctification—which is rooted in Pietism. The introduction of the doctrine of "entire" sanctification did not displace the early view. Instead it acknowledged that the seeker of Christian perfection could experience a divine act wherein the control of sin could be overcome.

Beyond this nourishment of a previously-held doctrine, there appear to be no additional doctrines or trappings of the denomination that can be confidently attributed to the Wesleyan tradition. Camp meetings, the altar of prayer ("mourner's bench"), and "revival meetings" were phenomena often associated with Wesleyan-type evangelistic efforts, but such trappings were not exclusively Wesleyan in their origin. Also, the occasional offering of praise to God by either "shouting" or manifesting physical demonstrations has mixed historic precedent. There were and are no conclusive influences on the denomination that can be attributed solely to Wesleyan influence.[59]

Since Wesleyan theology was strongly influenced by Pietism, wherein Christian perfectionism is a spiritual ideal, and since the Wesleyan emphasis on "entire sanctification" nourished rather than replaced the church's standing doctrine, and since the Brethren In Christ expression of the doctrine of sanctification, in more technical terms, may not be Wesleyan (more influenced by the American Holiness Movement), and since other Wesleyan manifestations in the Brethren in Christ have not been proven, this writer concludes **sub-thesis 3:** *The theological tradition of Wesleyanism does not warrant an ascription of being either a primary or root heritage of the Brethren in Christ.* Instead, Wesleyanism, a theological stream within the Pietist tradition should more accurately be considered a "deeper-life advocate/sharer" of the holiness tradition that contributed to strengthening the Brethren in Christ theological synthesis.[60]

The writer's failure to endorse Wesleyanism as a primary shaper of Brethren in Christ theology should not be viewed as a signal to draw away from current Wesleyan influence or reduce the denomination's emphasis on seeking Christian perfection. Nor should it be viewed as an indicator that the denomination is not sufficiently oriented toward the holiness doctrine. However, the recent decision of Christian Holiness Partnership to cease being an association because of lack of interest cautions that single doctrinal emphases, regardless of their merit, may fail to draw wide denominational participation in the future.[61] The lessening cross-denominational exposure to and visibility of the emphasis of being Wesleyan, in this writer's mind heightens the above conclusion that two primary theological traditions, rather than three, have been substantial shapers of the Brethren in Christ today.

Evaluating the Influence of Evangelicalism

The question has been raised in chapter 2 as to whether Evangelicalism has been sufficiently influential in forming the identity of the Brethren in Christ to be considered a major shaper of the denomination.[62] In 1949 the denomination joined the National Association of Evangelicals, an organization comprised of conservative and moderate denominations and churches committed to fostering evangelical ministries.

When one evaluates the impact of a theological movement on a given denomination, a logical starting point is to examine the primary doctrines that the movement promulgates. The diverse groups that constitute the National Association of Evangelicals are committed to the historic Christian faith. While no exclusive claims can be attached to the term "evangelical," several foundational concerns form the message to which the movement is attuned. Evangelicals have clearly shown themselves to be committed to the authority of the Bible, to conversion, and to evangelism—all concerns that coincide with that of the early Pietists.[63] In joining the National Association of Evangelicals, Brethren in Christ identified with other Pietist dispositions such as spiritual fellowship with other believers, and they affirmed a concern for social action (differing in this respect with more exacting Fundamentalists).

It appears indisputable that during the past half-century the evangelical community has been important in supporting the values and improving the ministries of the Brethren in Christ. The church's connection with the National Association of Evangelicals is only a small part of that influence. Evangelical books, magazines, journals, seminaries, para-church organizations, and college and mission associations have been meaningful to the denomination. These varied mediums and organizations have assisted Brethren in Christ as they seek to minister in today's varied cultures. The church body has found common cause with and benefit from evangelicalism. On the other hand, Brethren in Christ have been of direct witness to the broader movement regarding world peace and reconciliation concerns.

Two qualifying statements are offered regarding the denomination's evangelical identity: First, while the church is closely connected with evangelicals theologically, they have not identified with political causes or special-interest groups that go under a banner of "Christian" or "evangelical," whether to the right or to the left. Second, as members of the National Association of Evangelicals (United States) and Evangelical Fellowship of Canada,[64] the benefits accrued to denomination appear to be largely strategic and informing regarding mission in the changing times, rather than influencing the denomination in any new theological direction.[65]

The rationale for evangelicalism not wielding a decisive theological influence on the Brethren in Christ follows: Both historic Pietism and Evangelicalism have been committed to the ultimate relationship of the individual to Christ. The essence of evangelicalism is a continuation of the key truths of Pietism.[66] Therefore, because of similar values and truths, evangelicalism has not modified the church's understanding of the Christian faith. In a case like this when similar traditions influence a group in parallel ways at different times, it seems that an original shaping makes the more decisive impact. This later influence of Evangelicalism is reinforcing rather than foundational in its effect.

This leads to consideration of **sub-thesis 4**: *The Evangelical movement has exerted facilitating, informing, collaborative, and reinforcing influence on the Brethren in Christ, rather than contributing any new theological insights that changed the content of its* Manual of Doctrine and Government.[67] The one exception to the *Manual* change proviso was the effect on the denomination as it discarded certain legalisms of an Anabaptist character, i.e., "separation from the world." Separation was previously viewed as a highly important doctrine. However, according to new insights being viewed as more ethos in their character there was a calling for doctrinal amendments to the *Manual* in order to remove certain requirements thought to verge on being legalistic.[68]

In connection with **sub-thesis 4**, it should also be noted that early chapters of this work tie the identity of the denomination quite closely to its initial doctrinal values, while later chapters deal with church identity according to other analyses. Evangelicalism, in historic respects, is an extension of Pietism,[69] and Pietism is expressed in the idiom of the centrist form of evangelicalism—"neo-evangelicalism."[70] General theological discourse tends to steer clear of using Pietism for describing current attributes and truths that are defining of the Brethren in Christ. However, evangelicalism in its best light is descriptive of these truths, it therefore seems reasonable, if not obligatory, that Brethren in Christ be referenced as an evangelical group, even though no new theological insights from that source have been added to the church's *Manual*.

Part of the Original Vision is Revised

As theological changes to the Brethren in Christ founding vision are reviewed, section one of the early *Confession*, conversion and regeneration, has remained rather constant except for the added understanding that Christian perfection can be attained as God grants entire sanctification to those fully surrendered to Him. The concept of the church, section two of the *Confession*, continues to be quite similar to that of the founding period. The third core section of the *Confession*, "separation from the world," on the other hand, has undergone significant change over the denomination's history.

The wide variety of "worldly" items which were designated as being "inconsistent" by the church are clear indications of the denomination's seriousness about its "separation from the world" theme. Items deemed to be inconsistent for Christians changed with the times. Some initial prohibitions of the church were deleted, with other directives added and then later withdrawn.[71] After continued wrestling with "separation" issues in the first half of the twentieth century—especially to uniform apparel for men and women, there came a major attitudinal transition in the church body. The denomination's overall attitude toward the world and general culture also encountered significant change.

This attitudinal shift was accompanied by a new set of understandings about the world. The church moved from pronounced separation (fleeing the world), to a non-conformed stance of being "in the world, but not of the world." Obedience to God was beginning to be interpreted as a Christian presence in the world so as to be "salt," "light," and "leaven."

The change of orientation from pronounced separation to non-conformity was not abrupt. It appears to have evolved over a number of years and differed in time and place within the denomination. There became less emphasis on what to be separated from, and higher expectations as to what the Christian should be separated unto—set apart, but unto the gospel of God, and unto Jesus Christ. This change put increased value on making connections and less emphasis on divisions. Separation came to be no longer characterized by isolation, meager social interchange, and the perpetuation of uniform personal appearance. Even though use of the term "separation" continued, a new discernment directed toward what is right and good came into play.

This dawning of a new perspective was more than a different slant on separation. New biblical insights were unfolding a new world and life view. As Anabaptists, the church's concept of separation was based on two distinct realities—the kingdom of God and the kingdom of Satan manifested historically in the church and the world. The church was good and other structures and things were bad. The church tended toward a dualism that compartmentalized life into the spiritual and the ungodly. As Pietists they had held their guard high against the dangers of scholastic Christianity. As Anabaptists they kept isolated from society. But, it was becoming apparent that not everything outside the church was necessarily bad.

Missions and church outreach were imperatives to be carried out for the Pietist-inclined group. But, as cultural and international borders were crossed, new questions were developing about the strict interpretation of non-conformity and separation issues. "The Great Commission" was a command from God that might be more effectively fulfilled by reducing restrictions on engagement with the world. In addition, their "evolving vision" on separation was starting to consider more than the singular objective of seeking those who were spiritually lost. While the Christian's citizenship was still in the kingdom of heaven, people in the church were beginning to wonder about His will being "done on earth as it is in heaven." There was a growing sense that Christians as "light" and "leaven" needed to increasingly assist in caring for others and for the world around them. An historic Pietist principle of "hope for the world" was germinating.

For more than a century the Brethren in Christ assumed little responsibility for the general society and no apparent responsibility for improvement of the culture. Anabaptism was culture-denying. The church which had considered itself a safe shelter from the world turned a corner in the late nineteenth century and the early twentieth century. A new insight emerged—the church as a refuge from the world about them came to be viewed as a betrayal of its calling. As a result, the church started a "rescue and benevolent home" for the aged, opened several orphanages, and started an educational institution to train missionaries and provide other study opportunities. Also, through its mission programs in several British colonies of Africa and India, the church took on broader social and cultural responsibilities as part of efforts to "extend the kingdom of God."

While "the Great Commission" provided substantial biblical guidance for moderating any propensity toward isolation that may have accompanied their separation doctrine, a new biblical perspective informed them that the world was not entirely evil. The biblical basis for a revised Christian worldview that would come to have significant impact on the Brethren in Christ was affirmed in a corporate action, not made by the Brethren in Christ corporate body, but instead was incorporated in a resolution acted upon by one of the denomination's colleges. It was made in by the Messiah College board of trustees, the governing body for the oldest and largest church educational institution, when it adopted the motto, "Christ Preeminent." Although this resolution was not an official denominational act, it was a determination by a board made up entirely of Brethren in Christ members and, as such, held both direct and indirect implications for the church as a whole.[72]

The college's new motto was taken from Colossians 1:15-20 (KJV). Verse 16 of the passage says "by Him were all things were created," and verse 17 adds "by Him all things consist." Verse 18 gives the motto basis, "that in all things He might have the preeminence." This text sets forth that Christ is one with God as the creator, and that all truths are His truths. A new insight was dawning—truth from God is available to humans outside of God's special revelation. This text and the motto were the theological and philosophical grounding for Messiah College to broaden its offerings and to become a college of arts and sciences.[73]

One consequence of the "Christ Preeminent" interpretation was that God's created world came to be viewed not as evil, not as Satan's realm, but as God's good creation. A further implication was that even though the two-kingdom theory is descriptive of spiritual domains, and of the millennium to come when Christ shall reign, this figurative language is not well suited for categorizing and dividing truth in the present world. The Colossians text gave support for the denomination's emerging worldview. It enlarged the church's vision of the world, and broadened its understandings about God's truth. Both concepts, special and general revelation were beginning to be accepted. The earlier definition of the term, "the world," was modified.

This shifting of the Brethren in Christ vision regarding "separation from the world" raises a question as to how the alterations affected the original two-part synthesis of the denomination. In the case of early Anabaptism the answer seems obvious. The transition fit less with its long-held Anabaptist views that were premised on a separation doctrine somewhat allied to a visible church concept. Nor was it compatible with a two-kingdom theory. Movement away from pronounced separation ran counter to certain historic Anabaptist views.[74]

As for Pietist views, the separation changes appear to be more readily accommodated. Early Pietists emphasized a unified worldview even though they usually separated themselves from the political realm (believing the way to change society is through God changing men's hearts). Also, while Pietists voiced opposition to evils in the fallen world, they looked for transformation of the world to be accomplished by God's work in converted lives. Therefore, the newly revised worldview was more consistent with Pietist views.

In one sense, alterations in the "separation from the world" concept could be partially described as a shift from an Anabaptist to a Pietist interpretation of separation. But this would not account for the foundational premises that accompanied the shift—especially those pertaining to defining "truth"—which is not a Pietist premise. For the source of these new views about the world and truth, one needs to look outside the denomination's primary traditions. However, in looking to other traditions to determine an added source of influence, there are dangers. Any admission that external "incursions" have penetrated a denomination is generally met with great reluctance. "Outsiders" can be viewed as encroachers on the tradition(s). Naturally, under these conditions one needs to apply special care in proposing a new thesis.

As one reviews the separation and worldview changes that transpired in the brotherhood since 1950, deciding on the source of the changes may seem easy to discover. Wouldn't one first look at the company closely associated with the denomination? It is not that simple. The denomination's formal contacts and its informal circulation are quite diverse. Fraternal exchanges and cooperative efforts have been distributed among Anabaptist, Holiness, and Evangelical meetings and fellowships. Also, it appears that no single tradition was sought out or granted preferred association during the period when the changes were made.

Therefore, pinpointing specific external theological impact on the denomination seems out of the question. As one looks internally it appears that a combination of new biblical understandings and a growing sense that legalisms were hampering ministry of the church were the primary factors leading to change.

The church now possessed a clear biblical basis for the new views (Colossians 1:15-20 and John 1:1-14).[75] With such a grounding, and assuming that the changes originated internally from fresh biblical insights, a question might be—why should one give further effort to determine if the thought system of a theological tradition is related to these new concepts of the world and of truth? However, in the interest of identity clarification, this question should not be ignored. Even though the change appears to have been more through internal factors, and the origins of the understandings connected to a Christian worldview are mixed (including Catholic and Pietist contributions, among others), this writer proposes the denominational worldview shifts made during the latter half of the twentieth century, had their most lucid interpretive sources in Reformed ideas.[76]

The Brethren in Christ have never been closely associated with corporate groups of the Reformed tradition. Perhaps any relationship could be characterized as "we" "they" in view of Reformed Calvinistic theology. In sharp contrast, the tenets of the Brethren in Christ are strongly Arminian. For this reason one's confidence increases that the new interpretations, deemed to be prominent in the thought system of the Reformed tradition, were biblical and consistent with internal Brethren in Christ views, rather than an "outside" incursion.

In granting that the Christian worldview and life is stressed by the Reformed tradition, one need not wonder about other potential baggage such as curbing man's free will or possibly devaluing obedience to God's truths becoming newly adopted as marks of the Brethren in Christ. A worldview that avoids dualism and a principle that all truth centers in Jesus Christ are quite different from issues of human choice or the security of the believer. Since foundational groundings for the new views of world and truth are mediated through its colleges, a short analysis of the theological traditions perpetuated by the church's colleges is presented.[77]

Brethren in Christ Colleges Transition to a Christian World and Life View

Messiah College in Grantham, Pennsylvania, and Upland College in Upland, California, from their founding to well into the 1940s, provided secondary education and some programs in higher education that were quite Pietist in nature. The initial name of Messiah Bible School and Missionary Training Home clearly marks it as being Pietist in purpose. Beulah College (later called Upland) had similar programs to Messiah and would fit the same classification. They possessed additional common traits such as strong emphases on evangelism, Fall and Spring revival meetings, parietal rules, regular dorm prayer meetings, and daily chapel services, all of which were Pietist in nature.[78] At both colleges the co-curricular and curricular lives of students were thoroughly Pietistic.

Theological influences can have significant bearing on the degree of community that exists within a college. Although success in maintaining a sense of community is difficult to assess, both Messiah and Upland, (as small colleges) perpetuated community relationships among their staff, as well as between staff and students. A deep love for each other (koinonia) was manifested. They had a common religious commitment.

The sense of community at the church's colleges could be classified differently at various times in their histories. The relative composition of each community had some bearing on whether it tended to be Anabaptist or Pietist in character. An Anabaptist definition of community would correlate best with collegiate times that were more sectarian and denominationally focused. On the other hand, Pietistic expressions of community evolved at the colleges as students from other communions demonstrated a heartfelt and obedient faith in Christ. Both colleges became increasingly open to other Christians and this open spirit was one factor preparing the denomination for potential transition in the area of separation.

Another way that colleges presented themselves as Christian was through curricula content and their success in integrating faith with learning. This is where Reformed understandings enter the picture for both the colleges and the church. A brief statement about the Christian world and life view, a holistic view that is basic to Christian liberal arts colleges, is offered.

Most Bible colleges[79] treat truths of special revelation (God's Word) and those of general revelation (God's creation) in somewhat of a dualism. Christian liberal arts colleges, on the other hand, invariably treat all of God's truth as coming together in Jesus Christ (according to Colossians). The integration of faith with learning is axiomatic to presenting a "Christian worldview."

Some Christian colleges (as well as denominations and congregations) fall short in conveying an adequate Christian world and life view. At times there is a tendency to see life in a dualism or to compartmentalize the faith (in terms of God's truths and one's personal commitment). Christian colleges and individual scholars in particular can often learn a great deal about the integration of Christian faith with the various academic fields from scholars who have studied in the Reformed tradition, since such scholars have typically done serious integration work in their respective academic disciplines.[80]

As Reformed proficiency in integrating the Christian faith with academic disciplines is acknowledged, it by no means implies that Christian liberal arts colleges in general representing varied denominations need to consider hyphenating the Reformed religious tradition to that of their own founding tradition(s). For the Brethren in Christ and its colleges, however, the case may be different because of its pronounced change related to separation from the world tendencies that were to come about within the church and its institutions. The colleges made such pronounced transitions that it well-nigh requires that a philosophical or theological source be identified in order to validate its magnitude. The church for nearly two centuries, and its colleges for three to five decades, had functioned according to understandings that emphasized dualistic realms, and "separation from the world" perceptions. There had been little or no previous hint that for Christians to render full service to previously divided realms that Christian truths should ideally be integrated into a world and life view. For the Brethren in Christ church and its two young colleges, vast changes were in process.

Messiah and Upland colleges, in the early years of their baccalaureate offerings, were surely weaker in faith and learning integration areas (Reformed) than in other areas—the student's personal faith and practice (Pietism)—and providing a community characterized by love, and a separated life (Anabaptist). This does not insinuate that students failed to get a sound education. From the start the colleges required students to take courses in the humanities and sciences, but these views were not brought together as God's truths. As the two colleges broadened their liberal arts offerings there was increasing effort to set forth a Christian worldview. Both colleges became much more serious about integrating the Christian faith with learning—integrating them instead of projecting biblical truth and the academic disciplines as being separate entities—all of truth centering in Jesus Christ.

Reference was made to Messiah College adopting the motto, "Christ Preeminent" (in all things). This Scriptural admonition was the ground for deepening its academic offerings and adding new fields of study. The Upland motto, "Vision for Service" also conveyed wholeness and bridging-to-the-world themes. Service was intended for God and others, and the scope was enlarged to serve societal and cultural needs (a reaching beyond the "walls").

Both colleges believed in a liberated mind that must be renewed by Christ.[81] A liberated mind tends to question barriers and divisions. The colleges also sought to have each student wrestle with what it meant to bring Christianity into one's chosen vocation. As a result, the college's students began to consider diverse fields of study and increasingly began to enter graduate education. The more lofty aims of these colleges were not fully attained in every student, but still a high measure of student development was accomplished. In turn the learning often translated into a broadening that produced in graduates a newly felt or latent sense of tension about the church's separation doctrine.

Faculties of the two colleges exhibited a consistent loyalty to the denomination. Dress patterns varied and thus indicated a span of commitment to that part of separation. But those who served in the church's schools did not promulgate change, nor did the respective faculty personnel exhibit contentiousness regarding separation issues. It appears the church's colleges were sending forth many students who had been sufficiently liberated in their minds and commitments to join with others in their home congregations in considering revision to separation policies of the denomination.[82]

In the middle of the twentieth century, the denomination decided to adopt a new interpretation of "separation from the world" as it acted to remove restrictions perceived to be legalistic, relaxed guidelines thought to be inwardly focused, and built bridges to other Christians by joining trans-denominational associations. Without design or duplicity to move from the basic concept of separation, the church's colleges became a contributing force in leading the denomination toward significant change by offering biblical and philosophical foundations that altered its belief system. The colleges were agents of a new set of world and truth views just as the several camp meetings served in spreading the doctrine of entire sanctification.

Upland College closed its doors during the mid-'60s. As Messiah College developed and grew its emphasis on faith-learning integration became intensified. One indication of this turn in direction was a significant strengthening of the faculty and offerings in the area of philosophy, including an advancing of the requirements that all students needed to fulfill in the field of philosophy. This was quite a difference from what historic Pietists offered at Halle University. Another indication was that additional majors were introduced that helped to round out its offerings as a Christian college of arts and sciences. Messiah College, throughout its history, diligently endeavored to follow its founding church. However, in the area of the wholeness of truth the college moved into a lead role.

The cohesion of these world and truth insights from Colossians was not always given priority attention by either early Anabaptists or Pietists. Attaching the Reformed tag to such views signifies only that these understandings are integral to the theological thought of that tradition. Just the same, there was a growing awareness within the college and the church regarding the wholeness of truth, the importance of the Christian mind, and the need to integrate faith with learning.

Again, it is recognized that there were multiple forces at work in both the church and the college for them to transition toward broadened world and life views at the same time. A "new day" was sensed for the college to develop a more holistic and integrated education, while the sons and daughters of the church were becoming more interested in getting an education that the larger world would take seriously, such as training for professions of various sorts. There were other factors as well that prompted the church to engage the world more vigorously. World Missions development needs, MCC endeavors, church leadership demands for personnel, and the newly perceived need for seminary-trained pastors, called for a broadened vision of the world.

When Messiah College transitioned to become a College of Arts and Sciences, it acknowledged a new approach to learning based on a worldview that all truth is God's and that His truths (both natural and revealed) should be integrated with the varied academic disciplines. The college in every stage of its history—first as Messiah Bible School and Missionary Training Home, and then Messiah Bible College, and later Messiah College—always sought to follow biblical principles. With the newly interpreted unity of truth principles they continued on that track.

Within these potential borrowings there was one thing that was somewhat different about the Brethren in Christ adopting a more integrated Christian world and life view. Adopting the new tenets would essentially involve moving from what had been a pronounced "dual kingdom" theory that had built a formidable wall between the church and the world. In other words, both the church and the college were being confronted with serious change issues. The magnitude of change was considerable. And it meant that the church would become more open to impacting the general culture around them. However, even though the new understandings replaced the traditional rationale for separation, an amended interpretation of separation and non-conformity continued in the brotherhood. It appears that no other Reformed earmarks, including a modified emphasis on God's providence, were tied to the new world and truth understandings. This leads to another thesis:

Sub-Thesis 5: *Although Reformed views were significant for redefining the church's long-standing interpretation on separation from the world, the Reformed influence on the denomination should not be viewed as determinative or primary.* Any understandings acknowledged as Reformed in nature should be considered highly ancillary. The non-conformity concept continues today (in different form and intensity),[83] and there appear to be no significant Reformed influences in other areas of the church (or within the college). Moreover, it was new scriptural understandings that incited both the denomination and its colleges to express amended insights, thus more fully defining the meaning of the Christian worldview, and interpreting the role of Christians in today's world.

In summary, the findings concerning basic truths and values of the Brethren in Christ denomination lead to the following five sub-theses:

Sub-thesis 1

The early *Confession* of the Brethren in Christ presented a concept of the church that was both Anabaptist and Pietist in nature.

Sub-thesis 2

It appears that Pietism was more determinative of who the Brethren in Christ were at their time of founding. An example of this is the repeated citing in the original *Confession* of the doctrine that all are "poor sinners," (a Pietist term) in need of redemption and regeneration through Christ. Also, its placement (along with reconciliation to God) as one of the first doctrinal exhortations, thus causing it to be among the premier and controlling doctrines, is quite Pietistic. This is something very different from Anabaptist emphases at this time. The formation of the new body appeared to be driven and motivated by their Pietist imperatives and empowered by Pietist emphases on spiritual edification. Perhaps the clearest Pietist indicator was that as a group they essentially "gave up" on the idea of joining the standing churches of their area, including one of the church bodies that historically professed to follow both Pietist and Anabaptist views, therefore, prompting their formation as a new and distinct body, putting them clearly within the classification of "radical Pietists."[84] It follows that as the first indigenous denomination to be formed in America they were in the "radical Pietist" tradition—just as were the Moravian Brethren, German Baptist Brethren, and the Lutheran Brethren who were formed in Europe more than a century before.

Sub-thesis 3

Even though Wesleyan-type insights on sanctification have nourished the Brethren in Christ doctrine on the "holy life," the Wesleyan movement, *per se,* has not been sufficiently influential to be classified as a primary or shaping heritage of the Brethren in Christ. Instead, Wesleyanism should more accurately be recognized as a theological stream within the Pietist tradition that has contributed to the Brethren in Christ "holy life" message and to its theological synthesis.[85]

Sub-thesis 4

Since the Brethren in Christ in 1950 officially identified with the National Association of Evangelicals, and since neo-evangelicalism represents the belief core of historic Pietism, and since Brethren in Christ perceive the term *evangelical* to be most descriptive of who they are, it is incumbent that *evangelical* be used as a current descriptor. However, from a historical perspective, Evangelicalism, *per se,* has not contributed any original theological insights to the Brethren in Christ.

Sub-thesis 5

During the mid-twentieth century new world and truth views based in Reformed thought became grounding to the arts and sciences programs of the church's colleges. These interpretations later became implicit reality in the life of the denomination when it altered its stand on "separation from the world." However, Reformed theology should not be understood as being a shaping or primary influence on the denomination.[86] The rationale is that the Reformed interpretations are isolated to these views, and Brethren in Christ continue to maintain an amended doctrine of "non-conformity to the world"— somewhat different from the Reformed view— which throughout their history have from time to time incorporated civic or political action positions as part and parcel of their corporate religious view.

A Composite Thesis

These five sub-theses evaluate the influence of specific religious traditions and movements on Brethren in Christ theological interpretations and contribute to the expression of the general thesis of this study an overriding judgment consisting of three parts. They are: First, the basic historical identity of the Brethren in Christ church is rooted in Pietism and Anabaptism (not three or four traditions that have been suggested in various studies).

Second, additional theological insights have essentially been appropriated or assumed. Entire sanctification was somewhat allied to the Wesleyan tradition—adopted by the denomination in 1910. The Reformed tradition's "Christian world and life view" was fused into academic life of the denomination's colleges and has become the worldview reality for a significant portion of the Church's membership. However, since no additional enduring insights or widespread influences from the Wesleyan and Reformed theological streams have been either formally or informally appropriated by the body, the Wesleyan and Reformed traditions are not deemed to be primary shapers of theology or practice of the Brethren in Christ.

Third, this part of the thesis relates to how the identity of a Church body can be comprehensively analyzed. In order to attain a thorough review of identity factors it is proposed that several additional segments or steps be incorporated in the analysis. First, one should historically trace the given theological streams that have flowed into the life of the body, and make judgments that analyze their impact. Second, one should seek to discern the most obvious qualities evidenced by the body. Third, attention should be given to evaluating and ordering its historic priorities. Beyond these several steps, and depending on there being sufficient clarity to discover the decisive principles of life for the denomination, I have sought to get at the heart of a key issue—what is the soul of the church body?

---

[1] Several studies were made during the latter decades of the twentieth century from which this conclusion is derived. This most recent twentyfirst century study, however, may have less comparative longitudinal significance because of a diminished number of Anabaptist-related denominations participating in the study. This comparison problem is further compounded by the rather recent merger of two major Mennonite participants. However, the addition of the Church of the Brethren to this recent study is positive in the sense that they, just as the Brethren in Christ, acknowledge that both Pietism and Anabaptism influenced their heritages. At the same time there is another loss in the longitudinal comparison in that another Mennonite body that has claimed both Anabaptism and Pietism as root heritages, the Mennonite Brethren, chose not to be part of this most recent study.

[2] E. Morris Sider, "From the Editor," *Brethren in Christ History and Life*, Vol. XIX, No. 1, April, 1996.

[3] Luke L. Keefer Jr., *Brethren in Christ History and Life*, Vol. XIX, No.1, April, 1996 p. 38. Also, within this same volume is the opening address of the study conference by Moderator Harvey Sider. In that presentation he raised the same question as to whether a fourth stream, Evangelicalism, should be added to those of primary theological influence on the denomination.

[4] The German Baptist Brethren divided into a number of "Brethren" groups. The largest of these groups today is known as the Church of the Brethren.

[5] The United Brethren in Christ church was formed (officially organized) after the Brethren in Christ (the River Brethren). Prior to the formation of the Brethren in Christ, a number of the

initial members of the new body had spiritual fellowship with an informal society of revivalist-type believers. These spiritual fellowship meetings, it appears, were ministered to by Martin Boehm, a Mennonite minister (who after being silenced by the Mennonites became associated with the Methodists, and subsequently was elected to be an overseer of the United Brethren in Christ denomination when it was formed in 1800).

[6] A. W. Climenhaga, *History of the Brethren in Christ Church*, E. V. Publishing House, Nappanee, Ind., 1942, p. 33.

[7] The River Brethren borrowed trine immersion baptism, the love-feast, deacon visitation, election of officials (rather than by lot), and other practices almost directly from the German Baptist Brethren. C. O. Wittlinger, *Quest for Piety and Obedience*, Evangel Press, Nappanee, Ind., p. 19.

[8] In 1748 a German Baptist tract entitled "The Humble Gleam" (thought by historian Verland Eller to be written by Alexander Mack, Jr.) stated on the matter of "the true conversion" that "the Christian life begins with true repentance of the heart and conversion to God." Donald Durnbaugh, *The Brethren in Colonial America*, The Brethren Press, Elgin, Ill., 1967, pp. 429-432.

[9] A translation of the early *Confession* is in the appendix of this work.

[10] Although an analysis of the comparative Pietist and Anabaptist influences on the doctrinal contents of the early *Confession* was not made by them, these three parts were deemed to be logical divisions of the *Confession* by both Owen Alderfer, *Mind of the Brethren in Christ*, Claremont Graduate School, 1963, p. 56, and Martin H. Schrag, *The Brethren in Christ Attitude Toward the World*, Temple University, 1967, p. 24.

[11] Climenhaga, op. cit., pp. 23, 24.

[12] Alderfer, op. cit., p. 56.

[13] C. O. Wittlinger described the decision by the Brethren in Christ to start a new church as involving "deep soul-searching." op. cit., pp. 23, 24.

[14] Wittlinger, op. cit., pp. 23, 24.

[15] Lines 20 to 24 of the *Confession*. The "poor sinners" term was particularly emphasized by the early Pietist group, the Moravians, who had a strong settlement of believers in the town of Lititz—not far from where the "mother congregation" of the early River Brethren began.

[16] Lines 9 to 12 and 16 to 32 of the *Confession*.

[17] Lines 3 to 5 of the *Confession*.

[18] While the Munster radicals were not typical, the diversity of Anabaptist groups is borne out in the fact that some advocated violence to achieve religious ends.

[19] Schrag, op. cit., pp. 10, 11. From an Anabaptist perspective the question might be raised as to whether Martin H. Schrag ties spiritual intensity to a more evangelical-type conversion experience—this writer is inclined to think that he does, and further believes it was at the crux of any River Brethren differences (at their time of starting) with both the German Baptist Brethren as well as Mennonites. Furthermore, such an interpretation should not be considered anachronistic with either Menno Simons, or with more modern era Mennonite evangelism efforts such as the Brunk Brothers of Virginia, and that of native Ohioan, Myron Augsburger—in both instances, forming organizations to help them carry out numerous evangelistic-type campaigns, largely to heavily Mennonite populated areas.

[20] Donald Durnbaugh, *Brethren Beginnings: The Origins of the Church of the Brethren in Early Eighteenth Century Europe*, (published by the author, 1960), pp. 63-65.

[21] Terry Brensinger and E. Morris Sider, eds., *Within the Perfection of Christ*, p. 299.

[22] "Wesleyan-Anabaptist Dialogue Insert," Feb. 10, 1976, p. 26.

[23] "Wesleyan-Anabaptist Dialogue on the Nature of the Christian Church," Fred D. Layman, pp. 8-14, and Cornelius J. Dyck, pp. 15-20.

[24] The Brethren in Christ followed the brand of Pietism promulgated by Boehm and Otterbein, two local evangelists. It seems that the original German Baptist Brethren brand of Pietism may

have become more diluted than that propounded by founder Alexander Mack in Europe, and later his son—who migrated to Philadelphia.

[25] It was typical for Pietists to use the name "Brethren" as was the case for groups such as the Moravian Brethren, Lutheran Brethren, German Baptist Brethren, River Brethren, and the United Brethren in Christ.

[26] For additional information on this baptismal request see later footnote of this chapter.

[27] See *Confession*, in the Appendix.

[28] Ibid.

[29] The River Brethren viewed repentance of the sinner as God's open door to grace, redemption, regeneration, and salvation (all preceding and leading to the rite of baptism). They did not perceive of a "proof of good fruits" obedience test prior to regeneration. They likely would have contended that with God's help (and assisted by the Spirit) I will obey Jesus—John 15:4 (NIV), Jesus said: "No branch can bear fruit by itself; it must remain in the vine. Neither can it bear fruit unless you remain in me."

[30] Lines 32 to 37 of the *Confession* at the close of this chapter.

[31] Line 33 of the early *Confession*.

[32] The United Brethren in Christ, a Pietist group, failed to emphasize the Anabaptist views to which the Brethren in Christ were committed.

[33] For more information on the seeming preference of the infant Brethren in Christ church to closely relate to the German Baptist Brethren see footnote regarding that subject at the outset of chapter 8.

[34] From lines 52 to 54 of the *Confession*.

[35] From lines 62 to 85 of the *Confession*.

[36] Schrag, op. cit., pp. 10, 11.

[37] Augustine was the first to make a distinction between the visible and the invisible church. By the *visible* church he meant the church as an institution that has a list of members on its rolls. By the *invisible* church he meant all those people living in the world who had been renewed by the power of the Spirit.

[38] The initial group of River Brethren went to a Dunker brother, Elder George Miller, and requested that he baptize them in the mode of the German Baptist Brethren. Since the group was not ready to join his church, Elder Miller declined and reportedly advised them to baptize themselves. See C. O. Wittlinger, op. cit., p. 22. and Owen Alderfer, Part II: "The Brethren Mindset. Part II: The Brethren Mindset and the Brethren in Christ" *Brethren in Christ History and Life VIII*, 1, April, 1985, pp. 3-13.

[39] The first hymnal known to be Brethren in Christ contained twenty-one hymns from a 1795 edition of a German Baptist Brethren hymnal. H. Royce Saltzman, *A Historical Study of the Function of Music Among the Brethren in Christ*, University of Southern California, 1964, pp. 98, 133-136, 146.

[40] For more information on this subject consult an early note to the text of chapter 8, "Three Meaningful Qualities of the Brethren in Christ."

[41] Lines 55 to 58 from the *Confession*

[42] Lines 52 to 55.

[43] Alderfer, op. cit., p. 101, (The U. S. Department of Commerce Report of 1926 indicates membership of the Brethren in Christ church in 1890 was 2688. With the members in English Canada the total count in 1890 would have approached 3,000. This number shows that growth of the denomination exceeded a doubling in each decade from the start of the denomination to 1890.

On average, a minimal doubling of the Brethren in Christ church each decade from their beginnings to 1890 appears to this writer as being highly significant, especially when compared to the later growth of the Brethren in Christ denomination from 1890 to 1940—scarcely more than doubling during that half century (from 3,000 to some 6,000).

While a significant part of this church growth from 1778-1890 surely came from retaining family converts, this seemingly good record of both retention and growth for the River Brethren, during this period, when compared with the Yorker branch of the River Brethren (known today as Old Order River Brethren) who from the time of their "separation" to more recent times have registered little or no growth, is somewhat stunning in comparison. While both of these church bodies, along-side each other, for more than a century continued to emphasize "separation from the world," the Old Order body clearly demonstrated less intent toward outreach and church growth. Comparatively, the less-evangelizing Old Order River Brethren body which "split-off" in the mid-19th century with some 500 to 600 members, about a century and a half later (in 1996) were reported to have "fewer than 350 members." (Membership data as cited in *Plain Women: Gender and Ritual in the Old Order River Brethren*, Margaret C. Reynolds, Pennsylvania State University Press, 2000, pp. 15 and 33.

44 The final lines of the *Confession*, 115-117.

45 Only a decade after the founding of the new church body a group of Brethren in Christ went from Lancaster County to "colonize" in southern Ontario, Canada. While the basic intent of the colonists presumably was economic, and their grouping together as a body with a common faith was to maintain the church, these settlers to Canada and the emissaries who came to minister to them, surely had some awareness of their Confessional mandate "to build and plant and keep His church in healthy growth."

46 See *Confession* lines 100 to 107.

47 One indication of being "world negating" for Pietism was this: At Halle University, where Pietism began under scholars such as Johann Arndt—in order to ensure the spiritual stability of the church, they supported the study of theology but were against what was called "Theological Scholasticism." This term was interpreted by Pietists as manifesting an overly rigorous concern regarding theological systemization.

48 The persecutions inflicted on Anabaptists in Europe by the respective governments and territorial churches would have strongly encouraged the development of their separatist tendencies. The fact that other "Christians" were seeking to kill them would undoubtedly have made their separation from "the world" more pronounced. These pronounced tendencies clearly carried over to their "new world" experience where they exercised fuller religious freedoms.

49 Another endnote of this chapter lists Pietist-oriented denominations, contemporary to the early Brethren in Christ that used the "Brethren" tag. The early body at origin initially called themselves Brethren, then River Brethren, and later Brethren in Christ. The fact that the name Brethren was commonly used by Pietist groups seems to say something about their theological preferences and their closer identification with the German Baptist Brethren at that time. While this fact is not fully consistent with all Anabaptist groupings, that is, one such group at a given point being referenced as the Swiss Brethren, it is surely well-known that the early Anabaptists differed greatly in particular areas of Europe—according to varied times and general locations, as well as leadership—and that different groups of Anabaptists represented varying degrees of pietistic inclinations at different times in their history.

Also, while the concept of brotherhood historically has had pertinence to both Pietist and Anabaptist traditions, it seems instructive that the newly accepted name of Brethren, rather than some form of Mennonite name, was chosen by the body.

50 See *Brethren in Christ History and Life*, Vol. XVII, No. 3, Dec.1994, p. 285.

51 Strands of historical writings about the early Brethren in Christ appear to be based on the assumption that the initial group was predominately Mennonite in background—Anabaptist/Mennonites who simply acquired the "new birth"—with an overlay of Pietism—thus diluting sub-thesis 2, as stated above. This dominantly Mennonite theory, at

times, is cited as fact without offering evidence or rationale to support it. For example, one reader/advisor of this manuscript simply commented "they (the early BIC's) were Mennonites who came under the influence of Pietism." Another, commenting in the same vein, referenced the early *Confession* by saying "The Anabaptist qualities were underplayed (in the *Confession*) because the group accepted their Anabaptism." However, there are a number of factors that raise questions about holding such a premise. The following five considerations are offered:

(1) While it is known that Jacob Engel came out of a Mennonite background, only two additional Mennonite individuals have been confirmed as being signers of the original *Confession*.

(2) From the start, the early body adopted the essential ordinances and practices of the German Baptist Brethren, including modes of baptism, the "love feast," the "charity kiss," deacon's visits, and voting for the appointment of leaders. It seems highly probable that there was a diversity of church religious backgrounds represented in the mother congregation. Also, this seeming bias against German Baptist Brethren modes strongly implies that individuals from that background were part of the composite membership. (In addition, see additional notes in chapter 4 that cite other connections, showing that the Brethren in Christ seemed to appropriate much from the German Baptist Brethren.

(3) Within the Donegal area, the place where the spiritual revivals that gave birth to the Brethren in Christ were held, there were additional religious groups (both Pietist and other Protestant types)—who may, as well, have attended the local revivals, with some becoming newly revived Christians—and thus preparing other "new birth" Christians to be potential candidates for the "mother" Brethren in Christ congregation. Evidence of such was forthcoming from a Lutheran writer in a work entitled *Gestalt des Reichs* (1814, p.135) where he noted that Jacob Engel founder of "a new group at the river (was) fishing away (not disparagingly) many of their best congregational members (as cited in *Plain Women*, Peggy Reynolds (1993, Pennsylvania State University Press, p. 27).

(4) There were perhaps, as well, secular people not associated with any previous church body who became new Christians in this revival setting and in such an event could have become potential prospects for the newly formed Church body—as was typical with the first and second Great Awakenings that transpired across the Colonies during this era (from the mid-eighteenth to the mid-nineteenth centuries).

(5) There appears to be no indication that the mother congregation of the Brethren in Christ was formed by a "split" or schism from another given body—which would have likely been necessary (during these times of sparse population, and limited travel) if the new mother congregation were to be largely composed of Mennonites—or for that matter any other single group such as German Baptist Brethren.

These five indicators lead this writer to deduce that the composition of the initial mother congregation probably included Anabaptist/Mennonites, Pietist/Anabaptist/Brethren, and that the overall initial body may have been more diverse in makeup than has been previously envisioned by some theorists.

[52] Johann Arndt, *Evangelical Visitor*, p. 317.

[53] The three individuals generally considered to be the "fathers" of historic Pietism were Johann Arndt (1555-1621), Philipp Jakob Spener (1635-1705) and Augustus Hermann Francke (1663-1727). Arndt was the theological father to Spener, and Spener to Francke. Each of these Pietist leaders, in varying degrees, were protagonists for cleansing from sin through conversion-regeneration, and of a collective pursuit of perfection in the church. It was Johann Arndt, however, who was the most articulate in pressing the ideal of Christian perfectionism. His widely read book, *True Christianity*, was particularly attuned to Christian sanctification. Jakob Spener published an introduction to Arndt's writings, later published separately under the title, *Pia*

Desideria: or Heartfelt Desires for a God-pleasing Improvement of the Protestant Church.

Arndt expressed concerns for the "new birth," the "new life" in Christ, and for sanctification to enable one to follow Jesus. He characterized sanctification as follows in *Paradiesgartlein*, (p. 67): "so perfectly clean hast thou washed us with thy blood . . . that no speck is left." He continued in *Wahres Christentum*, "Christians need to reach the stature of the perfect man in Christ" (p.174). "The new life" implies, on the one hand, "dying to the world" (p. 315), and "dying to self" (p. 282).

[54] The *Confession* as cited at the close of the Appendix of this work.

[55] Sin eradication was never officially accepted by the denomination and was preached only by a few ministers.

[56] While the denomination has not used "a second definite work of grace" language to describe its "Life in the Spirit" understandings, it appears that completed sanctification of the believer can be attained gradually or within a defined period. See *Brethren in Christ Manual of Doctrine and Government, 2006.*

[57] Luke L. Keefer Jr., op. cit., pp. 33, 34, 36. It is noted in this connection, that John Wesley never claimed the doctrine of entire sanctification (sinless perfection) for himself; but he professed that he witnessed it in other believers. Wesley, however, did claim sanctification at death, termed "glorification"—to be saved from judgment and the presence of sin (Acts 15:11).

[58] The denominational description of sanctification is called *Life in the Spirit.* An explanation of the deeper life doctrine wherein "God's grace provides more than forgiveness of sin" is made in the church's *Manual.* One paragraph renders a doctrine that can be interpreted as "entire" sanctification, and a second paragraph on the subject can be interpreted as progressive sanctification. *Manual of Doctrine and Government of the Brethren in Christ church*, 2006, p. 17.

[59] Pietist groups of varied stripes, including some influenced by Calvinistic theology, held protracted revival and camp meetings during the nineteenth century—well before the first Brethren in Christ camp was founded in the 1930s. Such nineteenth century groups included the Church of God (Harrisburg and Winebrenner in origin) who had a camp-meeting site at Central Manor (Lancaster County); the United Brethren in Christ whose camp-meeting campus was established south of Chambersburg (Franklin County); and the Evangelical church with a camp-meeting location in Upper Dauphin County—and others. But it was not the Pennsylvania brethren alone who were exposed to the earmarks that accompanied camp-meeting revivalism. In fact, the doctrine of entire sanctification in the Brethren in Christ experience was most ardently sponsored by western sectors of the Church who were also exposed to the camp-meeting phenomena within their own regions, but a half-century prior to the designation of camp-meeting sites sponsored by Brethren in Christ.

[60] Another note of this chapter accepts the finding of Luke Keefer's that the Brethren in Christ holiness interpretation is of a different lineage than Wesleyan. In a later memo from Keefer to this writer, dated 10/18/07, he, an accomplished Wesleyan scholar, wrote, "Two things need special attention: First, Wesley did not believe entire sanctification had to be a big, "red letter" experience. He believed one could approach it in small degrees in such a way that it was hard to detect the moment that "inbred sin" had ceased to live and one was completely filled with the love of God. He used the analogy of those whose natural death is so gradual that it is hard to fix an exact minute for their death. Second, Wesley taught that most Christians who were not taught about entire sanctification experienced its equivalent as they approached death and said goodbye to everything that was not of eternal consequence." This characterization of sanctification, from the perspective of John Wesley, does not appear to closely correspond with the way "holy living" has been preached, described, debated, and repeatedly acted upon by the Brethren in Christ—thus lending further credence to the conclusion that the Wesleyan tradition has wielded markedly less influence on the history and life of the Brethren in Christ than did Pietism and Anabaptism.

[61] The Christian Holiness Partnership was initially called the National Holiness Association, later adopted the name Christian Holiness Association, and then settled on their present name several years ago. One wonders whether the frequent name changes may have been a harbinger of diminishing vision or purpose of the group itself.

[62] Luke L. Keefer Jr., (op. cit., p. 38.) proposed that Evangelicalism might be considered as a fourth impact stream, and Harvey Sider cited it as a fourth influence, to that of Pietism, Anabaptism, and Wesleyanism. For additional analysis of their views and the reasons offered for considering Evangelicalism to be a significant contributor to the Brethren in Christ, see chapter 10, "Descriptive Designations to Identify Who the Brethren in Christ Are."

[63] These were concerns that early Anabaptists appear to have closely identified with, but as times change the emphases of denominations often become altered. The tendency of Anabaptists today would not be to use the evangelical language that Menno Simons used, and few of their numerous denominations demonstrate close fraternal relationship with Evangelicals—for example, only the Mennonite Brethren branch of the United States has held membership in the National Association of Evangelicals. For information on the spiritual terms used by Menno Simons see chapter 2.

[64] The Canadian Conference of the Brethren in Christ relates to the Canadian Evangelical Fellowship which is a vibrant organization as manifested by its budget of $2.6 million and a staff of more than twenty. (*Christianity Today*, July 18,1998, p. 41.)

[65] The major theological point that might be questioned is whether evangelicalism had a hand in the denomination moving toward a Christian (unified) worldview and away from a stance of pronounced "separation from the world." However, the denomination's action to join the Association appears to have been part of an array of "outreach" and "wholeness" decisions that were jelling within the denomination, at both the leadership and laity levels, and within its colleges. (The place of its colleges in this transition to a more broadened worldview is more clearly sourced in the Reformed tradition than in Evangelicalism, and such views are specifically considered in the next section of this chapter.)

[66] For a listing of the historic truths of evangelicalism see the section on evangelicalism in chapter 2, and review the George Marsden note in chapter 10, "Descriptive Designations to Identify Who the Brethren in Christ Are."

[67] A reader-advisor of this manuscript commented: "I am a bit surprised that you hesitate to add evangelicalism to the streams affecting the Brethren in Christ. I'd say that the growth of the churches today is because of the wide influence of evangelicalism and our commitment to principles of the evangelical movement." In response, I agree that the effect of evangelicalism has been significant to the denomination, but as stated above, since the essence of evangelicalism, from a doctrinal standpoint, is a continuation of the key truths of Pietism, it would be theologically duplicative to displace the founding tradition of Pietism with the more modern evangelicalism. This also follows the previously cited understanding that the initial introduction and appropriation of given theological or spiritual emphases should be recognized as being more shaping of the denomination than a later expression that is deemed somewhat repetitious.

[68] The new insights that came to the Brethren in Christ about their being somewhat constrained in effectiveness as Christians, due to legalisms, not only became apparent to them as they began to move more closely with evangelicals, but it also was increasingly evident in their close involvements with many Anabaptists who had already discarded "dress legalisms." These involvements with Anabaptists put many scores of Brethren in Christ into close association with other Christians in Civilian Public Service, Mennonite Central Committee relief work, Council of Mennonite and Affiliated Colleges programs, such as study abroad groups, and international student consortiums, etc.—all of these happening during the 1940s—a decade of beginning to work more closely across denominational lines.

[69] A full rationale on Evangelicalism being a descendant of Pietism and standing for corresponding principles and values to Pietism is offered in the section on defining Evangelicalism in chapters 2 and 7.

[70] Originating in the 1940s, the Brethren in Christ become part of the Association soon after its formation.

[71] Examples of separation-type issues that were found by the General Conference "to be inconsistent" for members included the following: 1871, "it is not consistent for members to have their likeness taken" (photograph); 1873, "It is not consistent for brethren to put lightning rods on their buildings;" 1878, "It is not allowed for brethren to grow a mustache without a full beard," 1878, "It is not consistent for members to have bride servants (brides-maids) on wedding occasions;" 1890, "It is not consistent for members to hold weddings . . . making a display, both in setting tables and presenting gifts;" 1895, "Members are advised not to take part in street parades or other excitable gatherings."

[72] It needs to be recognized that from all appearances the church and its colleges were moving in complementary directions at this same time—toward a more integrated Christian world and life view. Both the church and its colleges, it appears, were ready to seek amendment to their "separation from the world" understandings.

[73] The transition of Messiah College into a four-year liberal arts college came about in the decade of the 1950s. Upland College preceded Messiah, by several years, in granting baccalaureate degrees. Prior to the time Messiah College granted degrees its junior college graduates who wanted to continue at a church-related college largely went to Elizabethtown College, Wheaton College, Houghton College, Goshen College, or Greenville College. Two of the more prominent church-related colleges for Upland Junior College graduates to attend were Pasadena College and Westmont College.

[74] When a denomination makes significant doctrinal modulations it seems important, for the sake of both integrity and historical accuracy, to trace such change well beyond its biblical groundings by fully examining it according to theological consistency (tradition-wise).

[75] Both are renderings of the creation story from New Testament sources.

[76] The Reformed tradition views on integration stress God as the creator of all and all truth centering in Jesus Christ.

[77] Other things were also happening that reached beyond the denomination's colleges to make the church aware that their truth and world views may be truncated. Institutions, media, and agencies including other Christian colleges of the arts and sciences, the publication *Christianity Today*, Educational Journals, the higher education associations, the Council for the Advancement of Small Colleges—all of these—surely contributed to the new sense regarding the need for an integrated Christian worldview that relates to all of God's truth. Carl F. H. Henry, editor of *Christianity Today*, and author of *The Uneasy Conscience of Modern Fundamentalism* also was a strong protagonist for adopting a Christian worldview. However, in 1950 the most functional way of exposure for Brethren in Christ to more holistic views of the world was through its colleges where many of its youth enrolled.

[78] Most colleges that were founded by church bodies, either have today, or have had in their history, strong Pietist emphases in their programs.

[79] Initially the four-year programs at both Upland and Messiah were essentially Bible college programs.

[80] The Reformed proficiency for integration of truth with the Christian faith in numerous academic fields has been well demonstrated. For example, in the field of philosophy, an area where Christian scholars in recent years have exerted unusual leadership and have done so alongside their secular counterparts; two of the lead Christian scholars in philosophy are from Reformed backgrounds—Alvin Plantiga at University of Notre Dame and Nicholas Woltersdorff at Yale University.

[81] The "Christian mind" and "thinking Christianly" are Biblical concepts emphasized within the Reformed tradition.

[82] Since there was much overlap in leadership personnel between the colleges and the church, it is hard to know exactly how much the colleges influenced the church and vice-versa. In all likelihood they were traveling parallel tracks. Again, the term "leading", on the part of the colleges, should be interpreted as that of providing biblical and philosophical foundations for such a transition to new world and life views.

[83] "Nonconformity to the world" for the Brethren in Christ is no longer interpreted as "separation from the world" *per se,* since positive engagement in the world for acts of goodness, on the part of the believer, is considered both positive and Christian—its ideal is for the Christian to be "in the world," but "not of the world." The "nonconformity to the world" concept seeks to avoid injurious and harmful acts to either the self or to the general society and would pertain to things such as self-indulgence, materialism, and prideful conceit.

[84] As cited earlier, E. Morris Sider considered Pietism to be the decisive factor in the formation of the Brethren in Christ church (See *Brethren in Christ History and Life,* Vol. XVII, No. 3, Dec. 1994, p. 285.). Also, as pointed out by Martin H. Schrag—from European times forward there were both churchly and radical Pietists. "Churchly Pietism was the form of Pietism that remained within the standing churches. The major thrust within Pietism was churchly Pietism. In contrast, the radical Pietists were those who had given up on the standing churches and separated themselves from those churches." (Quoted from a letter written by Martin Schrag to this author, dated March 7, 1974.)

[85] "Holy life," the term used in the Church *Manual,* to speak for the Brethren in Christ regarding "deeper life" considerations for the Christian, could have just as appropriately been referenced by the term "holiness," since it appears that the primary influence (beyond Pietism) in this area came to the denomination from camp-meeting related sources (rather than from Wesley). However, since the Brethren in Christ church as well as its college, Messiah, and many of its scholars, have continually referenced the Brethren in Christ holiness views as Wesleyan (tradition-wise), this writer, for communication purposes chose to place these considerations in the same manner—as Wesleyan.

[86] This consideration of worldview issues could have been treated as a new worldview and simply referenced as a fresh biblical insight that came to Messiah College (as it was initially treated)—and thus fail to trace its close association with Reformed theological and philosophical interpretations. But the effort to reach beyond its biblical foundations was added because the Brethren in Christ scholarly practice is to fully acknowledge theological traditions that have nourished its religious insights or understandings. Regarding this particular theological worldview consideration, it has given an opportunity to more closely examine additional questions raised by Brethren in Christ scholars—is there evidence of Calvinist influence affecting Brethren in Christ thought or doctrine? And, if there is such evidence, what is its extent? The expression of sub-thesis 5 has sought to respond to these questions.

Chapter IV

The Founding Vision of the River Brethren
(1778-1865)

More than two centuries ago a new nation was formed in North America. The creation of one nation out of thirteen colonies of diverse peoples had never been done before.[1] Heretofore nations had grown to oneness by a process of ethnic, religious, territorial, and political assimilation over centuries; instead this was a nation "brought forth" by "our fathers" (as cited by Abraham Lincoln). But the creation of the nation out of a mix of peoples, in a short span of time, was not the only noteworthy political precedent. They wrote a constitution, elected a federal system, set their domestic affairs in order, and won the respect of the nations of the world—all precedents that were achieved prior to 1800.

The new nation's population at the time of its founding and of the new denomination's beginning was less than Philadelphia today. That setting produced an amazing set of early political leaders. Out of approximately one million males who were eligible to participate in government the nation produced Washington, Franklin, Jefferson, Hamilton, Adams, Madison, John Marshall, and a number of other distinguished statesmen. The historian, Henry Steele Commager, contends that during this period, from a comparatively small pool, "the new nation produced the most remarkable galaxy of political leaders in their own history and perhaps in the history of the Western world."[2]

Far less spectacular, but nevertheless unprecedented, was the formation of the first free-standing religious body in America that has sustained its ministry to the present—the Brethren in Christ. But in contrast to the striking political accomplishments and the noted eminence in which these early political leaders are held, their contemporaries, the founders of the first religious body, were quite common within their community and were ordinary in their lives. The original church had a mere handful of congregants. They had experienced a Christian conversion and within their spiritual bonding searched for a way to be baptized, but eventually felt led to baptize each other. They named a leader, provided mutual edification and service, and then formulated a *Confession*. Their beginning as a new body was without pretense. They exhibited little theological creativity. They took God and his Word seriously, but not themselves. They copied the churchly forms of the German Baptist Brethren, but in all things they sought to imitate the Scriptural church, and to reflect a likeness to Christ.

While the new government and the new church differed substantially in originality of ideas and in the size of the regions and populations initially affected by them, these two political and religious creations—parallel in timing and equal as new precedents—were historic hinges for coming major transitions. The new political creations became models for other nations in pursuit of liberty and democracy. The new denomination, somewhat small and separated to be a visible model, marked the beginning of a parade of new American religious denominations. Even though the newly formed Brethren in Christ were not primal in their theological interpretations, they introduced fresh accents to a theological synthesis and created a new and unique religious heritage. That heritage bequeathed to its later generations a distinct identity that was transmitted to communicants world-wide.[3]

The new body appears to have been committed to independence, but not for its own sake. They did not split from a denomination, and they showed no allegiance to a single theological source (except the Bible). It seems they had clear convictions about faith and doctrine that could not be compromised by joining any similar, neighboring group. There was no designated minister from another church body within the founding group. Although initial leaders were respected, there remain no traces that the clergy exerted control over the body. The polity of the early group appears to have been highly democratic.

The Brethren in Christ time their beginning as sometime between 1776 and 1778.[4] The denomination started at least a decade prior to George Washington being sworn in as the first president of the United States in April 1789.

The initial Brethren in Christ body lived along the Susquehanna River[5] in Lancaster County, Pennsylvania. They resided among other Anabaptist and Pietist groups that met in the vicinity. German Baptist Brethren (later to be named Church of the Brethren) and Mennonites espoused doctrines and followed practices that the newly formed Brethren in Christ valued.[6] There was one salient belief in which the new body of believers differed with existing Anabaptist groups. They strongly believed a conversion-regeneration experience was the critical first step for a new Christian to cross the "threshold of faith." The long-standing Anabaptist groups were apparently not prepared to accommodate this position to the satisfaction of the new church body. The doctrine of a conscious conversion from sin, prior to the ordinance of water baptism, was a Brethren in Christ "non-negotiable."[7] In addition, the Anabaptist groups were reputed to be spiritually-lukewarm, a condition that likely reinforced the newly-converted brethren to start their own group.[8]

On the other hand, Pietist groups in Lancaster County that early Brethren in Christ presumably could have affiliated with included loosely connected conventicle-type assemblies that later organized as the United Brethren in Christ in 1800, and the Moravian Brethren who had their origins in Europe.[9] However, these groups were less inclined to a consistent emphasis on "separation from the world," a doctrine to which the river-located believers were committed.

The new church group perceived the conversion experience to involve more than saving grace alone. A life of faithfulness to God and the availability of divine assistance for right living through ministry of the Holy Spirit were viewed as integral parts of conversion-regeneration. Becoming a Christian and being a Christian were joined. This crucial doctrine brought into unity the new birth with a new life and it coupled similar concepts such as salvation and obedience; inner experience and outward walk; knowing God and serving God. One's faith in Christ was wedded to a changed life in Christ—dual evidences of the Christian. The obedient Brethren underscored, however, that salvation was through God's grace—not earned by obeying God's laws.[10] As true Pietists, they also believed in sanctification—wherein the Holy Spirit enabled the Christian to possess a living faith.

Both parts of the Christian life—faith and conduct—were essential to the early Brethren in Christ, just as both were intrinsic to the heritage of classical Pietism and to major strands of historic Anabaptism. Clear evidences of the dual understandings exist in writings of Menno Simons and the literary contributions of Alexander Mack, Sr. and his son Alexander Mack, Jr. While the views of the founding brethren of the new body, as stated in their early *Confession,* indicate they diligently studied the Scriptures, one might surmise that some of the early Brethren in Christ were exposed to writings of the Macks and Simons, or with other thought leaders who represented the two theological streams.[11] We do know, for example, that one of the early Bishops of the brotherhood from Franklin County, Christian Lesher (1778-1856), converted in 1803, and chosen as Bishop in 1825, possessed three books in his library authored by Johann Arendt (1555-1621), a forerunner and foundational to the rise of German Pietism.

Classical Pietists and historic Anabaptists possessed the distinctive faith-life synthesis that could provide examples and hold up ideals for the early Brethren in Christ. Over time many individuals or groups from these traditions lost sight of one or more of their distinctive ideals. In the case of Pietists, they failed in being consistent on the biblical obedience side of the standard, while for Anabaptists the salvation/new birth element of the ideal has, at times, been less than fully portrayed. Although Brethren in Christ have neither individually nor collectively always attained the dual-dimensioned ideal, it appears that the church has kept the full scope of the vision as an objective to be pursued. It has consistently set forth both vital faith and right conduct as being norms for the Christian.

The Brethren in Christ interpretation of the dual standard of conversion-obedience as spelled out in the *Confession* appears to be most akin to Pietist theology because of its stress on divine access and assistance. Brethren in Christ acknowledge the ministry of the Holy Spirit in transforming and empowering the believer. Values from classical Pietism affected the early Brethren in Christ in their worship, service, and outreach, as manifested in their emphases on spiritual edification, individual morality, and spiritual sharing ("public meetings" and "private meetings"). The Anabaptist influence on the early development of the group was expressed in community accountability, reconciliation and peace, and non-conformity concerns.

Adjustments to the denomination's identity are examined according to five historic periods. The time spans of the periods are: Period One, from *circa* 1778 to 1865, the era when the church was identified as the River Brethren. Period Two, from 1865 to 1910, was a time of transition when the church acquired a new doctrine and began new ministries. Period Three, from 1910 to 1950, a second transition era when the denomination's attention turned toward making internal adjustments (bounded in 1950 by the church making a significant identity shift). Period Four, from 1950 to 1980, was a time when the denomination began to demonstrate the implications of a new "worldview." Period Five was from 1980 to the present, when the church modified its ministry to a society transitioning to what is often described as "late-modern," or "post-modern."

The River Brethren Era (1778-1865) Begins

The fledgling denomination came into being on the heels of the first "Great Awakening"[12] and just as the early waves of the second "Great Awakening" were about to start.[13] Of special note, however, there is another denomination that has claimed to be the first religious body to start in America (not transplanted from Europe).[14] It is a body contemporary to the early Brethren in Christ that continues today—the Church of the United Brethren in Christ (referenced later as UBIC). Both denominations came out of the same Pietist/Evangelical movement and began in the same general area.

When two different bodies claim to be the first to become established a question arises—what determines when a religious denomination begins? At minimum, three key conditions and dates should be analyzed and compared when seeking to determine an official beginning for a new denominational body: First, the time when there is clear independence or separation of both leadership and laity from other distinct religious bodies—thus terminating prior religious connections. Second, is the time when authoritative leadership was formally determined and officially assigned. Third, is the time when the new group's initial *Confession* or doctrinal order statement was formulated.

Regarding the first, a clear independence and separate identity from other religious bodies, historians of the UBIC have repeatedly emphasized that the initial Pietistic happenings, including the broadly attended meetings in barns and the smaller gatherings in homes, were heterogeneous occasions for evangelistic or spiritual edification purposes. One prominent UBIC historian states that the intent of such meetings was in "no way designed to lead to the formation of a new denomination."[15] The 1998 denominational booklet of the Church of the UBIC states: "Gradually the movement developed into a full-fledged denomination." No specific date was cited as to when the UBIC discontinued being part of a general revival movement (crossing multi-fellowship lines) to declare their intent to become an independent denomination.

Looking back, a number of different Pietist-type fellowships, later to form as denominations (though not initially intended), were jelling during the last two decades of the eighteenth century. In addition to the "to-become River Brethren brand" and the "to-become UBIC brand" there was the "to-become Evangelical Association brand" under the leadership of Jacob Albright.[16] Regarding the specific development of the "to-become UBIC brand," preachers or pastors representing various religious groups met together from time to time. The first such religious leaders' conference of the "to-become UBIC brand" recorded was in 1789 in Baltimore. It was attended by leaders from both German Reformed and Mennonite churches (as yet indicative of being part of a movement rather than a denomination). This 1789 meeting and a subsequent meeting held in 1791 were billed as "promoting ecumenical fellowship." Again in hindsight, this gradual genesis for the UBIC is understandable in light of their often cited purpose to serve as a renewal arm for varied Christian groupings—especially intended to minister to colonists of German-speaking background.

Regarding the first indicator cited above, the Brethren in Christ established a new and independent body around 1778—compared to the UBIC becoming established by action at a conference held in 1800 at the house of Brother Frederick Kemp in Frederick County, Maryland. The 1800 conference was composed of thirteen German-speaking pastors (or itinerate preachers) from varied denominations. This was a third such meeting of the so-called "to-become UBIC brand" clergy spanning an eleven-year period (meetings of 1789, 1791, and 1800). Only four of the thirteen attendees in 1800 participated in all three meetings. It was at the 1800 conference that participants acted to become a new body. Two actions were made which indicated a new religious body was officially organized: two presiding Bishops were elected, and it is presumed that the name UBIC was chosen. *In Trials and Triumphs: A History of the Church of the United Brethren in Christ*, the writer states that "though not given in the minutes, it is certain that the name, 'United Brethren in Christ' was adopted at this (1800) conference"). Therefore, as one compares the two beginning dates it seems unmistakable that in terms of a given group acting to form a new and independent body, the River Brethren were the first.

The process of union for the River Brethren may have been simpler than for the UBIC. The UBIC formation made by 13 clergy-type leaders implied a decision and the convincing of more then the respective clergy.[17] It, of necessity, involved a corporate consensus on the part of the congregations to follow their clergy into the new churchly associations, which surely would have been more complicated than starting the Brethren in Christ grouping composed entirely of laity (who upon forming a new religious entity acted to name a fresh leader). Also, in contrast, the River Brethren began their new body by founding a "mother congregation." Therefore, the task that faced the new UBIC body was a large one—that of melding diverse bands of believers, most of whom had perhaps only met sporadically in either a revival meeting or in smaller conventicle-style worship and devotional exchange.[18] Perhaps this challenge of fusing together numerous scores of members representing a mix[19] of religious backgrounds contributed to the author of the definitive history cited above choosing the title, *In Trials and Triumphs*.

With respect to the second indicator, the approximate time when formal leadership of the new body was designated—for the UBIC, it is presumed to have transpired at the Fredrick County, Maryland conference of 1800. Two of the most prominent evangelists of the general revival movement were named bishops of the newly formed church. William Otterbein, a long-standing minister of the German Reformed church, and Martin Boehm, a former bishop of the Mennonite church, who had previously been silenced by his fellow bishops.[20] Jacob Engel was elected to be the first minister of the River Brethren in the mid-1770s and was advanced soon thereafter to be the first overseer for all congregations. Engel served in an overseer capacity until his passing in 1833.

In evaluating the third indicator, the time when formulation of a confession or order of doctrine was officially approved, it is noted that a doctrinal declaration is essential to the establishment of a new religious body. The UBIC performance was most sluggish. Again, slower movement is somewhat understandable because of the high diversity of backgrounds of both the new body's clergy and its members. It was not until 1815 at a conference held in Mount Pleasant, Pennsylvania that a "Discipline" was passed containing the doctrines and rules of government of the church.

A recent booklet produced by the UBIC describes the historic journey of their body as first being part of the colonial-Pietist movement and highlights Otterbein and Boehm as luminaries in that movement—which they surely were. The account recognizes the forming of their denomination as being "gradual." It appears true that the Brethren in Christ church is the first Christian religious denomination indigenous to America to be founded.

The infancy years of the denomination were times of national religious disunity the likes of which had never been seen before. Gordon S. Wood has referred to the period of the early republic as "the time of greatest religious chaos and originality in American history."[21] W. R. Ward saw the period of 1790 to 1830 as "the most important single generation in modern (religious) history of the whole Christian world."[22]

Nathan O. Hatch in his book, *The Democratization of American Christianity*, argues that between 1780 and 1830 as the young nation extended new horizons of freedom, an indelible imprint was left on the structures of American Christianity and political life. People not only began to think for themselves in matters of civic life, they were also becoming free thinkers about religious issues.

Hatch further points out that as the early republic embraced religious liberty, common people were challenged to take religious destiny into their own hands, to oppose central religious authority, and to question the elevation of the clergy as a separate order of men.[23] He referred to these times as producing an "explosive conjunction of evangelical fervor and popular sovereignty" and called the period, "the heyday of religious Populism."[24] A mood of religious disunity would soon be moving to its zenith in the nineteenth century.

At the vanguard of this religious-fragmentation was the River Brethren. It appears the denomination has had difficulty defining precisely the ingredients of its continuing tradition. And, heretofore, only minor attention has been given to comparative strengths of theological streams within the body.

The earlier parts of the church's history cannot be highly verified because the initial leaders were not writing individuals.[25] There are no official records of the church from its founding. Among the few written sources are several religious articles or pamphlets written by Christian Lesher and Jacob Hershey and David Landis, Lesher contemporaries in the early nineteenth century.[26] Of the three writers, Christian Lesher was the most productive, with three major works. They were entitled, *Witness to the Truth* (about the church and church discipline); *Spiritual Clockwork,* an eighty-five page manuscript, the original of which is located today in the Kittochtinny Historical Society Museum, Chambersburg, Pennsylvania. The third work is *A Small Spiritual Magazine (or Storehouse) as a Witness to the Truth*. He wrote this book in 1847 at seventy-two years of age and published it in 1849.

In addition to the above three writers, who represent the religious ethos of the River Brethren during this period, there are a number of references to the group by individuals outside the brotherhood during these earlier years. There exist, as well, several general publications that offer relatively short historical accounts or contemporary descriptions regarding the denomination. The most valuable source from this period is a number of copies of an early statement—the initial *Confession.*

The scarcity of early writings seems to be matched by the absence of an abundant oral tradition. Since there was no standing lay minister or church leader from an outside religious body to assist in leading the newly-formed body, and since the elected leader, was apparently not a dominant person, the group may have lacked a public spokesperson.[27]

The decisive nature of the "new birth" doctrine indicates the first individuals to join the new church were exposed to some form of the new Pietist/Evangelical ethos appearing in the colonies just before the Brethren in Christ came into being.[28] In similar fashion to the Great Awakening that started in New England, evangelistic services affected German-speaking communities of Lancaster County. Since the original River Brethren had individual, but mutually held, conversion experiences, the early members were exposed to the language, theology, and ethos of Pietism.

Theological interpretations of the early Brethren in Christ crossed traditional religious lines. The new denomination was not likely shaped by original theological thought. The language and themes of preachers who led revivals in Lancaster County contributed to the core language of the River Brethren. The new birth doctrine and other spiritual emphases were representative of the Pietist tradition. Even though many German Baptist Brethren no longer preached the importance of an initial conversion experience, some of the language of that tradition continued to be perpetuated by them.[29]

Religious Populism, Revivalism, and Anti-Creedalism during the "River Brethren Era," 1778-1865

As one endeavors to sort out the group identity during their formative years, one should examine the young body in relation to historian Nathan O. Hatch's view that the splintering of American Christianity, and the rise of new denominations, should be understood as the uniting of a quest for religious liberty and political freedom.

The Brethren in Christ start, however, does not appear to correlate with the Hatch thesis. While there is clear evidence of a democratic upsurge in religious matters during this period, and while the newly formed Brethren in Christ appear to have formed a democratic polity, their beginnings lay in belief and doctrinal issues rather than anti-clerical or church governance issues. A good portion of individuals constituting the first group lived among lay-governance religious traditions, including lay-ministry. Although the new group avoided formation of a religious hierarchy, the early Brethren were not revolting against ecclesiastical forms *per se*, and were not breaking away from a specific denomination.

Also, since "separation from the world" was one of the Brethren in Christ core doctrines, political goals and cultural ends were not co-mingled with their religious purposes. Such earthly objectives were more anathema to them than of even secondary importance. They were greatly concerned about a "right church" but little about "right politics." Their motivation was not a desire for political power and their evangelical fervor was not tied to popular culture. They were truly committed to being part of the kingdom of God and to extending His realm. Although the democratization of Christianity may have been a passion for many new Protestant groups during this era, it was not a decisive factor for starting the Brethren in Christ. The Hatch view does not account for the origins of the Brethren in Christ.

On the other hand, some historians point to revivalism as the key force for religious change during the early republic. Both the young nation and its churches, including the new River Brethren, were surely affected by spiritual stirrings throughout the land. It has been acknowledged that religious awakenings were the source of Pietist views of early Brethren in Christ. However, it is not known with certainty when the first Brethren in Christ members came into their respective experiences. Public meetings were the likely route for most of the original members to experience a spiritual encounter.[30] Martin Boehm and William Otterbein were preachers of German descent who served in evangelistic efforts in southern Pennsylvania areas. For an extended period the early River Brethren seemed to put high trust in Martin Boehm.[31]

While it is assumed that some individuals within the Brethren in Christ mother congregation became converted in the special revival efforts held in Lancaster County, and their *Confession* called for "public gatherings where the word is preached and people are exhorted to repent," the group evidently became cautious about concerted meetings. In spite of showing clear marks of being evangelical in doctrine and intent, the new church members, prior to the 1870s, did not subscribe to popular revivals. Perhaps they viewed the institution of revivalism as a device of "worldly" Christianity. American Protestantism, in general, was considered to be part of the world by the Brethren in Christ.[32] Therefore, throughout this formation period popular revivalism was not a significant help to them in gaining converts as it was for other new denominations.[33]

In spite of their restrictive stance and comparatively rigid positions about life of the believer, steady growth of the group during the River Brethren years indicates they were sufficiently strong in their evangelical commitments that revivals, *per se*, considered as instruments of men, were not needed to bolster their life.

The writings of Jacob Hershey in 1825, included a letter addressed to "fellow believers" which stressed "the depravity of the carnal mind," the importance of "the divine nature," "that this work of grace (needs to) be carried forward," and "what we attained yesterday we (can) lose again today." Hershey's sentiments indicate that the church's Pietistic/Arminian positions continued during this early period. A River Brethren pamphlet written by David Landis in 1825 emphasized conversion-regeneration when he wrote, "whoever says the new birth is not necessary there is evidence that he himself is yet in blindness." Christian Lesher also reflected a clear Pietist tendency in his writings. Martin Schrag who gave careful study to the life of Lesher characterized him in this way:

> Lesher's use of Pietist and Anabaptist sources indicates that he was in the tradition of the founders of the Brethren in Christ in bringing together elements of the two movements. His purchase of Pietist sources (some radical). . . and his use of Pietist language and ideas suggests he was strongly influenced by Pietism. (Schrag added) It may be of some significance that he wrote his name in and the price he paid for each of the Pietist books, but not for those with an Anabaptist orientation.
>
> (Further regarding Lesher's "Pietist bent," as Schrag termed it, he wrote), Lesher's crisis conversion experience, his flexibility regarding individual experience, and his emphasis on personal spiritual growth clearly show the impact of Pietism on him and his writing.[34]

Although intermittent church-sponsored revival methods of the mainstream churches were not used by the Brethren in Christ until the 1870s, concerns about salvation and turning from sin, long-time concerns of the brotherhood, seemed to continue during the era. A sense of mission, as well as maintenance, was evident as the church made migratory moves (in the form of groups) to Canada, to new areas of Pennsylvania, and to other states such as Ohio, Illinois, and Michigan. While the essential reason for "colonizing" appeared to be economic (land opportunities), Morris Sider reported that more serious efforts were made toward evangelization after the time of the migration to Kansas.

As soon as a group of River Brethren were settled a congregation could quickly be formed since a lay-minister would be named to serve the flock. Church leaders such as Jacob Engel (1753-1833), John Engle, Christian Lesher (1775-1856), Abraham L. Eshelman (d.1867), John I. Gish (1800-1875), and Levi Luckenbach (1807-1896), all traveled for interest of the brotherhood—including service in preaching missions. Yet "revivalism," as an institution, was still to come in the brotherhood.

Nathan O. Hatch detected an increased turning to the Bible for direct guidance accompanying the general movement across America of religious populism and revivalism. This new emphasis on the Scriptures fostered a mood of anti-creedalism. The repeated standard of many new groups became "no creed but the Bible."[35]

Although a posture of strong biblicism and limited creedalism surely coincided with sentiments of the Pietist-inclined River Brethren, the pervasive biblicism of these times was often built on a strongly individualistic hermeneutic—premised on the inalienable ability of every person to understand the New Testament for themselves. Therefore, the denomination's Anabaptist interpretation of the church in which each member deferred to the counsel of the group protected them from the pitfalls of individualism that often accompanied an anti-creedal mind-set.

In sum, it appears that the Brethren in Christ in this early era were atypical of the other newly-formed denominations that Nathan Hatch references. Compared with numerous other groups of the same period, the River Brethren did not portray a strong sense of individualism, nor did they wed the concepts of religious liberty and political freedom to their theology. They refrained from marching to the tunes of the times. Just as they perceived Jesus as refusing to allow public opinion to steer or direct His ministry, they sought to follow the mandates of the Father in heaven.

An Interplay of the Denomination's Root Traditions during the River Brethren Era, 1778-1865

Even though Pietism was deemed to be the most determinative of the beginning Brethren in Christ, careful analysis of the *Confession* reveals the heritages of Pietism and Anabaptism were rather equal in influencing day-to-day life. However, their conversion-regeneration doctrine leads one to conclude that the Pietist priorities were of the highest order.[36]

Due to the scarcity of sources, it is hard to evaluate the relative intensity of Anabaptist and Pietist values. It is even more difficult to determine whether one heritage controlled the other. Martin H. Schrag, however, felt that the denomination's interpretation of the church and its stance on separation from the world (Anabaptist ideas) dominated the church during this period.[37]

One strong indication of Anabaptist influence was the church's separation principle which at times took precedence over that of a more strident Pietism, that is, the denomination refraining from agreeing to hold more conventional-style revival meetings. While we don't know the particular source of its new members, the growth seems to indicate some form of evangelism, and outreach was going on, even if it was mostly from the retention of family members.[38]

Regarding war and peace, an Anabaptist concern, it seems almost unfathomable that there is scant, if any, record about individual member attitudes regarding the Civil War struggle between the North and the South. The "blood-soaked terrain" of the Civil War cost over 620,000 lives and over a million maimed and wounded,[39] of an approximate 25,000,000 United States population. This is more dead and wounded than most of the nation's wars, including World Wars I and II, combined.[40] Even this event drew little more than meager United States membership reaction, although the church as a corporate body did register with the government in opposition to participation in the war.[41] It seems that beyond the previously referenced spiritual-life oriented writings by leaders such as Christian Lesher, Jacob Hershey, and David Landis (much of which conveyed Pietist-type messages), that a sense of concern related to war and peace either failed to be communicated, or failed to be preserved for posterity. It is surprising that there is no record from these three or others indicating either peace-loving reminders (in pamphlet or essay form) or lamentations of deep concern regarding the war's loss of life.

However, there are a number of basic things about church life during this period that are known. The young church "met frequently for prayer and mutual edification,"[42] and "experience meetings" were normally held on Saturday evenings.[43] Also the *Confession* instructed them to hold "public assemblages where the Word is brought for penance-calling, and private (assemblages) where such children (in the faith) often gather and reveal to each other, filially, one to the other."[44]

The above facts, and especially the extant religious writings, indicate that segments of the church were quite spiritually oriented. Their meetings had both edification and evangelization intent. It appears the degree of Pietistic intensity had not become cold.[45] While additional first-hand information would be useful for evaluating the dominance or subjugation of theological views, their separation from the world obviously continued to orient them in an Anabaptist direction.

From available information, one may deduce that both the Pietist and Anabaptist traditions continued with strength during the River Brethren era. In spite of the difficulty in documenting signs of spiritual zeal, one can infer the continuing strength of Pietism by the following: First, by comparing conditions at the time of origin of the denomination with that of the early 1870s when a regular flow of official information about the church began; second, by reviewing the dynamics of denominational choice for incoming and exiting members; third, by examining the causes of schism in the denomination during the period. These inferential analyses are expanded upon in the pages that follow.

Clear markings from Pietism include the importance they placed on the conversion experience, the provisions they made for spiritual edification, and their unmistakable emphases on the need for evangelization and righteousness (perfection).[46] When these early characteristics are compared with those surviving at the end of the period one gets a picture of the degree of continuity of Pietist values. Several denominational decisions made in 1871 and 1872 offer strong indications about the values and general mood of the church that existed earlier. Two noteworthy actions indicate a persisting Pietist inclination after the closing of the River Brethren era. The church set up its first missionary fund in 1871 and it relaxed its stand against protracted revival meetings in 1872.[47] Therefore, we might conclude the Pietist views[48] that pervaded the group around 1778 remained in durable form in the early 1870s. "Spiritual warmth" and "concern for the lost" are not phenomena that groups can generally turn on or off at will.

One also senses that the denomination's steady growth (more than doubling of members in each decade to the nineteenth century) would not have been possible during these times without the continuation of its dual-founding tradition.[49] Membership numbers indicate the denomination continued to maintain a unique niche and identity by attracting new church members. If they had made a turn toward dominating Anabaptist views the denomination would have lost its original identity and essentially duplicated its branch of the Old Order River Brethren—which failed from the mid-eighteenth century to the present time to record any continuing growth.[50] By the same token, such individuals could have joined the Mennonites or German Baptist Brethren, who continued to grow—but again, Brethren in Christ growth appeared to be substantial.

If the denomination had swung in a more exclusively Pietist direction, it would have lost its dual-tradition identity. In such a case, the United Brethren in Christ, Methodist, and Evangelical churches, all of which continued to be somewhat Pietistic and revivalistic, but were far less restrictive regarding non-resistance and non-conformity, would have been formidable contenders for new members.

Maintenance of the church's dual identity held implications that reached beyond attracting new members to retaining standing members. Any serious movement away from either of the church's two traditions would likely have meant the loss of standing members due to abandoning its unique synthesis.

There is another inferential conclusion that one might tie to a strong dual tradition during the period. Several schisms were experienced by the denomination during the River Brethren era.[51] The two recorded schisms went in opposite directions as each departing group pursued different ultimate goals that reflected one founding Brethren in Christ tradition or the other. One schism transpired to the right of center. It stressed the need for greater church discipline and the will for the dissenters to preserve a more Anabaptist character. A second split toward the left was precipitated over outreach and church-growth concerns. This departing group was motivated to pursue Pietist values thought by the main body to be extreme.

The Yorker Brethren, known today as Old Order River Brethren,[52] exited from the parent body because they held more rigidly to time-honored practices and forms. They felt the rest of the River Brethren were becoming too progressive. They were reputed to have accused Brethren in other sections of the church as being too slow in disciplining progressives such as Matthias Brinser, of Dauphin County. Many years after the group exited, a member of the Old Order River Brethren reported his insights regarding the event as follows:

> In 1843 a number of the River Brethren withdrew from the main body, claiming that the original doctrines of the founders were being departed from, particularly in regard to non-resistance and non-conformity to the world. (Other sources, however, date the time that the "Yorker Brethren broke-away" from the main body as sometime in the 1850s).[53]

The division to the left came in 1855 as a group of Lancaster County brethren cut off an element of the Dauphin County church that had become progressive. Matthias Brinser and his followers wanted to erect a "meetinghouse" to care for their growing church group and then proceeded to build it. They were expelled as they attempted to fulfill a Pietist value—preparing for service and outreach to a growing number of communicants.

The Old Order River Brethren exited to the right and the Brinsers (later to be known as United Zion's Children and today the United Zion church) dissented to the left, but the majority body remained intact and continued its stand within Pietism and Anabaptism. Just as the church found its way among other denominations by retaining its unique identity, it was now treading an internal course between liberal and conservative schisms. These dividing experiences not only underscore the durability of both theological traditions, they also demonstrate the emergence of a cohesive identity. The denomination showed it could straddle the divide and stand simultaneously in two boats of tradition.

Despite few records from this period to help determine the denomination's self-understanding, the church continued to build upon its original identity of Anabaptism and Pietism. Both the right and left break-away schisms and denominational growth in the face of stringent membership requirements disclose positive feelings among insiders about the church and its dual-theology practices.

After nearly a century of informal existence as the River Brethren, in 1865 they chose an official denominational name, Brethren in Christ. The denomination then put its signature on the two traditions by continually confirming them as synthesis. Surely the church's very own tradition, along with its new name, could now be declared reality.

A People Dispersed but With Uniform Characteristics (1778-1950)

The period from post Civil War in the States to following World War II was marked by tremendous social change in both the United States and Canada. In 1788 the denomination became bi-national as a number of members emigrated to southern Ontario.[54] These Brethren, seeking land opportunities, took their unique brand of Christianity with them. There were also early migrations westward to Ohio, Indiana, Illinois, and Michigan; with later migrations to Kansas, Oklahoma, and California.[55]

The independence demonstrated by many Brethren as they moved to distant frontier areas did not sever their continuing identity as River Brethren.[56] They were known as "Tunkers" in Canada,[57] but in other areas they retained the "River" designation until 1865. In that year the church as part of an effort to represent members opposed to taking up arms in the Civil War, registered with the United States government under the official name, Brethren in Christ.

In spite of many social changes in the two nations where Brethren in Christ lived and a continued westward scattering to set up new religious outposts, there was an amazing cohesion in the dispersed group. The practice of sending visiting ministers from established districts to new areas contributed substantially to maintaining a unified identity. There were other cohesive factors that contributed to oneness of the body, including a common language, similar work, and coherent doctrines of the church and of separation.

The background and common language of early members of the Brethren in Christ was German.[58] Their ethnic ties were similar to those of other sectarian[59] and "worldly"[60] groups that had settled in southern and eastern parts of Pennsylvania. The early generations of Brethren in Christ often held to their ancestral language. As time passed, the older members especially continued to be drawn to their German Bibles and hymns as they worshiped in the manner of their forbears. *Geistlichen Liedern*, the church's hymnal published in 1874, still had 397 German hymns along with 616 in the English language.[61]

Another means of unity was their common commitment to the occupation of farming. While agriculture was the primary means of livelihood for society during the first century of the denomination's life, virtually all Brethren in Christ were connected to the soil. This pattern continued well into the twentieth century. The uniformity of occupational interests meant that the Brethren in Christ were largely rural people. Although not segregated as a group, their rural character provided a social isolation that tended to foster homogeneous perspectives. They not only gathered as like-minded Christians, but as workers with common understandings and sentiments.

Rural people tend to be characterized as simple and unsophisticated. They appreciate common sense and seem to opt for the less complex. Prior to the twentieth century the completion of basic education at a grade school level was sufficient for most church families. They were apparently convinced of their ability to get along without the benefits of extended formal knowledge; indeed, in some cases they felt they might get along better.

The greatest single factor for unity of the group appeared to be its doctrinal interpretations about the church and its precept of separation from the world. The church was governed by scriptural principles which were specific and abiding.[62] As a tightly knit community, both their doctrinal beliefs and their ways of life were often prescribed. Practices of the faith were emphasized and ordered by mutual agreement of the members as, for example, among Amish today.

Brethren in Christ throughout their "dispersion times," as they had in the River Brethren era, sought to pattern themselves after the early church. They continually strove to be "the true people of God." This Anabaptist principle was instrumental in synthesizing their dual-tradition theological views. The transforming aspect of conversion-regeneration and perfection ideals they gained from Pietism (later reinforced by a holiness doctrine that came to be termed Wesleyan),[63] meshed well with the non-conformity beliefs of Anabaptism.[64]

The issue of the church being a community of accountability was taken seriously. The church expected a high degree of conformity among its members. As late as 1941, the denomination passed legislation controlling attire for men and women.[65] Although there was individual deviation, the defining of the church as a covenanted community and actions that detailed patterns of life for its members, came together to produce a sameness that was unmistakably Brethren in Christ.

Accompanying the strict and detailed observance of church principles and practices was an exclusionary view about fellowship with other believers. A Brethren in Christ General Conference action in 1876 stated that "promiscuous communion . . . with other denominations . . . is not considered consistent." This legislation indicates a strong sectarian premise to the faith had developed in the brotherhood.

A few Brethren in Christ in the latter nineteenth century are known to have taught school (little training beyond grammar school was required). However, individual members did not begin to consider professional work until much later in this transition period. Even agricultural training was viewed as unnecessary. Enos H. Hess studied the science of agriculture at the graduate level, but he then used his science training to serve on the initial faculty body of Messiah Bible School and Missionary Training Home when it opened in 1910.[66] As a people of similar occupation who avoided the complexities of urbanism and saw little benefit in the upper levels of education, conditions that tended to reduce divergent thinking, the Brethren in Christ were ideal candidates for single-mindedness.

By 1950, a year that ended the second of two "transitions eras" (1865-1910 and 1910-1950, periods of identity issues that will be treated separately), there existed within this relatively small denomination that stretched from Pennsylvania to California, and from Florida to Ontario to Saskatchewan, an astonishingly high degree of unity and an amazing uniformity.[67] By 1950 even the church's thriving mission programs in what are today Zimbabwe, Zambia, and India, with certain cultural differences, showed similar signs of uniformity to the parent body.[68] The Brethren in Christ church appeared to be truly one body in mind, spirit, and action.

---

[1] They had no common tradition, religion, or head of state to draw them together.

[2] "A Requiem for the Spirit of 1776," *The Miami Herald*, July 4, 1976, section E.

[3] In 2005 there were 111,374 members worldwide in the denomination, with 27,630 located in North America.

[4] The Brethren in Christ denomination celebrated its bicentennial in 1978, two years after the bicentennial of the United States. C. O. Wittlinger, the writer of the most definitive history of the denomination, informed Robert Ives that the year of the denomination's beginning was probably 1776, but to avoid confusing the church's commemoration with that of the nation's the church's anniversary was celebrated at the General Conference of 1978. Perhaps this timing was a precautionary measure to avoid tying "God and country" (civil religion) together. (Information from an interview with Robert Ives on Oct. 15, 1998.)

Laban T. Brechbill in his book, *History of the Old Order River Brethren*, says that "about the year 1776 the mother congregation of the River Brethren was formed" (p. 28). Brechbill also, on page 31, cites the *History of the Engle Family* written by Morris Engle as follows: "The River Brethren Church was organized 1773 to 1778, published by Brechbill and Strickler. However, historian E. Morris Sider advises caution in regarding the authoritative nature of both the Brechbill and Engle reporting dates.

Oscar Kuhns, in his 1971 reprint of *The German Swiss Settlements of Colonial Pennsylvania*, placed the date of origin for the Brethren in Christ in 1776. On p. 179 he says: "Since the deed to the Engel property was dated 1775, and early meetings were reputedly held in the house on the property, this date seems a likely origin (Ann Arbor, Mich.: Gryphon Books).

[5] For nearly eighty years the group used the name River Brethren reflecting their founding location by the Susquehanna and their practice of baptizing in the river.

[6] The new body's ordinances (the chosen mode of baptism was especially critical) and forms were largely copied from the German Baptist Brethren, a group also standing within the same theological traditions. For an analysis of divergencies between the early Brethren in Christ and the German Baptist Brethren on "baptismal regeneration" and the salvation merit of "good works," and differences with the Mennonites regarding "total depravity" and water baptism mode, see chapter 2, "Theses Concerning Essential Truths of the Brethren in Christ."

[7] C. O. Wittlinger, *Quest for Piety and Obedience*, p. 23.

[8] Rev. Philip Boyle, a German Baptist minister, in 1848 wrote about the German Baptists (a group born in Pietism) coming to America, and explained that their dispersion into varied areas hindered their meeting in public worship, which in turn made them lukewarm regarding religious things. Winebrenner, (*History of All the Religious Denominations in the United States*, Harrisburg, Pa., 1848, pp. 91, 134.) This explanation does not follow the pattern in Acts where dispersion of the early Christians had the opposite effect. Donald Durnbaugh, an historian of the German Baptist Brethren, concluded that the group's decline in spiritual zeal was connected with the German Baptist Brethren's increased emphasis on Anabaptism (life-style and obedience issues) as another explanation offered.

[9] Moravians first came to the United States in 1735.

[10] The early River Brethren *Confession* emphasizes that "all this (salvation) is of grace and not of works."

[11] We know, for example, that one of the early Bishops of the brotherhood from Franklin County, Christian Lesher (1778-1856), converted in1803, and chosen as Bishop in 1825, possessed three books in his library authored by Johann Arendt (1555-1621), who was a forerunner and foundational to the rise of German Pietism. Other books in his possession included *Pilgrim's Progress* by Bunyon, John Arndt's *True Christianity* (a Pietist writer), the German Baptist Brethren Hymnal (1844), and the Anabaptist work, *The Bloody Theater of Martyr's Mirror of the Defenseless Christians* (from Martin Schrag's work, *Christian Lesher: 19th Century Brethren in Christ Bishop*, pp. 86, 87.)

[12] The first "Great Awakening" was led by preachers such as George Whitefield, and Jonathan Edwards. This "Awakening" had its rise in New England in the 1740s, spread to the central colonies and reached the southern colonies in the 1750s, and doubled back into the southern and eastern Pennsylvania areas in the 1760s.

[13] Roger Williams, born in Wales in 1599, formed the first Baptist church in America in 1639 (as the first dissenting religious body in America), and was then banished from the Massachusetts Bay Colony. Even though Williams established the first colony (Rhode Island), as well as a new denomination on the principle of religious freedom, his brand of Baptists claimed their origins to be English. Thus their own interpretation rules them out as a denomination indigenous to the New World, and opens the door to view the Brethren in Christ as the first church body indigenous to North America.

[14] This claim was made on page 5 of a booklet entitled *Getting Acquainted with the Church of the United Brethren in Christ*, 1998, Dept. of Church Services, Huntington, Ind.

[15] *The United Brethren in Christ*, Drury, p. 102.

[16] In 1802 the Evangelical Association clarified its inter-church ties to become a denomination.

[17] The two elected Bishops or overseers, however, continued to maintain their memberships, credentials, and associations with their standing denominational connections. Martin Boehm, a

former Mennonite Bishop who upon being banished by his fellow Mennonite Bishops, united with the Methodist church, and William Otterbein with the German Reformed church continued their previous denominational affiliations a substantial number of years beyond the 1800 beginnings date. It is not known whether the other eleven clergy of the original 1800 group may have relinquished their prior official religious connections.

[18] *Continental Pietism and American Christianity*, Stoeffler and Schrag, p. 91.

[19] The record shows that the UBIC membership consisted as follows: "some were Presbyterians or German Reformed, some were Lutherans, others Mennonites, and some few Methodists." Quoted from Winebrenner's *History of all the Religious Denominations in the United States* (1848, p. 561).

[20] The diverse backgrounds displayed by the new leaders were surely accentuated by the fact that the German Reformed church was Calvinistic and the Mennonites were Arminian in their theological orientation.

[21] Gordon S. Wood, *Evangelical America and Early Mormonism*, New York History 61, 1980, p. 362.

[22] W. R. Ward, "The Religion of the People and the Problem of Control, 1790-1830," in *Popular Belief and Practice*, ed. G. J. Cummings and Derek Baker, Cambridge, 1972, p. 237.

[23] Nathan O. Hatch, *The Democratization of American Christian*, Yale University Press: New Haven and London, 1989. p. 58.

[24] Ibid., p. 15.

[25] Alderfer, op cit. p. 259.

[26] One article of Lesher, the Franklin County Bishop, particularly emphasized the order of the church, an Anabaptist theme. Written in 1841, it was entitled, "How to Keep Order in God's House" and appeared in the June 1, 1904, issue of *Evangelical Visitor*, p. 14. The Jacob Hershey articles appear in the June 1, 1895, issue of *Evangelical Visitor*, pp. 280, 281, but both were written several generations earlier. Hershey's articles indicate that the subjects of sin and salvation continued to be of high concern during the early nineteenth century. In Pietist form he warns against the "carnal mind" and "Satan" and calls for a "work of grace" and for "spiritual-mindedness." The David Landis writings consist of a number of pamphlets written between 1825 and 1830. The pamphlets supported Pietist views and were printed by J. Bauman, Ephrata, Pa. These are in the possession of the Brethren in Christ Archives at Messiah College, Grantham, Pa.

[27] The first leader named by the group was Jacob Engel who apparently was highly respected and gave effective leadership until his death in 1833. However, the founding of the Brethren in Christ does not appear to have been precipitated by a highly dominant individual, as was often the pattern in many new religious bodies. Laban Brechbill reports that Jacob (Yokeli) Engel was born in 1753, and in 1767 joined the Old Mennonite church. Engel was "converted to God, experiencing the new birth" in 1771. (The order cited by Brechbill was that Engel experienced the new birth in 1771, four years after he had become part of the Mennonite Church.) Brechbill continued, that "while in the beginning no attempt was made to form a separate organization, about 1773 such an organization was affected . . . Jacob became the first Bishop of the new church." (Ibid. p. 30)

[28] The "Great Awakening" like its Wesleyan English counterparts has been identified as a wave of Pietism. Wm. Warren Sweet, *Religion in Colonial America*, New York, Harper and Brothers, 1903, pp. 281, 282.

[29] Alexander Mack Jr., son of the German Baptist Brethren founder, served as an itinerant preacher in Pennsylvania and produced writings permeated with Pietistic language.

[30] The technique adopted to spread the "Good News," according to Martin H. Schrag, was the

"big meeting" where preaching was carried out in homes, churches, or in big barns to accommodate the large crowds. The meetings were held on Sundays and week nights and usually lasted two to three days. *Continental Pietism and American Christianity*, Edited by F. Ernest Stoeffler, Grand Rapids, Eerdmans, 1976, p. 83.

[31] The early Brethren in Christ may have lost some confidence in Boehm as he formed a group that was less restrictive, the United Brethren in Christ, who were first known as an "un-sectarian society." The group eventually organized as a denomination and held their first annual conference in the year 1800. John Lawrence, *The History of the Church of the United Brethren In Christ, vol. 1*, 1868, pp. 263-299.

[32] Churches that failed to pursue separated lifestyles and other "obedience" principles were considered "worldly." See Martin H. Schrag, op. cit., p. 216.(that is, Morris Sider reported that George Eliot, a minister in Canada (died 1919) recounted that the church did not have revivals until later because they did not like the emotionalism of the Methodist revivals.

[33] New denominations that benefited most in acquiring new members through revivals of the "Second Great Awakening" included Methodist, Baptist, United Brethren in Christ, and other "less restrictive" groups.

[34] Quoted from pages 87 and 106 of *Christian Lesher: Nineteenth Century Brethren in Christ Bishop*, pp. 87 and 106.

[35] Hatch, op. cit., p. 213.

[36] For more information on this conclusion see chapter 3, "Theses Concerning Essential Truths of the Brethren in Christ."

[37] Martin H. Schrag op. cit., pp: 77, 299.

[38] Gains in membership for the River Brethren group would not have been easy. In addition to requiring that the potential member testify to a saving knowledge of Christ, they needed to meet specific and, it appears, rigorous expectations about a "life of obedience" that most denominations did not require. For data on denominational growth see footnote XX of chapter 3 on "Theses Concerning Essential Truths of the Brethren in Christ."

[39] Data cited in *Mennonites, Amish and the Civil War*, James O Lehman, Johns Hopkins University Press.

[40] Comparatively, the twenty first century war in Iraq—over five years from March 2003 to March 2008—3,990 U.S. soldiers had died and 29,395 had been maimed or wounded. (U. S. Dept. of Defense data cited in the March 18, 2008, issue of the *Fort Myers Press*, p. 1.) In contrast, in the Civil War Between the States, at its Battle of Gettysburg there were 51,000 casualties, including 7,000 deaths. Reported in *USA Today*, April 11, 2008, p. 5D.

[41] In the fashion of Jacob Hershey, David Landis, and bishop Christian Lesher who a decade or two prior to this time were sufficiently inspired or sensed a responsibility to write on other religious subjects, apparently no clergyman or bishop stepped forward to write on the subject of war and peace.

[42] H. Royce Saltzman, op. cit., p. 303, from an article describing the early Brethren in Christ—the article initially appeared in an 1887 issue of the *Evangelical Visitor*.

[43] Ibid.

[44] From the early *Confession* statement of the Brethren in Christ. See the appendix for a copy of the early *Confession*.

[45] Suggestions have been made that the religious services of the present day Old Order River Brethren may provide an indication of the spirit and tone of the original body because this was the era that they departed from the Brethren in Christ. But they left for the purpose of preserving the older forms—an Anabaptist-oriented concern. On this score it may be that the United Zion Church provides a better basis for such a study—since their exit was due to more Pietist-type goals.

[46] For elaboration on Pietist emphases see chapter 3 entitled, "Theses Concerning Essential Truths of the Brethren in Christ."

[47] Some of the more "worldly" denominations that had domesticated revival meetings to an ecclesiastical routine were by this time discontinuing such meetings.

[48] These are called Pietist views in light of being classified as such during the founding years of the Brethren in Christ. It needs to be recognized that some Anabaptist groups, during the middle to late nineteenth century, also became more pietistically/evangelically oriented—much in line with their earlier European forbears. By the late nineteenth century, Mennonites were beginning missionary work as were the Brethren in Christ.

[49] While Brethren in Christ growth was not explosive as it was for many denominations during this revivalistic period, their growth was substantial for a "sect" type denomination committed to "separation."

[50] Regarding this particular analysis, as one compares the nineteenth century growth of the Brethren in Christ with the twenty first century Amish church experience, which has maintained and in some areas grown by retaining their youth in the church (without intentional outreach), some may wonder about the logic used in relation to church growth. In defense of this analysis, the Brethren in Christ were then and are today quite different religiously and sociologically from the Amish. A better analogy, for this period and later would be between the Brethren in Christ church and the Old Order River Brethren church, both of which came out of the same background and religious family. The Old Order River Brethren who historically have been more highly Anabaptist in their separatist ways and surely less Pietist than the Brethren in Christ—in fact declined several hundred members to around 350 members today (from approximately 500 members initially in the mid-nineteenth century).

[51] The first of three schisms in the denomination occurred between 1838 and 1841 in southern Ohio. It was called the Wengerite schism. Due to conflicting oral accounts, the details of the schism are obscure. See Wittlinger op. cit., p. 133.

[52] The title "Yorker Brethren" was used because the main faction of the group, at their time of leaving the original body, was located in York County.

[53] From an interview with a Yorker member in 1926. Owen H. Alderfer, op. cit., p. 89.

[54] This was due to the direct effect of moving in colonies. John Winger and Jacob Sider were the first to emigrate. C. O. Wittlinger, *Quest for Piety and Obedience*, Evangel Press, Nappanee, Ind., p. 131.

[55] By 1887, when the publication of the *Evangelical Visitor*, the official periodical of the church was begun, articles, letters, and testimonials from members were contributed from nine states: Illinois, Indiana, Iowa, Kansas, Maryland, Michigan, New York, Ohio, and Pennsylvania, and from the Province of Ontario, Canada.

[56] This was affected by their moving in colonies.

[57] The name referred to the manner of baptism used in which candidates were immersed (dunked) in a river or stream.

[58] Beyond their common language, the German people had other characteristics. Benjamin Rush, member of the Continental Congress, physician, and educator, who lived in Philadelphia, helped to found Dickinson College in eastern Pennsylvania. In his travels to Carlisle Rush often encountered people of German ancestry. He may have even encountered Brethren in Christ as he passed through the region. In his 1790 Journal he described how those of German descent differ from others. He wrote, "A house built by a German could even at a distance be readily distinguished from one erected by a Scot, Irish, or Englishman." The chimney occupied the center of the roof . . . a house with a chimney at each gable end was erected by an Englishman." Also he wrote, "The Germans take great pains to produce in their children, not only habits of labor, but a love of it . . . to fear God and to love work are the first lessons they teach their children."

And he said, "the hungry or the benighted traveler is always sure to find a hearty welcome under their roofs."

[59] Mennonites and German Baptist Brethren.

[60] Lutheran, Reformed, and Moravian Brethren (The Moravians at times displayed sect qualities but they eventually became highly supportive of ecumenical efforts.)

[61] H. Royce Saltzman, *A Historical Study of the Function of Music Among the Brethren In Christ*, 1964, p. 312.

[62] An example of a scriptural interpretation about which there was a high degree of conformity in the brotherhood during the nineteenth century was the expectation that male church members wear beards. The scriptural rationale for beards was that man was created in God's image (Gen. 1:26), and hair on a man's face is part of God's creation. *History of Old Order River Brethren*, Laban T. Brechbill, Brechbill and Strickler, 1972, p. 29.

[63] At the point of becoming more theologically sophisticated regarding religious traditions (which came to the denomination in the mid-twentieth century with advanced schooling for both the denomination's scholars and increasingly trained pastors) the "holy life" for Brethren in Christ was simply referred to as the holiness doctrine. At the same time some preachers described it in the idiom of "the second work of grace,"—though not officially defined in that fashion. For further consideration of the importance and pertinence of the term *Wesleyan* to the life and theology of the Brethren in Christ see chapter 3.

[64] An example of this meshing of beliefs is that as the Wesleyan insight of entire sanctification became domesticated to the brotherhood, it was not unusual for seekers at the altar of prayer to testify they needed self to be crucified and pride removed in order to go the plain way (wear plain clothing).

[65] In 1941, after nearly one and a half centuries of the church's existence, the General Conference passed its most restrictive action regarding attire.

[66] Hess later became the third president of what was then known as Messiah Bible College.

[67] It is not unusual for a denomination to have some variance in its emphases when the church is widely dispersed to distant regions, and a degree of disparity could surely be discerned within the Brethren in Christ. But in general, the normative statements and expectations appear to have been rather close to reality in the denomination. An example of variance was that the Western frontier of the church tended to be more open to new doctrinal ideas, such as the doctrine of entire sanctification (holiness), than was the original area of the church.

[68] In vastly different cultures uniform dress patterns were honored and observed by both men and women (consistent with the church's stand on the head-covering for women and the plain vest for men).

Chapter V

The Brethren in Christ, the Vision Becomes Supplemented (1865 to 1910) and Specified (1910 to 1950)

The forty-five year period, 1865-1910, was a time when major innovations came to the denomination. It ventured into new forms of ministry (a church periodical and Sunday schools), added agencies (home and foreign boards for missions), and founded institutions (a home for the aged, orphanages, and a Bible school) to facilitate the work it was called to do. These changes were clear symptoms of another distinct change. The body was opening itself to the wider American evangelicalism of the era. The church was now apparently being modified by dialogue with and borrowing from the larger religious culture of the nineteenth century. The church also encountered a significant theological interpretative change as it extensively deliberated and eventually adopted a new doctrinal insight—entire sanctification.

But during this period the society's religious outlook in general also began to change. The popular mood toward itinerant evangelists,[1] camp-meetings, and revivalist scenes that accompanied the second Great Awakening was now shifting.[2] During the latter half of the nineteenth century most of the larger denominations began to reduce their emphasis on enthusiastic- and experience-oriented religion. The Evangelical Alliance, an interdenominational association that included mainline groups, encountered a rapidly diminishing allegiance to its "heart-change" endeavors.[3] In their quest for respectability, the trend for mainliners was now to stress religious form rather than heart-felt religion.

While in the religious mainstream there had always been a contest between the forces of revival and those of the Enlightenment, between revealed and natural religion, and between the heart and the head, new views arrived from abroad that introduced theological liberalism to many of the mainline churches. By the end of the Civil War mainstream Christian religion, which had previously been quite evangelical, diverged into two distinct tracks. One branch consisted of those who attempted to hold to standards and approaches drawn from the evangelicalism of the ante-bellum era, while the other branch was ready to adjust religion to the tenor of the new times.

Religious leadership in both the United States and English Canada was ready to consider new theological views such as evolutionary naturalism and higher criticism of the Bible. As a result a new theology took root within a generation and became a dominant force in major ecclesiastical circles. Theology, as an academic discipline, was no longer viewed as a fixed body of eternally valid truths. Many teachers and churchmen came to perceive theology as being in flux. They sensed that modern religion should adjust to the standards and requirements of modern culture.

But the Pietist-inclined Brethren in Christ were not affected by the new thinking. Their deep supernatural commitments would have caused them to deplore critical rationalism as being contrary to their own spiritual experiences. Doctrines were largely viewed as being self-evident. The Brethren attitude was that even the untutored could understand issues of faith. Also, they may have remained sufficiently separated from "modern" religious thought so that new theological ideas did not immediately affect them.[4]

In spite of the denomination's somewhat oblivious and perhaps "sect-like" attitudes toward general religious trends, the church experienced phenomenal change during this forty-five year period. One striking manifestation of denominational transition was its "about-face" toward revivalism. Just as many of the mainline churches were becoming cool to the revival idea and discontinuing the holding of protracted meetings, the Brethren in Christ in 1872 gave official approval to such meetings. This marked change of direction was astonishingly followed only nine years later by a revivalism reinforcing action. The General Conference approved rather forcefully that protracted meetings should be held throughout the brotherhood.[5] The resolution declared it to be "the duty of the members in several districts to encourage, and bear expenses of holding protracted meetings."[6]

Revival meetings were not the only evangelistic tool the Brethren sought to use. The new periodical of the denomination, the *Evangelical Visitor*, was viewed as being a means of outreach for the church. The initial purpose of the paper as stated in its masthead was: "Devoted to the spread of evangelical truths and the unity of the church." Also, an evangelistic intent appeared in the editor's "Salutatory," when he wrote, the "intention is to make the *Visitor* a blessing both to saved and unsaved."[7]

Additional dramatic changes for furthering the Gospel included the erection of the church's first meeting houses[8] (1870), the starting of the church's first Sunday school (1876), and publication of the denomination's first periodical, the *Evangelical Visitor* (1887).[9]

The church continued its practice of dispatching visiting ministers to more remote areas of the denomination. With a new emphasis on protracted meetings, evangelists were sent forth both singly and two at a time. It seems that going forth two-by-two was particularly useful to penetrate new outreach areas, and it followed the biblical pattern.[10]

There were other unprecedented developments in the century-old religious body that gave new impetus to the church's outreach and scattering spirit. A denominational mission board was organized (1872). It planned and supported varied ventures such as a mission to Native-American territories, a mission migration to California, and the daring cross-cultural undertaking of entry into urban missions settings in Chicago, Des Moines, Philadelphia, and Buffalo.[11] The mission board report repeatedly became the largest section of the annual General Conference minutes.[12] The denominational mindset was strongly missions oriented. An article in the first issue of *Evangelical Visitor* referring to "the Greek church" (Orthodox) epitomized the pro-missionary mood of the Brethren. It deridingly reported that the Greek church was not sending missionaries, and stated: "they do not obey the injunction, 'Go ye into all the world and preach the Gospel to every creature.'" As the nineteenth century closed, the addition of a foreign mission board to home missions served as the foundation for what was to come—a growing dominance of the church's mission theme at ensuing General Conferences.

Further evidence of this being a shifting denominational period was the founding of church institutions. A home for the aged called the Messiah Rescue and Benevolent Home was begun in 1897. A separate institution for children was started and titled Messiah Orphanage in 1905.[13] Messiah Bible School and Missionary Training Home was chartered in 1909.[14]

The denomination made its first major theological change during this transition period by adopting the doctrine of "entire sanctification," a supplement to its previous position on the holy life. For many years varied positions on the doctrine of sanctification were presented and debated in the church's General Conference. The church marked a milestone in 1910 when it approved a doctrinal statement embodying much of the substance of perfectionism, as advocated by the American Holiness Movement.[15] This addendum to the original interpretation of sanctification did not arrive without some stress. Consideration of the doctrine yielded heat as well as light.[16] Although the new statement specifically repudiated the provision of a "second definite work of grace" to describe sanctification, the provision for "completed cleansing" of the believer was clearly affirmed.[17]

Despite the church going through deep waters of adjustment on the holiness question, enacting unprecedented structural change, and enduring further scattering as distant mission points were opened, the denomination seemed to be highly unified.[18] The church formalized a bi-national status in 1879 when the

Tunkers of Canada and the Brethren in Christ of the United States, officially joined to become one General Conference. This union was symbolic of the sense of oneness and mutual identity that prevailed in the group.

The Brethren in Christ theological concepts during this period of adding a new doctrine and new organizational and institutional structures appear to have continued to be aligned with the two primary traditions. Its new spiritual insight on "holiness" enriched the church's Pietist core. Its goals of missions and evangelism, both historically Pietist in nature, dominated the church's attention. The new emphases on service to society evidenced by establishing orphanages, a benevolent home, and a new educational institution were both Pietist and Anabaptist. But again, their long-held German-Pietist views were now becoming affected by the wider American evangelicalism of the era.

Another way to assess the outlook and perspective of the denomination during this period is to review what grass-roots members said to each other via the denomination's periodical, *Evangelical Visitor*. Pages of the *Visitor* were used to maximize personal interaction and individual expression about the faith. This small, dispersed denomination was like a close-knit family.[19] The overriding themes that appeared in member's letters, testimonies, and short articles were accounts regarding repentance, regeneration, and Christian experience—dominantly Pietist in character.[20] For example, between November 1, 1894, and April 15,1895, the bi-monthly publication included personal testimonies as follows: Nov. 1, "Born Again," by C. H. Balsbaugh of Union Deposit, Pa.; Jan. 15, "Regeneration," A. Bell, Stayner, Ont.; Jan. 15, "Experience," C. A. Hoover, Mansfield, Ohio; Feb. 1, "Experience," Alice J. Lenbaugh, Yocumtown, Pa; Feb. 15, "Experience," Sarah E. Bitner, Ont., Ca., Mar.1; "Experience," Sarah Nigh, Stamford, Ont.; April 1, "Experience," H. B. Musser, Mt. Joy, Pa.; April 15, "Experience," Mamie Hoffer, Columbia, Pa; and Frank Perkins, "Experience," (no address given).[21]

During this late-nineteenth-century period Anabaptist-type themes in the denomination's periodical portrayed virtually no articles on the subject of nonresistance. However, there were a number of articles or statements about "the separated life," especially as it related to plain clothes. This 1888 statement in *Evangelical Visitor* stressed the importance of separated living:

> A minister must not think his work is done, when he has been successful in persuading sinners to come to Christ and make a profession. He has a further responsibility in relationship to his converts. He should teach them to come out from the world, to be a separate people, to take upon them the yoke of Christ, and follow Him, and become obedient to the gospel.[22]

The greater magnitude of the church's attention during this time of pursuing spiritual perfectionism (entire sanctification) was focused on mission concerns, and the church opened its doors to American evangelical ideas. It seems logical to conclude that the denomination veered in the direction of its Pietist roots, even though the church's Anabaptist commitment to "separation from the world" continued with force. Issues such as nonresistance, although scarcely mentioned in the denomination's periodical, were assumed to be part of the "obedient life." Accountability to the church as community was evident in prohibitions that ranged from mustaches, to lightning rods, and bridesmaids, to nonparticipation in political elections.[23] The identity of the denomination during this period of innovation, although tending toward Pietism, continued to maintain the dual vision.[24]

The Vision Becomes Specified (1910 to 1950)

During the latter part of the nineteenth century, a new kind of theology entered the Americas (from European Universities) that would impact the religious scene. At the same time a new science was emanating from the newly-fashioned modern research universities. It was a model of thinking that tended to dismiss Christian conviction. Concurrently, the new theology took on social emphases that came to be called the "Social Gospel." As the new tendency toward scientific truth joined with social concerns a formidable religious liberalism was produced.[25]

The message of the Social Gospel had an inherent secular bias and it raised doubts about a faith based on divine revelation. The popularity of Christian piety was displaced and new evolutionary ideas of Charles Darwin gained prominence. Religious skepticism began to pervade mainline Protestantism. In reaction to this sharp movement to the left a fundamentalist coalition began to form on the right. Its adherents moved on two fronts. One segment fought against the penetration of liberalism within the major denominations. Simultaneously, William Jennings Bryan and other fundamentalists campaigned to ban teaching Darwinism in public schools. The fundamentalist coalition seemed quite strong, but the ridicule that came to Bryan in the 1925 Scopes trial in Tennessee and his subsequent death moderated the groundswell of appeal toward the fundamentalist cause.[26] Although weakened and somewhat alienated, Fundamentalism continued to be a steadfast subculture on the religious scene.[27] Consequently, the years from the mid-twenties to the early forties became recognized as the "age of Fundamentalism."

As a result of early setbacks to Fundamentalism, its followers retreated to sectarian and separatist patterns, which further hindered them from exerting substantial influence on the religious community around them. But even more disastrous to their cause, fundamentalists became noted for inconsistencies, pugnacious attitudes, and a reactionary stance on intellectual matters. George M. Marsden points out that "most fundamentalists were unwilling to accept the principal assumptions and conclusions of recent science and philosophy."[28] They exhibited great apprehension regarding things of the mind and became rather distrustful of reason.

In response to the polarized positions of liberals on the left and fundamentalists on the right, a new movement began in 1941 that sought to represent evangelical concerns for Christians. It was composed of numerous small denominations as well as individuals and congregations from mainline churches, including para-church organizations. This group purposed to be less militant, more engaged with society, and more open to intellectual discourse than the fundamentalist version of Christianity. The forming group called themselves "new" (neo) evangelicals as they forged a coalition of denominations and churches under the name of National Association of Evangelicals.

The Brethren in Christ essentially remained on the tracks of its shaping traditions from 1910 to 1950. The church's efforts during these times could be characterized as soul-winning and culture-denying—traits consistent with the church's roots. In contrast to the preceding period (1870-1910) engrossed with new structural and expansive ideas, this period (1910-1950) was occupied with proceedings that were regulating in nature. The church's attention became directed toward internal adjustments. Even though several new educational institutions took form within the denomination and fresh mission points were launched, the denomination was far less evangelically aggressive and bold than in the previous period.[29] The church devoted much of its attention to the separation side of its heritage. Considerable time and energy was placed on issues related to members' adornment and appearance. For the first time in the church's history attire regulations were enacted that went beyond the stating of general standards for dress. Legislation was passed that rendered specific expectations about attire for both male and female members.[30] Evidently, the brotherhood came to believe that reliance on the admonition of principles and on living examples to preserve the non-conformist traditions would no longer stem a perceived drift toward worldly conformity.[31]

Beyond the matter of attire there were additional conformity questions that came to the General Conference. The two World Wars during this period produced issues about direct and indirect involvement in the military by denominational members. In addition, there was a decline in the primal vocation of agriculture as new technologies brought more diversity for earning a livelihood. These changes created new topics for the church concerning Christians and their relationship to labor unions. Also, there were nonconformity worship issues that came to the fore, such as the use of musical instruments.

As the denomination became more specific on issues of non-conformity it attempted to convey clearer understandings of the faith by instituting an indoctrination program. In 1941 the church created an agency called the Indoctrination Committee. This kind of indoctrination effort, formalized with a church-wide committee status, was unprecedented in the denomination.[32]

Alongside the church's attentiveness to conformity issues, the Brethren in Christ maintained their strong emphases on spiritual disciplines and evangelism. The launching of new home missions fields was pressed with vigor.[33] The foreign missions' arm of the church grew substantially in Africa and India, and the church seemed to be particularly effective when the missions programs were connected with school and hospital services.

Outside the brotherhood the "Fundamentalist" version of Christianity served as a united voice for many small, conservative groups like the Brethren in Christ. This movement was somewhat sectarian, separated, and distrustful of science (especially when heralded as the sole route to truth)—all characteristics with which many individual Brethren in Christ would have found common cause. Some individual Brethren in Christ members supported a version of Fundamentalism (with a small "f").[34] Dispensational theology and eschatology influenced parts the Brethren in Christ.[35] But the church as a corporate body remained aloof from the fundamentalist-modernist controversies and never courted any of the inter-church fundamentalist organizations for membership. It appears fundamentalists were not sufficiently non-conformed and were not giving attention to concerns that fully mattered to Brethren in Christ at this time.[36]

Neo-orthodoxy was another early twentieth-century Protestant movement during this very period, which reaffirmed certain doctrines of the Reformation. Among others, it involved Karl Barth, Emil Brunner, Reinhold and H. Richard Niebuhr. This movement contended that Protestant liberalism had illegitimately accommodated the gospel to modern science and culture, and in the process had lost the classical focus on the transcendence of God as well as the Word of God. This movement drew little attention from Brethren in Christ who were much engaged with internal adjustments on nonconformity-to-the-world issues and occupied with their efforts in missions and evangelism.

As time passed, however, the agenda and mannerisms of another cross-denominational body, the "new" evangelicals, was a different story. The "neo-evangelicals" who came on the scene in the 1940s were attractive to the Brethren in Christ. The business of this inter-church organization coincided closely with the strong missions and evangelism mandates of the Brethren. Their cardinal principles of biblicism, conversionism, and evangelism—constant themes on the Brethren in Christ docket—were clear points of mutuality. They also seemed compatible as brothers and sisters in the faith. Evangelicals didn't show the signs of belligerence that fundamentalist's contentions were prone to display. The denomination was also now approaching a turning point regarding an educated clergy, and was gaining new insights as to the breadth of God's truth and His world.[37] These factors helped prepare the church body for an increased emphasis on the Christian mind as promulgated by neo-evangelicals such as Carl F. H. Henry and Harold Ockenga.[38] The age of Fundamentalism made little impact on the Brethren in Christ and was now passing. The rise of the "new" evangelicalism presented a potential partnership for the denomination.

This era of concentrating on details and focusing on separation from the world abruptly closed when the denomination joined the National Association of Evangelicals in 1949. At about the same time the Brethren in Christ became more substantially involved in their standing trans-denominational relationship with the Mennonite Central Committee.[39] They joined the National Holiness Association in 1950. An active involvement by Brethren in Christ in interchurch endeavors marked a sharp turn from a somewhat sectarian, separatist stance to a more open spirit of cooperation and fellowship with other Christians. The denomination was now ready to close its chapter of attending to conformity details and consider opportunities for broadened outreach and service. They were also ready to amend their views about the world by exhibiting new attitudes and abandoning older forms that had persisted throughout the early life of the brotherhood.

Even though the church in the period 1910 to 1950 was highly occupied with internal concerns, and the denomination's attention veered sharply towards the Anabaptist principle of separation, the church's long-standing devotion to historic Pietist values was not diminished. The starting of holiness camp-meetings and significant attention to the doctrine of entire sanctification[40] reinforced the Pietist concern for righteousness and purity of life. Therefore, it appears that commitment to the denomination's basic theological traditions did not change during this time, and the church's identity as reflected in its two founding heritages remained uninterrupted.

---

[1] The ministry of Charles Finney as an evangelist had essentially closed. Although Dwight L. Moody in the late 19th century renewed the tradition of evangelism and revival, the strong intensity and the extensive scope of revivalism was then past.

[2] The wave of revivals had affected the broad religious scene in English Canada, just as it did in the United States.

[3] Although meetings of the Evangelical Alliance were on occasion announced in the *Evangelical Visitor*, the Brethren in Christ did not seek membership in the Evangelical Alliance. Even though the denomination changed its course and adopted the form of protracted meetings in 1872, they remained somewhat sectarian and presumably viewed the composition of the Evangelical Alliance as being too "worldly."

[4] There were exceptions to Brethren in Christ being insulated from modernist theological issues as was the case in the Oct. 15, 1898, issue of *Evangelical Visitor*, pp. 383, 384, where an article written by A. Ben-Oliel entitled, "Higher Criticism and Common Sense" appeared. In it there is an examination of the question whether the book of Isaiah should be attributed to several authors on the basis of differing styles in the book. The writer contended, "Why should he (Isaiah) not, like everybody else, change his mode of writing—his phraseology and expressions—with age, with subject, and with attending circumstances? Where is the logic, the common sense, of apportioning parts of the book of Isaiah to separate and distinct writers just because the style is different, when the subject matter is so varied and divergent? . . . It is a glaring illustration of the hollow and frivolous assumptions of the higher critics—higher in their own conceit."

[5] In just one decade the church moved from a stance of opposition to protracted meetings, to a position of essentially requiring that they be held. This seeming order that evangelistic meetings be convened in local settings, if not recompense for previously lost opportunities, was likely made to assure there would be no lost opportunities in the future.

[6] From the minutes of the 1881 Brethren in Christ General Conference.

[7] *Evangelical Visitor,* August 1, 1887, Vol. I., No.1, p.1.

[8] The building of the first meetinghouses in the brotherhood may have been an even more drastic about-face for the church than was the abrupt change regarding protracted evangelistic meetings. In 1855 Matthias Brinser and his followers were excommunicated from the denomination because they had erected a meeting-house. Within fifteen years newly erected meeting-houses appeared, first in 1871 at the Ringold Church (Maryland), later at Woodbury, Pennsylvania, and then near Canton, Ohio, (Valley Chapel). In 1874 the Franklin County Brethren began to build them, and they soon became commonplace in Lancaster County where the initial judgment to excommunicate the Brinser Brethren was made. C. O. Wittlinger, *Quest for Piety and Obedience*, Evangel Press, Nappanee, Ind., pp. 133-138.

[9] The new periodical served purposes of spiritual edification and sharing information to the brotherhood. In addition, it contributed to the unity and mutual identity of the small denomination that was scattered to the back country as well as the frontier of two nations, and would soon be launching urban-mission sites in America and new stations in foreign lands.

[10] Historian Morris Sider tells of T. A. Long, along with a minister from Stark County, Ohio, going on an evangelistic mission to Erie, Pennsylvania (1875). Two years later Long made a three-month missionary trip with Benjamin Gish of Lancaster County, Pennsylvania, (both of whom sensed a call to evangelistic work). Their 1877 preaching mission included ministry in Clarence Center and Buffalo, New York. From there they went to Canada for a short stay of meetings and then on to Michigan and Indiana where they had their most successful services. T.A. Long later paired up with Noah Zook of Kansas, who served as a prominent traveling evangelist during this period. The General Conference of 1888 named Long and Zook to hold meetings in White Pigeon, Michigan E. Morris Sider, *Nine Portraits*, Evangel Press, Nappanee, Ind., 1978, pp. 50-53.

[11] The new course was "daring" in the sense that virtually all Brethren in Christ were rural people at this time.

[12] The mission's enthusiasm at the 1887 General Conference was evidenced by the conference adopting a plan whereby each member of the denomination would be solicited annually for a

contribution to missions (no small endeavor for a brotherhood that was scattered geographically).

[13] Orphanages seemed to be a special interest of the brotherhood. The Brethren in Christ either sponsored or cooperated in sponsoring the Hillsboro, Kansas, orphanage (1889); Ishi Faith Orphanage, Lancaster, Pennsylvania, (1899); Jabbok Faith Orphanage, Thomas, Oklahoma, (1899); and Mount Carmel Faith Orphanage, Morrison, Illinois, (1900). Ray Zercher, *Brethren in Christ History and Life*, Vol. XIX, No. 3, 1996, p. 453.

[14] The three largest institutions founded by the denomination during this period all retained the name "Messiah" in their title. While no historic reason has been cited for use of the word, the meaning of Messiah—"anointed one"—was surely compatible with the strong Pietist views manifested denominationally, as well as the "holiness" views being debated in the brotherhood at that time.

[15] C. O. Wittlinger, op. cit., pp. 322-325.

[16] At a prior General Conference held in 1898, the question of a second definite work of grace and its necessity "for securing eternal salvation" was considered. The minute record emanating from the conference was "that on account of the diversity of feelings, opinions and even experiences in connection with the subject, as evidenced by the discussion, the different elements be kept under control by largeness of love and much forbearance," according to Ephesians IV, 1, 2, 3, 31, 32.

[17] This acceptance of the doctrine of holiness is a clear affirmation of the Pietist goal of purity of life. But the doctrine of holiness (perfection) also became a boon to the Anabaptist interpretation of the faith as it was used to promote conformity to the decisions of the church. Luke L. Keefer, Jr., *Brethren in Christ History and Life*, Vol. XIX no.1, pp. 35-36.

[18] Rural customs and German ethnic trappings of the scattered group continued. However, a reduction in German language use shows in that the denomination's hymnal published in 1906 only contained 16 German hymns compared to 599 English, and a second edition was available in English only.

[19] For a period in the late nineteenth century, the denomination issued an annual directory of its members and shared it with the membership.

[20] While these themes were inherently Pietist, the experience testimonies frequently related to obedience to God—regarding the wearing of plain clothes, which incorporated the Anabaptist dimension.

[21] The individual testimonials did not change appreciably in either frequency or theme when the editor post changed from Henry Davidson (1887-1897) to H. N. Engle.

[22] *Evangelical Visitor*, Vol. I, No. 6, p. 85.

[23] The seriousness of the denomination toward non-conformity issues was borne out in legislation the denomination passed at its annual General Conferences. Life-regulating proscriptions were invariably prefaced by the negative directive "it is not consistent to . . ." and included "to put lightning rods on buildings" (1873); "to commune with other denominations (promiscuously)" (1876); "to have bride servants on wedding occasions"; "for brethren to grow a mustache without a full beard" (1878); "for brethren to attend political elections" (1880); and in 1903 acted to discourage members from joining labor unions. While the church was concerned about an intrusive culture, and it appears that the above actions were taken rather seriously, invariably these areas failed to be discussed (even in a reinforcing manner) in the pages of *Evangelical Visitor*. The editors, church leaders, and the membership evidently felt that heart piety and evangelical subjects were more important.

[24] For more information on the early *Confession* see chapter 3 entitled, "Theses Concerning Essential Truths of the Brethren in Christ."

[25] Protestantism which had splintered into many groups was, in general, becoming spiritually cold and formal. The evangelical emphases that were previously in command had now become comparatively dormant.

[26] George M. Marsden, *Fundamentalism and American Culture: The Shaping of Twentieth Century Evangelicalism*, 1870-1921, New York, Oxford University Press, 1980, p. 6.

[27] Joel Carpenter in his book, *Revive Us Again,* argues that Fundamentalism was a stronger force during the 1930s and '40s than has been credited to it by scholars. His arguments seem especially convincing when he places Billy Graham and other conservative religious leaders of the '40s into the fundamentalist camp. It is this writer's view that the new evangelical movement which began in 1941 (The National Association of Evangelicals was formed in 1943.) should not be classified as part of the fundamentalist coalition because of significant differences between fundamentalists and neo-evangelicals as cited in the ensuing text.

[28] Ibid. p.7.

[29] Alongside several additional educational institutions being started during this period, another type of church institution entered the scene—the camp meeting. In the 1930s Roxbury Holiness Camp in Pennsylvania was the first denominational camp to be started. The timing for entering the institution of camp meetings was similar to the church's entry into the institution of revivalism. The Brethren in Christ, presumably due to separatist tendencies, entered the camp meeting field when it was on the way out in some of the other denominations.

[30] After repeated consideration of the dress question between 1904 and 1937, the General Conference of 1937 adopted a uniform expectation that included an "erect collar"(without tie) for men, and the head covering and a cape dress for women. An exception to the uniform attire standards was made for those in employment where the church's uniform standards were not permitted. (This meant that the cape could be discarded and the necktie worn while on duty in employment.) "The General Conference Minutes, 1937."

[31] C. O. Wittlinger points out that "time would wither these high hopes for the perpetuation of dress standards." op. cit., p. 356. (An amazingly small amount of time was required for the withering process to take place—fourteen years. By 1951 the Brethren in Christ completely dismantled the dress standards set in 1937 by deleting the description of distinctive church uniforms from the doctrinal statement, and introducing flexibility into wearing of the women's traditional prayer veiling.)

[32] The compelling motive for the creation of this committee was triggered by the war question, after some members chose to join the army.

[33] The new fields during this period were largely located in rural areas such as Kentucky and central Pennsylvania.

[34] While both Protestant Fundamentalism and liberalism may have been somewhat alien to the Brethren in Christ, numerous members of the church used a Scofield Bible, and some were attracted to millennial subjects. At the same time, Brethren in Christ would have unquestionably counted themselves as opponents of modernism and the Social Gospel. The denomination's mission included social-service ministries only when they were part of a holistic emphasis wherein evangelization received high priority.

[35] In a letter dated March, 1999, Dr. Sam Brubaker shared his recollection of, as a youth, sitting under the ministry of J. Lester Myers of Franklin County, Pennsylvania, in a preaching series "in which he presented dispensational eschatology with considerable impact."

[36] E. Morris Sider found that Messiah College and Upland College in the 1920s briefly held memberships with certain fundamentalist-type educational groups (Messiah with a group called Conservative Private Colleges, and Upland with one called The World's Fundamentalist Association), and representatives from the institutions attended at least one meeting of the re-

spective groups, but the Colleges did not appear to become actively involved with the associations.

During the late 1950s when fundamentalist, Carl McIntire, and The American Council of Christian Churches were ardently "fighting" anything even remotely connected with communist countries or causes, they put C. N. Hostetter Jr., who was serving as President of Messiah College, Chairman of the Mennonite Central Committee, and Chairman of the World Relief Commission of the National Association of Evangelicals, on their list of religious modernists and communist sympathizers because he had conversations and fellowship with a delegation of Russian churchmen. E. Morris Sider, *Messiah College, A History*, Nappanee, Evangel Press, 1984, pp. 84, 85, and E. Morris Sider, *A Vision for Service*, Nappanee, Evangel Press, 1976, pp. 86, 87.

[37] For more analysis of these academic views see chapter 3 entitled, "Theses Concerning Essential Truths of the Brethren in Christ."

[38] Carl F. H. Henry, at this time, was the editor of *Christianity Today*. During this period, Harold Ockenga was the senior Pastor of Park Street Church in Boston and served as President of Fuller Theological Seminary in Pasadena, California.

[39] Association with the Mennonite Central Committee began with World War II. Ties to the organization seemed to strengthen substantially in 1953 when C. N. Hostetter Jr., a Brethren in Christ member, was appointed its chairman.

[40] During a substantial segment of this period V. L. Stump served as editor of *Evangelical Visitor*. He was a strong spokesman for holiness principles.

Chapter VI

The Vision Becomes Engaged (1950-1980)

At mid-twentieth century, both Canada and the United States were still frequently described as being Christian nations. Modernism, however, was beginning to infiltrate the mainline churches. Higher and rational criticism was increasingly becoming the normative approach to the Bible for ecclesiastical leaders and for academics in many Protestant circles. The new thought process amounted to a growing faith that man, not God, was in charge of human destiny. Mankind had come of age and there was no longer a need for religion.[1] A theological liberalism was emerging that exhibited little concern about human sinfulness, God's grace, or the supernatural work of Christ. Throughout the United States and Canada, a dramatic secularization had advanced at a rapid rate. H. Richard Niebuhr described conditions accompanying theological liberalism as "a God without wrath brought men without sin into a kingdom without judgment through the ministrations of a Christ without a cross."[2]

In the 1950s people in general seemed preoccupied with the pursuit of material comfort. The inability of prosperity alone to provide meaning meant this complacent decade gave way to the turbulent 1960s—a time of ferment as people began to explore everything from drugs to political activism in a desperate effort to discover meaning. A theological view was trumpeted about "the death of God," and the secular spirit that had influenced society became intensified. Harvey Cox accurately depicted the mundane mood of the '60s in a best-selling theological work, *The Secular City*.

Simultaneous with the growing secularism a revival of religious sentiment emerged. Except for charismatic influences, the revival of religion was not highly evident in the mainline churches. The smaller denominations that held fast to the "Gospel" exhibited strength and vitality. This revival of faith gradually increased into the 1970s. After Jimmy Carter, a born-again Christian, was elected president, the media declared 1976, "the year of the evangelical."

Preceding this 1960s search for meaning in general society, the Brethren in Christ denomination had launched its own inquiry and reappraisal. The 1950 General Conference named a Church Review and Study Committee whose function was to examine the "state, function, and work of the general church."[3]

Some of the church's leaders had become dismayed upon learning that their denomination was viewed by other respected Christians as legalistic.[4] The church's rather strict practice of non-conformity in areas such as closed communion, its specificity on attire, its prohibitions of the use of musical instruments for worship, and its opposition to life insurance[5] were areas perceived to be legalistic.

Regardless of the outside views about them, Brethren in Christ, by 1950, had become more open to other Christians, especially those who gave testimony to God's grace working in them. Many of its members were potential candidates for substantial change. This growing openness apparently was influenced by favorable inter-church evangelistic experiences, high satisfaction with the many Christian students from other communions who had entered the church's schools and colleges, the warm Christian fellowship with "outsiders" who took part in its recent camp meetings, and recent experiences of members worshiping with other Christians in diverse settings during World War II.

The Church Review and Study Committee wrestled with complex issues—especially regarding separation-from-the-world questions and potential changes in church administration. The diverse Committee agenda seemed to center on two bottom-line alternatives: Should there be significant modifications so as to more effectively confront the world for Christ or, in order to preserve the church's purity, should it remain isolated from and minimally engaged in the culture? The Study Committee and the General Conference came out on the side of increased engagement with the world.[6] In doing so, the church pledged not to discard the doctrine of nonconformity. The basic truth of separation from the world—one of a number of cardinal beliefs of the founding members—was reinterpreted.[7] Although not without caution and reservation, the church now perceived that Christians should be engaged in the world so as to be a part of God's redemptive force and to be of greater service.

During the decade of the 1950s the Church Review and Study Committee led the brotherhood through sweeping changes in attitude and understanding. The General Conference debates that ensued often centered on the merits and perils of Brethren in Christ traditionalism. Concerns about church outreach and service were recurring themes in sponsoring issues that ran counter to certain historic traditions. Items reviewed by the church were quite diverse. They included concerns about the wedding ceremony, the mode of believers-baptism for previously baptized membership candidates, and a new plan of church administration. Considerations dealt with a broad span of faith, life style, and church governance issues.

Following World War II thoughts and outlook of the church regarding the world and service had changed. Civilian Public Service and military returnees again became part of the local congregations. Many of them had gained broadened insights. When freshly educated college students were added to the mix a more holistic worldview resulted. The church seemed ready for change.

A key and inspiring message (characterized by historian C. O. Wittlinger as such) that challenged Brethren in Christ to become more engaged with the world, was the General Conference Sermon of 1950, preached by J. N. Hostetter.[8] This sermon set the stage for significant changes to be proposed to the denomination by the Church Review and Study Committee. It presaged for the grassroots membership a key reason why major changes would be brought before the membership. It became a crucial turning point for the denomination. J. N. Hostetter, who at the time was editor of *Evangelical Visitor*, told of working with statistics at the University of Buffalo to see what the membership of the church would be if it had just retained its own children. The number was shockingly high because the church was nowhere near that membership figure.

The ensuing denominational changes that came in that conference and others that followed amounted to much more than doing away with previously-held standards that are now deemed legalistic. More positively, the Church now understood its role to be engaged with the world. The new Brethren in Christ attitude fit more closely to Niehbuhr's view of "Christ Above Culture" rather than their previous position which matched his category of "Christ Against Culture." It was now assumed that the Christian life should be lived in interchange with the world.

While John Hostetter's sermon was important to starting this new period of increasing involvement with the world, the Conference sermon by Alvin C. Burkholder in 1967 gave additional emphasis for Christians to communicate with the world around them. Burkholder quoted George Macleod as follows: "I simply argue that the cross be raised at the center of the marketplace as well as on the steeple of the church."[9] Burkholder's sermon reinforced the idea of engagement with the world as being the work of the church when he cited Richard Halverson. Burkholder stated:

> How many ministers does your church have? The traditional answer is "one" or "two" depending on how large the paid staff. But the true answer, he said, is "two hundred or two thousand," depending on how large your membership is! Every believer is a minister! When asked, "Where is your church?" the traditional reply would be, "On the corner of Broad and Main." But the correct reply is, "My church is in Room 511 in the Professional Building where Bill White, professional attorney, is practicing law. It's at 30008 Melody Lane, where Jane White,

Christian housewife, is making a home. It's at Central High, where Jimmy White, Christian student, is studying for the glory of God." There is the church in action.[10]

The Brethren in Christ amended their vision. They earnestly wanted to minister in a broadened scope and across cultural barriers. Dorothy Sherk, a member of the Canadian Conference, manifested this new spirit in an article entitled, "Exploring Brotherhood." She wrote:

The early church suffered cultural shock when it contemplated the possibility of sharing a meal with an uncircumcised Gentile. Cultural shock happens wherever a group of Christians begin to recognize the working of the Spirit in a setting where lifestyle and modes of thinking are different from anything they have been accustomed to. As we come up against situations which are new and strange, we must earnestly seek for the discernment to know what is of God and what is our role, particularly as it relates to the practice of brotherhood and the maintaining of standards.[11]

The Brethren in Christ, instead of forming cultural barriers, wanted to break them down so as to minister more effectively. The idea that God's mission to humans in their social and cultural particularities, in a non-compartmentalized church, had won the day. It now needed to be actualized. The church was ready to confess a Lord who is of this world and the world to come.

One of the most significant change was the shift from a multiple ministry in the congregations to individual pastors. The 1940 General Conference enacted legislation directing that "no pastoral service should be on a commercialized or professionalized basis." The 1950 plan was another about-face calling for financial support to enable pastors to give "the time, care, and attention deemed advisable to extend the borders, and pastor the flock, even to full time when necessary."[12]

At the same time, there was a growing awareness that pastors needed more educational preparation to adequately fulfill their ministerial calling. Members in the pews were no longer predominately agriculturalists, and the educational level of the laity was rapidly advancing. It now seemed necessary to have trained pastors to keep pace with the people they ministered to. Likewise, there was a new awareness that ministers needed specialized training to carry out distinct tasks.

During this period of precipitous change there was one very significant area that remained constant in the denomination. Spreading the Gospel continued to be the church's uppermost objective. As the church opened doors for more active involvement of its people in the general culture and society, it was to win new converts into the kingdom. The Brethren in Christ agenda, which was highly occupied with evangelization for nearly a century, did not change. The sentiments that C. N. Hostetter Jr., expressed in a 1947 "Missionary Supplement" to *Evangelical Visitor* under the title, "The Master's Program for the Church," emphasized the church's responsibility in the area of evangelization.[13] Using Matt. 28:19, 20 he stated:

> It is the first responsibility of the Christian Church to get the Good News of the Gospel message within the reach of each creature. That command stands as long as there are men and women who have not heard and who have not responded to the invitation.

Bishop Alvin Burkholder sounded the same priority twenty years later when he preached the General Conference sermon. He said (no doubt for emphasis), "I have intentionally left this area of our message for our conclusion"—his final point being about evangelism. After giving forthright attention to the need for evangelization he closed with the following poem:

> Give us a watchword for the hour,
> A thrilling word – a word of power;
> A Battle Cry, a flaming breath
> That calls to conquest or to death.
>
> A word to rouse the church from rest,
> To heed the Master's high behest,
> The call is given: 'ye hosts arise,
> The watchword is Evangelize!
>
> The glad evangel now proclaim
> Through all the earth, in Jesus' Name
> This word is crying through the skies,
> Evangelize! Evangelize!
>
> To dying men, a fallen race,
> Make known the gift of gospel grace,

> The world that now in darkness lies,
> Evangelize! Evangelize!

The frontal place that evangelism had in the life of the church was epitomized at Messiah College, where the "Doctrinal Position" section of its annual catalog continually averred, "evangelism is the supreme mission of the Church,"[14] The position that evangelization was the "primary mission of the church" was a truism with the Brethren in Christ.[15]

Returning to the subject of denominational change, the steps taken to improve the pastoral ministry at this time constrained the church to review its polity and administration structure. In 1957 the denomination enacted monumental administrative changes that called for Regional Conferences to replace districts, a sharp reduction in the number of Bishops, placement of local administration and policy-making in the hands of congregational church boards, limited terms for deacons, and made other changes that gave an entirely new face to the brotherhood. Twenty years after these enormous changes, Paul Nigh, a Canadian, in an article entitled, "The Character of the Brethren in Christ," gave his views regarding the denomination's ability to face change. He observed:

> In fellowships of lesser stature a major fracture might easily
> have occurred. It was no small matter to terminate the positions
> of approximately thirty bishops and re-work the church bound-
> aries to six regional conferences and five presiding bishops.[16]

As one reviews the church's emphasis on Anabaptist values during increased engagement with the culture, it should be noted that other Anabaptist groups at this time shifted their views about separation and interaction with the world. This analysis will not attempt to discover the theological or philosophical reasons that lay behind the changes in other communions save to say that one interpretation of the separation-from-the-world doctrine sees it as originating as a survival measure for early Anabaptists. Martin H. Schrag, in describing the impact of Pietism on Mennonites, observed that less emphasis was placed on the Great Commission because of their early survival choice between "possibly being exterminated" as opposed to being a "church of the remnant."[17] Under this interpretation, the long-held position on separation, which early Brethren in Christ borrowed from Anabaptist life, was conceived in a socio-politico context of persecution and discrimination.

Regardless of its source, the Brethren in Christ for over a century and a half perceived the fabric of culture and structures of society to be alien to Christianity. Most congregations and ministers emphasized a strong cultural separation. Martin Schrag later observed, the creation of a subculture can become rationalized as the "true church," and "discipleship can be construed as a matter of following the cultural patterns of a community."[18] Many members realized they had become somewhat legalistic as a body. By 1950 they were sensing that the general culture is not all bad and the practice of separation from the world can be unduly hinged to a subculture. The denomination decided their stance on the separated life had degenerated. They tended to maintain the separation principle because of tradition rather than according to biblical insight.[19]

The Brethren in Christ were ready to change. While their previous interpretations on the separated life had not dampened their fervor for evangelical dimensions of the faith, the denomination decided to discard any aspects of "nonconformity" that could be construed as merely sub-cultural uniformity.

The decisive actions that modified the church's position on separation were enacted and received by the church in convincing fashion.[20] The previously held church standards regarding attire, for example, continued to be perpetuated by only a minority of the church's members. From 1950 to the present, it appears that a small segment of Brethren in Christ continue to be troubled about a possible loss of key values on the part of the brotherhood. Fears are at times expressed that nonconformity or Anabaptist values of the faith (usually unspecified as to their precise nature) are slipping away from the denomination. The denomination, however, in two recent formal studies was not found to deviate substantially from other major Anabaptist groups in matters related to values and identity.[21]

At the same time the denomination adjusted its Anabaptist values on separation from the world, the Brethren in Christ developed a closer relationship to Mennonites than had previously existed. From *circa* 1778 to well into the twentieth century Brethren in Christ displayed closer affinity with the German Baptist Brethren (later named Church of the Brethren), a Pietist-Anabaptist group, than with the Mennonites.[22] However, after 1940 when the denomination became connected with the Mennonite Central Committee (to carry out world relief), and participated with Mennonites in Civilian Public Service and Mennonite Disaster Service, a much closer relationship to Anabaptist-oriented causes resulted.[23] Cooperative ventures have included joint efforts in the production of Christian education literature, and leadership cooperation and interchange with the more evangelical Mennonite Brethren.

Another indication that the Brethren in Christ turned toward Anabaptism after World War II is shown in the language and concepts they used to describe the faith. "Conversion" is a Pietist term that is basic to Brethren in Christ and continues in use. However, its corollary term, "regeneration" and the concept of "transformation" have been used less frequently after 1950.[24] The tendency today is to put an increased stress on Anabaptist concepts such as "obedience"[25] and "discipleship." Although both of these terms are quite compatible with and applicable to Pietist beliefs, they convey concepts that are particularly stressed by Anabaptists.

Just as Anabaptist symbols of separation Anabaptist changed in the brotherhood during the modern period, so did the Pietist trappings of evangelism. More emphasis was placed on individual evangelism and less on protracted meetings. The long-held pattern for local congregations to hold regular fall and spring revival meetings gave way to less frequent and shorter spiritual-emphasis meetings. The tradition of holding evangelistic services at annual General Conference meetings (typically located in a large auxiliary tent), scheduled with conference business and programmed inspirational sessions, was displaced in 1972 by a clinic on evangelism.[26] By 1974 the denomination moved away from the pattern of holding evangelistic sessions in conjunction with the General Conference and discontinued naming an evangelist for the conference.

The adoption of new and starkly differing interpretations regarding both the world and separation, which now appeared to be the case, suggests that the denomination was moving away from Anabaptism. Since other major Anabaptist groups during the post-war years also made drastic shifts in their expressions of "nonconformity to the world," one wonders about finding accurate ways to describe the change.[27] Perhaps one should simply acknowledge that in this area the Brethren in Christ, along with a number of other Anabaptist groups, were becoming less Anabaptist in defining themselves.

With the marked change regarding uniform personal appearance of church members and a growing interaction with the world about them, their increased trans-denominational engagement added significantly to their identity shift regarding relationships with other Christians. However, it appears that their basic beliefs and values did not change. The denomination continued its strong emphasis on the Pietist-evangelical dimension of its theological synthesis as it gave considerable attention to church growth and evangelism.

After 1949 when the church became identified with the National Association of Evangelicals its accountability for and cultivation of Pietist values and emphases were directed toward the evangelical coalition, called "neo-evangelicals."[28] This new coalition consisted of groups and individuals who professed social action, generated spiritual fellowship across denominational lines, and perpetuated core doctrinal values upheld by historic Pietists.

In summary, during this era the Brethren in Christ modified their revivalist Pietism, but in doing so continued to give first attention to Pietist/evangelical concerns. However, the church did not overlook its Anabaptist values. While the church's ethnocentric and tradition-focused traits were reduced, and it moved away from pronounced separation from the world, there was no substantive deviation from being a community of accountability or from valuing the importance of nonresistance. While the church's interpretations regarding non-conformity were modified, the concept itself continued to be recognized. Clearly, the church's Anabaptist values were shifting. In spite of its Pietist values being assumed under a neo-evangelical perspective, and even though the denomination displayed a broadened and increasingly integrated Christian worldview, the denomination, in principle, remained firmly attached to its dual heritage.

---

[1] This was largely an academic phenomenon, which touched the laity very little. Significant segments of the laity remained quite religious.

[2] From "Church Meets State" by Mark Lilla. *The New York Times Book Review*, May 15, 2005, p. 39.

[3] C. O.Wittlinger, op. cit., p. 483.

[4] Ibid., pp. 480, 481.

[5] The church's General Conference in 1951 acted to make life insurance a matter of individual conscience, which terminated debates on this issue that had been in progress for three-quarters of a century. *General Conference Minutes, 1951.*

[6] By 1950, only a small minority of Brethren in Christ continued to be in agriculture, and with society being much more mobile, church members no longer lived in isolated "religio-cultural pockets."

[7] The reinterpretation centered on new definitions of truth and the world that were holistic rather than dualistic in their paradigms. Also, the emphasis on nonconformity shifted away from separation *per se*, and matters of personal uniformity shifted in the direction of placing one's values on things eternal, as opposed to matters of time and sense.

[8] It was a specific time and place when a group of Brethren in Christ leaders came together to pray and intercede for the church and to gain God's guidance about the future direction of the denomination. The group discerned that the Holy Spirit was guiding them toward making major denominational changes in order that they would more effectively be the church.

[9] *Evangelical Visitor*, July 3, 1967, p.5.

[10] Ibid.

[11] *Evangelical Visitor*, April 25, 1977, p.4.

[12] C. O. Wittlinger, *Quest for Piety and Obedience*, Evangel Press, Nappanee, Ind., p. 483.

[13] Third Quarter Reports, Nov. 3, 1947, p. 1.

[14] Each annual Messiah College catalog, from the early 1940s to 1969, stated that evangelism is to be "the supreme mission of the church." In 1969 the statement was modified to designate evangelism to be "a primary mission of the church," and the statement continued for many years.

[15] Evangelism as "the supreme mission of the church" was a position that became rooted in the Brethren in Christ during the last quarter of the nineteenth century.

[16] *Evangelical Visitor*, May 25, 1977, p. 4.

[17] Martin R. Schrag and Ernest F. Stoeffler, *Continental Pietism and American Christianity*, Grand Rapids, Eerdmans, 1976, pp. 74, 75.

[18] Ibid. p. 76.

[19] A leading church administrator, in July 1967, nearly two decades after the "separation from the world" changes, reflected back on the need for substantial change in the denomination and stated in the General Conference sermon: "an awareness developed among us that the Brethren in Christ does not need to represent a dying facet of conservatism, but that we have a godly heritage of biblical doctrines that when scripturally presented to our generation not only will be accepted but will bring growth for the cause of Christ and the church." *Evangelical Visitor*, July, 3, 1967, p. 3. The amended nonconformity principle tended to leave more discretion regarding the Christian's degree of engagement with the world to individual members and their sense of calling from God.

[20] A concern was voiced by some individuals that the denomination compromised its concern for holiness of life when it deleted specifics on attire from the *Manual*, but these views were not voiced loudly. There was one congregation that departed from the denomination (the Philadelphia "mission" congregation "broke-off" and adopted the name Calvary Holiness Church). At a later time several "offshoot" congregations were formed largely on the basis of stricter standards of separation from the world. These were small from the start and continue to be so. The "dissenter-formed groups" are located in Pennsylvania and Ohio, and are reported to be using the name Evangelical Brethren.

[21] See later section of this chapter entitled, "Occasional Voices (1980 to the present) Call for More Emphasis on Anabaptist Values" and a later endnote in this chapter seeking further information on these studies. See note in chapter 3 regarding comparative limitations of that study.

[22] Beyond church ordinances and forms that were copied from the German Baptist Brethren the church's first hymnals followed in verbatim significant sections of an earlier German Baptist Brethren hymnal. There was both fellowship and interchange that included the promotion of and attendance at G.B.B. colleges (including Juniata, and Elizabethtown in Pennsylvania, and McPherson College in Kansas)—as examples, Frances Davidson, the daughter of Henry Davidson, the first editor of *Evangelical Visitor,* attended McPherson College; also, two sons, Henry and Joe, and a daughter, Emma, of the founding president of Messiah Bible School and Missionary Training Home, S. R. Smith, attended Elizabethtown and Juniata colleges. By another measure, the frequency of other denominational leaders being favorably cited in the *Evangelical Visitor*—German Baptist Brethren appeared to be more visible than any other denomination. During the nineteenth and early twentieth centuries male members even followed the G.B.B. pattern of wearing beards, which according to Old Order River Brethren sources, was not nearly so prevalent within the Mennonite church (*History of the Old Order River Brethren*, Labin T. Brechbill, Brechbill and Strickler, 1972.). Until the 1930s, there seems to have been more recognition of the German Baptist Brethren by the Brethren in Christ than any other group.

[23] One wonders why after 130 years of rather close association with the German Baptist Brethren the Brethren in Christ in the 1930s and '40s shifted their "Anabaptist group" attention from the German Baptist Brethren (Church of the Brethren) to the Mennonites. While it is mere speculation, the fact that the Church of the Brethren courted with more liberal church organizations such as the National Council of Churches (they became members of the NCC in 1950), and their general ranks gave lesser attention to separatist attire (than the cross-section of Mennonites with whom the Brethren in Christ moved) may have influenced their becoming connected with the Mennonite Central Committee, a body from which selective service issues for conscientious objectors were initially managed (World War II), and world relief issues could be cooperatively considered, instead of working with the Brethren Service Committee. Other collaborative efforts with the Mennonites soon followed the Mennonite Central Committee connection.

The fact that historian Durnbaugh shows that only 20% of Church of the Brethren young men took the conscientious objector position during World War II, in itself, may indicate that the Brethren in Christ judgment to relate to the Mennonites to administer their Civilian Public Service Camps, rather than the Church of the Brethren, or the Friends to do it, was probably an appropriate choice — in that Brethren in Christ of draft age were considerably more inclined toward that position than were those out of Church the Brethren backgrounds.

[24] This writer has vivid memory of frequent use of the concept of "transformation" in the church and recalls the familiar song that goes — "Transformed by grace Divine, the glory shall be Thine, to Thy most Holy will Oh Lord, we now our all resign." This was a song often raised in an impromptu manner and used in informal praise or commitment services. The phrase "transformed by grace Divine" communicates praise for Divine change and assistance to the believer.

[25] While the stress on "obedience" *per se* appears to be a theme of more recent use, the song "Trust and Obey" has long been an impromptu kind of song raised in informal religious settings.

[26] This clinic held in 1972 was administered by a new appointee in the denomination — a part-time Director of Evangelism.

[27] In view of the specter of a possible decline in Anabaptist values, an associated question might bear study — Are the founding political, economic, and social contexts when the Anabaptist movement formed (centuries ago), so dramatically different today that it makes some basic Anabaptist principles less applicable to present times and places? Classical Anabaptism was born in a hostile social setting of church/state political and religious hegemony. As a result, a number of highly distinctive parts of the historical tradition seem to be particularly tailored to, if not inflated by, an established or theocratic religious context. These parts include a two-kingdom theology, an expectation of suffering for the Christian, and a pronounced social separation from the world. Would these three principles seem more important or valid to a devout Christian community today in countries like Iran, Sudan, Pakistan or China than in countries where there is high toleration on religious matters, and where issues of church and state are separated? Does the application of these beliefs and their urgency depend somewhat on circumstances (e.g., times of war)?

[28] A rather obvious difference between neo-evangelicalism and historic Pietism was that matters of the Christian mind were given higher priority by evangelicals than they received with the early Pietists. Also, the early Pietists exhibited a stronger social conscience than do many evangelicals today.

Chapter VII

The Vision Confronts Postmodernism and Unfolds to a Distinct Identity (1970s to the Present)

The 1970s was a period in which the denomination gave increased formalized attention to church growth.[1] The 1970s are not singled out because of any specific events in either the denomination or within the general culture that makes it pivotal. Rather the 1970s are used as the hinge to signify the passage of Western society from modernity to post-modernity. The 1970s also signify the time in which a new phenomenon called the "information society" was becoming established.

This moving beyond modernity began in academia.[2] Postmodernism was spawned in the field of literary criticism and was in reaction to the tyranny of science (positivism). The most influential postmodern writers and their publications of the 1960s included Michel Foucault, *Madness and Civilization* (1961), Thomas Kuhn, *The Structure of Scientific Revolutions* (1962), and Jacques Derrida, *Of Grammatology Speech and Phenomena Writing and Difference* (1967). Other philosophical lights of Postmodernism were Rorty, Fish, and Baudrillard.

A paradigm shift from modernity to post-modernity either extended or introduced some relatively new societal emphases such as ethnic and cultural pluralism, deconstructionism, and a post-empiricist philosophy of science. These transitioning elements were added to a base of modernity (a term with multiple meanings).[3] The era of post-modernity introduced an entirely new intellectual climate wherein relativism and perspectivalism were advanced, and knowledge tended to become increasingly subjective. Since an assumption of this era frequently appears that there are few if any absolutes beyond one's own or one's groups' perspective, the quest for truth and knowledge for many becomes an endless process—and often self-revising.[4]

Paul Hiebert, in a presentation to the Brethren in Christ seminar on "Culture and the Brethren in Christ" held in October 1997, cited Anthony Glidden as follows:

> Post-modernity refers to a shift away from attempts to ground epistemology. . . The condition of post-modernity is distinguished by an evaporating of the "grand narrative"—the overarching "story line" by means of which we are placed in history as beings having a definite past and a predictable future. The post-modern out-look sees a plurality of heterogeneous claims to knowledge, in which science does not have a privileged place.[5]

As strange as it may seem, within the continuing context of modernity, which coexists with post-modernity, came a revival of religion. In spite of repeated claims from the 1960s modernity world that spiritual life and God are dead, the decade of the 1980s showed that both were making strong comebacks.[6] By 1984 Harvey Cox, who twenty years earlier wrote *The Secular City* affirming the "death of God," now was writing about an "artesian religious quality" and a "subcutaneous spirituality" that had reappeared in modern society.[7] In the 1980s there were clear manifestations the general culture was being influenced by religion, and the plural cultures of post-modernity were also experiencing religious stirrings.

This revival of religion in the general culture did not become evident in the regular services of mainline churches (the Charismatic renewals in historic churches, including the Catholic Church, were an exception). A spiritual resurgence, however, was transpiring in smaller denominations and in para-church movements such as the Promise Keepers, and other groupings such as New Age.

The impact of postmodern subjectivism also affected the worldwide Christian church, especially in Pentecostalism. The movement emphasized direct experience of the Holy Spirit and the renewal of spirit and soul in people's lonely lives. Its special appeal to the poor and dislocated, the space it gives to women in the church, and its non-hierarchical structure, are all positives that fit the general mood of subjectivity within society. Pentecostalism experienced unparalleled success in its outreach.[8] The fact that it is somewhat in concert with the times can also have its risks. If the timely sensibilities of Pentecostalism, which include a strong subjective sense, become single-dimensional, a proneness to error can result.[9]

Most writers use the "year of the evangelical" in 1976 as a sign of the rise of subsequent evangelical influence. One wonders whether the sense of mission and spiritual strength of the movement became increasingly vulnerable, if not dislocated, when the victory of electing a born-again president gave impetus to the conservative Christian cause. The evangelical movement became more recognized than before, but its new visibility may have compromised its spiritual mission and its primary message, the Gospel. The political success accompanying these times appears to have contributed to a distortion regarding what it means to be evangelical to the press and the pundits. More importantly it confused the church itself as to what it means to be truly evangelical.[10]

While it is difficult to make definitive judgments about the strength and influence of a large inter-denominational movement at a given time, the National Association of Evangelicals, the primary body representing evangelical denominations and churches in the United States, appears to project a much lesser voice for evangelicals today than it did thirty and forty years ago. To its credit the organization has avoided involvement in partisan politics.[11] The NAE, once characterized by broad interest, a sense of vitality, and a clear sense of direction, seems to exert less influence within the evangelical community itself.

One reason the National Association of Evangelicals may be less engaged in recent decades is because para-church organizations have displaced much of the previous work that involved NAE Commissions.[12] Also, it may well be that some denominations and mega-sized congregations have advanced their programming to the point that there is less reliance on the Association.[13] If one adds the fact that international organizations such as the Lausanne Movement siphon some focus away from the National Association of Evangelicals and the Evangelical Fellowship of Canada,[14] the vitality and priority held by these lead associations become affected. However, even though leaders may be less engaged in the workings of broad evangelicalism than they were from 1950 to the 1980s, the church remains thoroughly evangelical in its character, and its Pietist leanings are nourished through continued identification with the broader evangelical movement.

There was an even clearer diminishing attention toward the Christian Holiness Partnership during this same period. By 2007 the organization was discontinued.[15] While "holy living" may be taught by some Brethren in Christ and other Holiness groups, it appears there is little emphasis on a "second definite work of grace" and the "full eradication of sin."[16] Even though the "second definite work" and "sin eradication" provisos were never approved as part of the normative statements of the denomination, during the previous era (1950-1980) it would not have been unusual to hear a sermon in the denomination stressing both points. The denomination's continued emphasis on the holy life and Christian purity remain as manifestations of its Pietist roots and what many have termed to be the Wesleyan influence that entered the denomination in the late 19th century.[17]

By 1970 Brethren in Christ communities had changed in that many church families no longer lived in close proximity to one another, and social interaction with fellow church members became less of a focal point in their daily lives. On the other hand, across the denomination, there was a consolidating factor at work. The denomination's movement from districts to regions, operating under a Board of Bishops into the 1960s and beyond, had a uniting effect on both theology and practice. The eighties brought additional changes, but of special note is the long-term church leadership that transitioned from the ranks. In the late '70s a generation of key leaders including some who were perceived to be influential giants retired or were about to transfer the mantle of leadership. Such a high credibility stature of these leaders was presumably gained first through the visibility-trust that came from serving as evangelists across the brotherhood, and later filling critical roles as Bishops in the new administrative realignment of the denomination.[18] In addition, some individuals who might be classified as leader-catalysts (having given a lifetime of service to the general church in a variety of roles, often wearing multiple hats) either passed or retired from the leadership scene.[19]

These leaders passed the torch to other worthy and well-prepared leaders who followed. The new leaders coming out of a more specialized society to serve a different church organization generally could not duplicate the broad exposure that some of the previous generation had gained through cross-denominational evangelism and carrying multiple visibility roles. The new leaders generally possessed a more localized reputation gained from holding successful pastorates or doing more specialized church services. Leaders in the 1980s were committed and divinely gifted, but they were now serving under quite different conditions, and from different perspectives.[20] It was not just society and culture that had modified. The denomination, as noted earlier, had changed.

As one reviews the general church scene in the 1980s there were several areas that commanded the attention of the new church leaders. A more formalized promotion of church growth came through the newly formed Board of Bishops and Board of Evangelism and Church Planting. These boards enacted a considerable change of strategy from outreach efforts made under what was titled the Home Mission Board. Outreach now ideally involved planting congregations with starting groups,[21] providing significant starting facilities, and the recruitment of new pastors. The new process involved much time and effort in dealing with potential locations, personnel, and funding issues. Church leaders were concurrently highly occupied with varied theological questions, such as receiving divorced people into membership, and coming to increased theological unity by dealing with other questions reflected in a changing society.[22]

In addition to the church's significant challenge to raise financial support sufficient to accomplish its new strategy of church planting, the central church initially struggled to gain funds required to pay added employees retained at the general church and regional board levels. However, after moving in the early 1990s from a congregational assessment plan to a process called "cooperative ministries" more adequate funding for church operations was forthcoming.

Another area that beckoned the attention of church leaders during the last decade of the twentieth century was an increasing desire to cross cultural and ethnic lines in the North American body. Also during this same general time period the Board for World Missions became increasingly intentional to reach out and begin new ministries and church plantings in more countries.

The most ambitious North American cross-cultural outreach was toward the Hispanic community of South Florida. As a result numerous Brethren in Christ congregations were planted, and an associate overseer for Spanish language churches was named to give guidance to the new church plants. A testament to the church's development was made when the 2006 General Conference was held in the region of a cluster of new churches in Miami. This conference also provided a formal occasion for Eduardo Llanes, the standing associate overseer of Spanish-language churches, to be installed as Southeast Conference Bishop.

From 1980 to the Present, the Christian Mind and an Integrated Worldview Receive Increasing Attention

The Brethren in Christ have always believed the Gospel is communicated through lives of Christians. Acts of obedience to Christ are considered essential for the church to be the church. Living the faith is viewed as foundational to all forms of witness. Verbal witness and proclamation are also recognized as being important. In fact, the purpose statement of the denomination reads:

> The purpose of the Brethren in Christ church is to foster a fellowship of believers whose objective is to worship and obey the triune God and to proclaim His Gospel to all people.[23]

"To proclaim His Gospel" is consistent with the early vision when the founding members vowed "to have public gatherings where the word is preached" so that others will be "cleansed, sanctified, and saved by the washing of regeneration and renewing of the Holy Ghost."[24] The ministering brethren from the beginning were highly dependent on a literal translation of the Word and illumination through the Holy Spirit for the content of their messages. Prior to the twentieth century very few ministers had formal training beyond grammar school.[25] By the middle of the twentieth century ministers were encouraged to finish college and a goodly number completed seminary training.

With higher levels of education being attained by both laity and clergy, the denomination began to take a more critical and reflective look at the history of Christianity, and they started to look at their own history as the people of God. It was not easy for Brethren in Christ to critically assess themselves. They cherished their past and possessed strong loyalty to historic denominational positions. Besides, they had a penchant for unquestioning biblical literalism. In looking introspectively and historically, the very "literalism" that guided the denomination meant differing interpretations on issues at different times. By 1950 a new worldview that is more holistic, less privatized, and less compartmentalized was coming to the denomination. A more critical self-analysis helped the denomination facilitate major changes. Beyond 1980 it is obvious that the Brethren in Christ moved toward an increasingly integrated worldview—that their faith affects all of life—along with a growing recognition that God needs to rule over all aspects of life. There was a new realization that God cares for this world as well as the next. Therefore, His children should do the same.

From 1980 to the Present, a Time of Reduced Focus on the Christian Experience and its Accoutrements

The Brethren in Christ denomination was born in a time of religious awakening. The believer's conversion experience was a central factor in its vision regarding Christian faith and life. The church's understanding of itself, the Gospel, and the world, has always involved bringing the Gospel (Good News) to "poor sinners."[26] As the sinner comes to repentance and submits in obedience to Christ he or she the sinner become born anew. Through God's grace, the sinner experiences conversion.

While the manner in which the church's evangelization practices were carried out became modified during different historical periods, the purpose and content of its message remained rather constant. The Brethren in Christ view has consistently been that the true Christian is one who is conscious of a heartfelt, life-changing experience of faith. Apparently, the denomination never stated that each Christian should know precisely the time and place of their personal conversion, but its early practice of giving utmost attention to the Christian experience seems to belie anything less. The importance of the Christian experience, and some degree of uniformity regarding it, was evidenced in the early church, as it held spiritual gatherings called "experience meetings." The common practice was for individuals to recount and declare their personal Christian experience (by the latter part of the nineteenth century and during the twentieth century many would have reported multiple spiritual experiences because of a sanctification experience).

As time passed the term "experience meetings" was displaced by another term "testimony meetings."[27] These meetings were for avowing one's spiritual experience(s), and for sharing about one's journey of obedience. The giving of one's testimony could be part of a mid-week cottage prayer meeting (in homes of members), part of "love feast" occasions (in the district), given at a communion service (congregational), or as part of a preliminary segment to a regular service or evangelistic meeting in the congregation. Another collateral church occasion at which testimonies were given was at the close of an "altar service" (after seekers responded to a public invitation).[28]

Holding testimony meetings and emphasizing experience continued well into modern times. The focus of ministry in recent decades turned from closely monitoring personal spiritual experiences and progress toward Christian nurture and finding a sense of Christian direction in today's confused world. This does not mean the church at large has abandoned key values or overlooked opportunities.[29] Small Bible-study groups at many congregations continue to carry the former concerns, including personal sharing and spiritual discourse. Some aspects of earlier patterns are today markedly diminished. Conversion of the believer is less characterized by public sharing of one's spiritual experience(s), and there is little public emotion or travail. Lengthy and repeated public invitations to the faith do not characterize services as they once did.

During this late-modern period there was also an increasing recognition that personal conversion experiences can vary significantly between individuals—just as they differed in New Testament times. Contrasting routes to Christian experience are acknowledged in the denomination's *Manual of Doctrine and Government,* when it infers that sanctification (holiness) through the Holy Spirit as being attainable for the believer by different paths.[30]

Another difference regarding Christian experience in the late-modern period is that less detailed and forthright preaching is given to the doctrine of "entire sanctification" today than at any time since the doctrine was officially added to the Brethren in Christ vision (1910).[31] Between 1910 and 1970 the doctrine had its most positive and visible exposure. During that period the theme of holiness was widely and earnestly preached by many of the denomination's evangelists and ministers. The greatest impetus to the doctrine came via the newly formed Holiness Camp Meetings late in that period.

Luke Keefer, Jr., however, detected a denominational decline in the holiness doctrine well before the time suggested above.[32] By the 1980s there was a significant decline in the prominence of the doctrine of entire sanctification. Since support of revisionist preachers who previously urged the need for a second definite work of grace and for sin eradication for the believer has melted away, the doctrine of entire sanctification has lost some of its idealistic qualities.[33]

Advanced Traces of Division Regarding the Overall Vision

History shows that the theological vision of the Brethren in Christ has been both enduring and synthesizing. There have always been differing emphases between leaders as well as differing sensibilities among the laity. We all know that when the Gospel is illuminated, different people can preach from the same biblical text with one weaving in lessons on peace and the other inviting sinners to repentance.[34] It is surely valid that the truth needs to be spoken regardless of where it may lead. In a society that values free speech, and a denomination where the Holy Spirit leads its preaching, teaching, and writing, one may contend that openly sponsoring changes to the denomination's traditionally-ordered synthesis is being prophetic rather than dividing.

The late-modern period of the denomination has experienced increased theological fragmentation. Some divergences may be due to the denomination's pastors studying at various seminaries. Whatever the reasons, the melding of the church's theological streams into a unified whole, which had been facilitated earlier by denominational leadership giants and cross-denominational evangelists has shown signs of fragmenting. Although signs of fragmentation in the brotherhood would not be considered serious by most denominations, especially those whose pastors, church leaders, and members span the theological spectrum, the historically unified of the Brethren in Christ are sensitive to even the slightest signs of deterioration in unity.

For at least 150 years the essential experience of the denomination, including church leaders, evangelists, thought leaders, educators, and laity, has been to close ranks and be supportive after brotherhood decisions are made. However, as the title of this section suggests, it may be that a bit of splintering in emphasis has begun to show. Generalizations are dangerous, and particularly so if made about the edges of a group rather than its center. This writer senses[35] the theological "center of gravity" of Brethren in Christ pastors, church leaders, and laity tends toward the church's long-standing emphasis on Pietist-Evangelical-Wesleyan truths,[36] and the theological "center of gravity" of those in academia[37] and perhaps a few thought leaders tend toward an Anabaptist position.

Differences in emphasis among groups and individuals need not fragment the church's vision. Sensibilities vary and there are many disputable matters within the faith. Moreover, it is not a bad thing to maintain different sides on secondary religious issues. Signs of theological division were evidenced in presentations made at the denomination's November 1995 Study Conference on Brethren in Christ Identity, in Grantham, Pennsylvania.[38] A degree of conflict at the conference was shown as antithetical-type comments were made that related more to the circumference of traditions than to the heart. The antithetical comments seemed to fall into two categories: one, emphasizing differences between existing theological traditions, and positioning them as polarities, and two, employing questionable generalizations about traditions or caricaturing aspects of them.

1. Emphasizing Differences between Existing Theological Traditions, and Positioning Them as Polarities

The denomination's background theological streams not only have similarities but often overlap and reinforce each other. Several presenters at the identity conference stressed or acknowledged the interrelatedness of the church's root traditions. Luke Keefer, Jr., traced how three theological streams of the church became integrated, and especially emphasized that Wesleyanism and Anabaptism were mutually beneficial.[39] David Zercher concluded that the Wesleyan and Evangelical expressions are not a rejection of "obedience but a consequence of taking obedience seriously."[40] Harvey R. Sider pointed out the complementary and mutually supportive nature of the traditions.[41] But some writers did not see them as complementary.[42]

The overall tone of presentations at the identity conference showed a hesitancy to acknowledge that the theological traditions having greatest influence on who the Brethren in Christ are have been quite historically kindred. Even though Dan Chamberlain emphasized that Wesleyan, Pietists, and Anabaptists would agree that they "wanted no part of cheap grace . . . grace without discipleship,"[43] others seemed to disagree.[44] At strategic times there was silence on the fact that Wesleyanism, Pietism, and Neo-Evangelicalism all interpret conversion as involving life transformation, and each set of beliefs expects the fruits of changed living to follow conversion.

Another area in which theological traditions seemed polarized was that Evangelicals, Pietists, and Wesleyans, in different instances, were pictured as ignoring societal sin when throughout history there have been strong elements of social concern and action in the fabric of each of these traditions.

There is too much common ground between the denomination's various shaping theological traditions to portray them at odds. It seems irrefutable that various theological streams affecting the Brethren in Christ have tended to strengthen and encourage other traditional values. While tensions among traditions exist, these can be viewed simply as check-points.

2. The Use of Questionable Generalizations or Caricatures

Daniel Chamberlain, in his summary to the conference, gave a lengthy but appropriate response about the dangers of presenting Wesleyanism in caricature.[45] A similar complaint holds on presentations pertaining to Pietism and Evangelicalism. They were portrayed as being individualistic, which without qualification implies that no attention is given to corporate dimensions of the faith by denominations that manifest these theological streams.[46]

A question about accuracy was raised regarding a presenter's observation that the Evangelical movement tends toward Calvinism (implying that the security of the believer gets prominence).[47] The National Association of Evangelicals' statement of faith, for example, shows no bias concerning security of the believer. The most prominent historian on Evangelicalism, George Marsden, portrays "not a shadow" of Calvinistic leaning in the five theological commitments he cites as being integral to evangelicals throughout their history.[48]

The Brethren in Christ formal attachments to evangelicalism are through the National Association of Evangelicals (United States) and the Evangelical Fellowship of Canada. The claim that evangelicalism is tainted by mild Calvinism fails to coincide with my experience of serving on the Higher Education Commission of the NAE for thirty years. Neither did the claim of mild Calvinism seem factual with Arthur M. Climenhaga's NAE involvement for thirty-five years.

For clarification on the "mild Calvinism" claim Climenhaga observed that the chief executive officers of NAE through the years have largely been appointees who came out of the Arminian persuasion. He adds that historically the NAE presidents, were selected alternately from the Reformed and Arminian theological camps.[49] In the case of the Evangelical Fellowship of Canada, their recent past chief executive officer was Gary Walsh, a former Free Methodist bishop (Arminian). Their current lead person, Bruce Clemenger is presently part of the Pentecostal Assembly of Canada (Wesleyan in origin). These high appointments seem to be indication enough that there is no NAE bias toward the Calvinistic position.[50]

Another statement that stirs questions was offered by a conference presenter who referenced Evangelicals, without elaboration, as being characterized by "individualism, organization, and prosperity." One wonders how a positive quality such as "organization" should be interpreted when cited as a trait alongside "individualism." Also, one wonders whether distinguishing Evangelicals with the word "prosperity" implies that they subscribe to the "prosperity Gospel." If this is the case it would be somewhat exaggerated since exponents of the "prosperity Gospel" tend to come primarily from a segment of the Charismatic movement, which is not consistent with NAE interpretations.

Another conference statement that raises questions is portraying American evangelicals as holding values of "veneration of religious experience, personal fulfillment, do-it-yourself empowerment, and spiritual democracy." This statement places Evangelicals beside the "New Age Movement" as values bed-fellows.[51] In reality, most denominations within NAE define spiritual empowerment as being from God, with a requirement of self-abandonment.

There are dubious elements within the wide span of Evangelicalism, as there are some within the Brethren in Christ. Fragmentation of the denomination's vision is displayed when incorrect generalizations are made about the impact of "shaping" theological traditions. The mere labeling of a tradition according to extreme manifestations or abuses does not exhibit the care required for examining, establishing, or valuing denominational identity and divides the church's theological synthesis.

Occasional Voices (1980 to the Present) Call for More Emphasis on Anabaptist Values

Major nonconformity-type changes made by the church after 1950 appeared to be well accepted by virtually the entire denomination. However, in the passing of time some members are apparently troubled about a continued erosion of key Anabaptist values. Fears have been expressed that nonconformity or Anabaptist values (beyond peace and nonresistance, the nonconformity or separation issues are often not precisely specified) are slipping away from the denomination.

Concerns about diminished Anabaptist emphases have been voiced by a relative minority. They maintain the denomination's historic Anabaptist values should receive more attention. This was also demonstrated in the identity conference of the denomination held in November 1995.

The conference presentations appear to have been structured according to topics and presenters so as to give a balanced exposure to—Pietism, Anabaptism and Wesleyanism. While some concern was voiced about diminished attention to the Wesleyan dimension, there was a large voice decrying the perceived loss of Anabaptist principles. The late Owen Alderfer, for example, was quoted as saying "Anabaptism had become a burden" to the denomination.[52] Samuel M. Brubaker[53] and Naomi Stambaugh[54] expressed concern that "separation" and other Anabaptist principles were receiving declining attention. Also, Harvey R. Sider perceived community to be the church's weakest area of a three-fold historic vision—biblical, evangelical, and community.[55] One contributor declared that the church should return to a "two-kingdom" worldview, give more emphasis to love-feasts and foot-washing, become more engaged in mutual aid, and take more seriously its role of church discipline.[56]

These interpretations of the decline in Anabaptist values produced a number of unanswered questions based on two studies. One study was by Mennonites Kauffman, Harder, and Dreidger. The other was a Brethren in Christ study by Yeatts and Burwell. Both studies concluded that Brethren in Christ are in the Anabaptist mainstream in terms of values and identity.[57] Such research results, in direct opposition to certain expressed views, seem to raise several obvious questions: First, do these prevalent feelings about decline in Anabaptist values fully reflect the issue in its broad dimensions? Secondly, could it mean that other mainstream Anabaptist denominations have also moved away from long-held traditions?[58] Thirdly, if this is the case—why is it?

Beyond 2000 the Church Continues Its Pursuit of Church Growth and Reaching Beyond Cultural and National Lines

Evangelization, while expressed in different forms and methods at different times, has been a task fully embraced by Brethren in Christ. They would agree with Wilbert R. Shenk's observation that "evangelization and the integrity of the church are inextricably linked."[59] The denomination not only affirms Shenk's proposition, they have demonstrated it. Overseas membership, largely the result of missions evangelism, is nearly triple that of the church in North America.[60]

From their founding Brethren in Christ have exhibited signs related to principles of the Great Commission—perhaps initially indirect (because of economic motivations for land opportunities) but, in the course of time, fulfilling "the call." As brethren moved across central Pennsylvania county borders they started fresh gatherings of members. The earliest "colonization" of church families was to Canada.[61] Later migrations were to more remote areas in Ohio and Indiana—opening new opportunities for church outreach. Later colonizing to Kansas, Oklahoma, and California blended church outreach intentions more directly into missions.[62]

In the early 1900s the church began its first overseas mission effort. The greatest growth of the international church has emerged since 1980. In 1982 there were 11,702 Brethren in Christ communicants overseas. By 1997 the number advanced to 46,642 and to 77,558 in 2006. Numerical membership growth is not the only indication that world evangelization continues as a denomination-wide concern. In 1980 the denomination's Board for World Missions worked in six countries. In comparison, by 1998, the board, in association with internationally recognized Brethren in Christ churches, administered mission points in sixteen countries.

An indication of the intention to grow the church during the first decade of the twenty first century is clearly reflected in goals shared by Dr. Warren Hoffman in the "Moderator's Message" appearing in the May/June 2002 issue of *Visitor.* The following projection was offered:

> By 2010, we want to strengthen the health of 325 congregations in Canada and the United States. We plan to start or restart 100 congregations. We aim to deploy 100 missionaries, with outreach to the least-reached peoples of the world. Our vi-

sion calls for us to become enriched by ethnic, cultural and racial diversity — as a witness to the transforming power of God's love.[63]

The church in North America (currently about one-third the worldwide church) has not experienced the degree of growth of its international partners. This is surely not because of a lack of mission and purpose. Church planting and outreach have been constant and recurring themes in both Canada and the United States.[64] The Brethren in Christ church offices quarterly publication, *Seek,* dated summer 2006, reported on the 10-year-birthday celebration of the Community of Faith Brethren in Christ church in Roanoke, Virginia, describing it as one of 64 new churches planted over the past decade.[65]

Another denominational report recognized John Cressman, pastor of Pathway Community Church in York, Pennsylvania, who went from serving on the pastoral staff of a Canadian church of 500 to pioneer a church plant, with his family members the only participants in the beginning. "Our biggest accomplishment has been that we've gone from gathering seekers to building believers," Cressman said. "In the two years we've been here we've gone from just the five in our family to 100 people. Ours is a very seeker, inconsistent congregation. I'm not dealing with a church crowd that comes to church because that's what they do. . . I love it." He said, "We're just trying to reach peoples and love people, without being legalistic and stuffy and caught up in policy." The article continued: "Cressman, who is half-way through a master's degree in church planting, hopes to launch a pathway south congregation next fall in southern York County. Though he hopes it would eventually get its own pastor, he would start pastoring that congregation as well."[66] While this York experience is among other success stories, it should be recognized that numerous plantings have had more ordinary results.

Church planting and evangelization continue to be the denomination's most defining task. The North American church has manifested significant growth during this period — though again, not at the pace of the international churches.

Followers of the Bible, not Tradition; and of Purpose, not Image

The identity of a denomination is affected by more than its *Manual* of beliefs. Its conduct, outlook, and polity can have significant impact on the denomination's profile. But a denomination's identity is also shaped by its self-consciousness.

Throughout its history a hallmark of the Brethren in Christ seems to be a relatively low level of self-consciousness. Most denominations or movements have had one or more highly visible leader(s). However, at the start of this de-

nomination the founding individuals seem to have carried rather ordinary pro-
files. The group appeared highly democratic in polity. There is apparently no
indication that a highly prophetic leadership style was exerted. Jacob Engel,
the first leader of the group, did not portray a pattern of many initial leaders who
were part of forming a new church body, i.e., giving particular guidance through
writing and in doctrinal formulation.[67] This founding group adopted an amal-
gamation of scripturally-based doctrines that corresponded with their own spiritual experiences and understandings—often replicating views of neighboring
bodies regarding ordinances.

Even beyond individual leadership, the church as a whole maintained a
minimal profile. Almost a century passed before the denomination designated
an official name for itself,[68] and it was not until early in the twentieth century
(1904) that the denomination was chartered. When a denomination waits for
nearly a century to adopt a name and for more than a century to incorporate, it
appears there is more concern about building the kingdom of God than advancing a distinct religious group. Denominational ends or goals *per se* did not
appear to be a priority.[69]

Most denominations ground their authority in one or more of several
sources including religious experience, the Scriptures, tradition, and reason.
The two sources "emphasized by the early Brethren in Christ were the conversion experience (divinely granted) and the Scriptures." Harvey R. Sider observes, "It is instructive to note that Scripture is both implicit and explicit
throughout the early Confession." The Brethren in Christ understood that "both
theology and practice must be based on what God says in His Word."[70] A radical Bible-centeredness was the reigning theory among them.

As we currently reflect on the early Brethren in Christ we interpret them according to specific theological traditions. Prior to the mid-twentieth century
such analysis, and the dividing of the faith into systems of thought, other than
"worldly" and "non-worldly" churches, would likely have been viewed as im-
pertinent. In acknowledging the denomination paid little regard to theological
traditions, it needs to be recognized that they did give attention to certain non-
conformity traditions.[71] It was not until after 1950 that theological study for
pastors became prevalent and an examination of the church's theological traditions began.

The Brethren in Christ demonstrated openness to new truth wherever it
led.[72] They did their theology en route according to the discernment of new
light from God. They made significant and even abrupt changes when they
sensed deficiencies or inadequacies in their current beliefs, policies, or practices. However, they did not change for the purpose of conforming to any theological tradition *per se*. Their attitude toward tradition is stated succinctly by

the findings committee of a study conference on the "Brethren in Christ and Culture" when it said, "While we respect our heritage, we are not tied to it. We are open to critical evaluation and change."[73] The fact that the denomination's faith interpretations cross several traditions attests they have not been bound to any given tradition.

Also, the Brethren in Christ were not unduly concerned about the church's image.[74] Counter to observations by some writers that major denominational changes in the 1950s were motivated toward gaining "a new church identity" and were "a self-conscious attempt to alter the movement as it had developed in the 1930s and 1940s;"[75] and that movement away from churchly forms and "separation from the world" was because Anabaptism had "become a burden,"[76] this writer believes Kent Byer analyzed the situation more accurately when he disputes such conclusions. Byer made reference to what he called "church identity confusion" and used plain dress as an example. He illustrated that one of the main principles behind plain dress—a desire not to draw undue attention to oneself (to guard against possible pride of more pretentious dress)—came to a place of militating against that very principle. Plain dress, he observed, was eventually viewed as the "uniform" of the Brethren in Christ, "something that drew attention to them"—counter to the original intent. Byer questioned the idea that the church made "plain clothes" changes for the sake of image when he observed:

> What took place with the Brethren in Christ during the mid part of this century may have been not so much 'a deliberate attempt to change the nature and image of the movement,' but rather the natural process that takes place when core values (concepts and principles) cease meaningfully to support the practical expressions given to the same.[77]

This writer concurs that the basic purpose of the denominational changes in the mid-twentieth century was more substantive than to rid itself of a "burden" or "alter an image." The thought leader most strategically located for systematically reminding the church to review where it stood and where it should be going was J. N. Hostetter, editor of the *Evangelical Visitor*.

He wrote key editorials and included guest editorials on critical issues the brotherhood was facing. As a result, a growing sense of dilemma was building within the church. The issues were timely and lead into his General Conference sermon on July 3, 1950.[78]

In Hostetter's sermon entitled, "The Holy Ghost and Us," he emphasized "the whitened fields ready for harvest, pointed out that the first passion of the early church was 'to make Christ known,'" He then recounted the dangers of legalism by reflecting on the need to discern between law and grace. It was evident that he shared the sentiment of the church leaders who met in a hotel room at the 1950 Spring Indianapolis NAE meeting when reportedly, "there was unanimity within the group that we (the denomination) had come into legal bondage."[79]

In the General Conference business sessions following the 1950 sermon widespread changes were enacted by the body. In the process of repealing its standing legislation on plain attire and acting to become part of several trans-denominational associations—thus moving to a position of more worldly engagement—questions about the church "going mainstream" were raised. The concerns were centered on whether the denomination was losing its uniqueness or becoming too eclectic to stand for anything. But the denomination, now less tradition-bound than before, continued to follow its conviction of being faithful to God's Word and new biblical light.

This pattern of devout biblicism speaks volumes regarding an aspect of the church's identity—their not being married to tradition. One might well conclude that over time Brethren in Christ gained discreet theological interpretations *via* the Word—interpretations that could be assigned to other theological streams. Such gains could be construed as making them somewhat mega-traditional. However, in view of the clear affect that the counter-traditional movement of Pietism had on the Brethren in Christ from its beginnings, they were not strictly bound by long-held traditions or understandings. "A living faith" helped them as they sought to discern between biblical principles and mere conventions and to arrive at key judgments that were purpose driven rather than image generated.

Mind-set Theories and the Church's Identity

Two accomplished Brethren in Christ scholars, David Weaver-Zercher and the late Owen H. Alderfer, have produced different theories regarding the existence of a Brethren in Christ mind-set.[80] These mind-sets are briefly reviewed for their pertinence to the church's identity.

The Brethren in Christ mind-set, as described by Owen Alderfer, corresponds with a mind-set he attributed to the Brethren church, an off-shoot of the German Baptist Brethren. Alderfer's thesis goes beyond doctrines and ordinances. He contended that Brethren in Christ hold similar attitudes and thought patterns to those deemed characteristic of the German Baptist Brethren.[81]

The Alderfer mind-set theory consisted of four distinct parts: that Christian truth is open-ended;[82] that God illumines the believer with fresh insights; that a sense of trust among believers assures a measure of tolerance regarding doctrinal concerns; and recognition that the body is more important than its parts.

If for purposes of examining church identity one assumes the Alderfer mind-set principles are highly applicable to Brethren in Christ, we should analyze them for their theological implications. "Truth being open-ended" fits with Pietist interpretations in that Pietism crossed territorial church and sectarian lines. While certain key truths could not be compromised by the Pietist, such as biblicism and the importance of conversion, most other doctrines are considered open to interpretation. Indeed they subscribe to some truths as being primary and others as secondary.[83]

"God will illumine the believer with new truth" coincides fully with the Pietist position on illumination through the Holy Spirit. "A sense of trust in fellow believers" conveys a measure of toleration of differences between bodies of believers, and is consistent with the Pietist interpretation of the invisible church. "The body is more important than any of its parts" aligns closely with the Anabaptist concept of the church. While Alderfer's German Baptist Brethren mind-set theory presents a blend of inclinations compatible to both Pietist and Anabaptist elements, three of the four seem clear reflections of Pietist values.[84]

David Weaver-Zercher's Brethren in Christ mind-set theory originates with a question regarding the denomination in the mid-twentieth century. What, he asks, did the National Association of Evangelicals and the National Holiness Association have in "common" and offer to the denomination "to their liking" to cause them to join their ranks? Zercher concludes both associations offered "revival," and then he presents a special definition for the term. According to Weaver-Zercher, revival (the mind-set) is "a heightened sense of God's activity in the lives of individual believers."

It appears to this writer that Weaver-Zercher, in presenting his mind-set theory provides a cogent and accurate insight as to who the Brethren in Christ were and are today. This perception seems to concur with much of the church's activities throughout its history. It helps describe spiritual happenings and distinctive qualities surrounding the founding period and the denomination's two primary transitions—the turn of the twentieth century when the church became part of the holiness movement (to incorporate "entire" sanctification), and at mid-twentieth-century when it joined the National Association of Evangelicals (to facilitate evangelization).

Weaver-Zercher maintains that the Brethren in Christ church shows strong inclinations toward spiritual fervor, and as a whole has not "strayed far from (its) Pietist roots."[85] The mind-set he describes is thoroughly Pietistic.

Dispositions of the Brethren in Christ and Their Relationship to Denominational Identity

There may be another distinct area of Brethren in Christ life that gives further understanding or clarification regarding the church's identity. It is a Brethren in Christ disposition. While collective dispositions could be considered as yet another mind-set theory, there is justification for distinguishing between a disposition and a mind-set.

A group's mind-set is driven and affected by group goals, while a disposition is a reflection of group values. A mind-set involves the will and purpose of a set of individuals. A disposition, although tempered by logic, centers on feelings and emotions involving collective affections and aversions. The mind-set theories presented above expressed a denominational leaning toward openness and toleration as Alderfer maintains, and a penchant toward personal and group spiritual growth and activity, according to Weaver-Zercher.

Any disposition attributed to a denominational or theological tradition must reflect the values its members proclaim and live out. Several distinct Anabaptist values such as peace, reconciliation, and nonconformity provide ingredients for an Anabaptist disposition. The Anabaptist concern about service to others is not perceived to be an exclusive Anabaptist value because service receives a prominent place within other Christian traditions. While other Anabaptist values might include humility and simplicity, these elements are neither paradigmatic of the tradition nor are they stressed to the degree of peace, reconciliation, and the non-conformed life.

Features of Christian faith that received special attention within the historic Pietist tradition such as biblicism, conversion, evangelism, missions, and social service are not truly dispositional values because they are also prominent in parallel traditions. Other underlying values unmistakably tied to the Pietist tradition and contributing to a Pietist disposition are illumination through the Spirit, reliance on spiritual disciplines (i.e., prayer, Bible study, and communion with God), non-traditionalism, and a thirst for holiness (God's purity).

One process for analyzing the theological identity of a denomination is to study the frequency and/or intensity of key themes in sermons or literature produced by denominational sources. From the Reformed tradition, for example, one would expect religious discourse will have either direct reference to the providence of God or will make allusions to it. For Anabaptists it is not unusual to find pastors, teachers, and writers considering subjects about peace, reconciliation, and nonconformity; placing them as primary doctrines instead of contributory doctrines. The recurrence of special theological themes and values defines a denominational disposition.

Having read Brethren in Christ literature, witnessed its denominational leaders, and mixed with its grass roots members, I am impressed that the denomination has strong dispositional tendencies toward Pietist/Evangelical values that seem to be of underlying importance. Brethren in Christ seemingly do not shun or avoid faith issues and tenets that are close to the heart of other religious traditions. Yet, it seems clear that most Brethren in Christ tend to consider non-Pietist-centered doctrines of only contributory importance.

Hints regarding the dispositional views of a religious body appear in the subjects they consider and their frequency. They are especially exposed in the presuppositions, the conclusions, and in the ancillary observations that emerge in their discussions. One only needs to read one or two of the Brethren in Christ periodical, *Evangelical Visitor*, to find many value statements and inferences highly supportive of the Pietist legacy.

Specific illustrations about a dominant Pietist disposition by Brethren in Christ are cited from papers given at the previously mentioned denominational Church Identity Study Conference: Luke L. Keefer, Jr., offers perspectives that one might judge to have a relatively equal weighting toward several Brethren in Christ theological streams. His paper demonstrates a three-part theological synthesis. Keefer could be typed, from the article, as a holiness-believing, separated Anabaptist, with a Pietist disposition.[86]

Luke L. Keefer's disposition shows when he writes, "We must allow pastoral leadership (in our churches) to emerge from the body . . . redefine training (theological) . . . not equating it with degree programs or ministerial schools . . . emphasizing the ministerial call and not the profession."[87] A similar sign of a Pietist disposition recurs when Keefer suggests that to recapture and renew the Brethren in Christ heritage: "It is more a matter of prayer than of theological formulation."[88] These statements affirm that illumination through God's Spirit is of greater importance than reason or study. This particular insight into his disposition is of special note when one recognizes that this is the inclination of an academic—a theological seminary professor.

Another illustration is from the presentation by Kent Byer. The final paragraphs of his essay offer conclusions that contain Pietist values. They are as follows:

> First, it is important that we (Brethren in Christ) find ways to articulate our core values. At the same time, we must seek to maintain those dynamics that were present with our forefathers, who in faithful response to what they observed in the world around them became true movements for God.

Secondly, we must allow for changing expressions of how we give evidence to those core values in a rapidly changing world. In fact, we should encourage creative and relevant expressions that are meaningful to each new generation.

Thirdly, having strengthened our self-image as Brethren in Christ, we must do our part in offering the unique gifts that God has given us toward the broader work that God is doing through the global body of Christ.[89]

Byer's first two conclusions indicate commitment to "core values" which support the Pietist belief that there are primary doctrines and secondary doctrines. His second conclusion implies that "God's transformation" applies to succeeding generations. The third conclusion shows a commitment to the Pietist interpretation of the wide fellowship of believers (God's invisible church) and to the bestowal of divine help and gifts to God's people.

Jeffrey Garis closed his article, "Small Denomination," with comments that indicate a Pietist view of the importance of God's assistance in building His church:

Though we will need to experiment with new strategies, innovative structures and as-yet-unrealized modes of communication, the future of the Brethren in Christ church as a denomination is ultimately to be found in the presence of Christ Jesus living in and through His church. May we seek this above all else.[90]

This statement sees the church as an internal work of the divine rather than an external way of human life where God works within the believer. Both views are strongly Pietist in nature.

There are other examples of a Pietist disposition from the Identity Study Conference. Doneen Dourte observed that "we do not need to be denominational in the way we live our faith; we need to be Christ-like."[91] And she adds:

Our distinctives (of the church) will survive and flourish only to the degree that we can demonstrate that they are based on biblical absolutes, not tradition or preference. I, for one, am ready for pro-active decisions to be made that will ensure that future generations of Brethren in Christ will treasure our biblically based "peculiarities."[92]

These illustrations demonstrate that Brethren in Christ continue to have strong predilections toward values, or perhaps more appropriately, convictions, that are Pietistic. Interestingly, three of these people were younger conference contributors. Their views offer evidence about the denomination's current identity. These dispositional views may also tell something about the direction the denomination is moving. The views they cite are consistent with the prominent dispositions of the founding brotherhood.

The general dispositions that currently permeate the faith and practice of the Brethren in Christ, leaders and members alike, appear to be values rooted in Pietist principles. Dispositional signs of Anabaptist values are present within the Brethren in Christ. However, with the exception of peace, non-resistance, and reconciliation they are not generally portrayed as surface dispositions. There are faithful Brethren in Christ who show strong dispositional predilections toward Anabaptist concerns such as reconciliation and nonconformity, but such individuals are comparatively few in number.

Summary of the Unfolding Church Identity

Throughout more than two centuries the denomination was intertwined with Pietist and Anabaptist views, values, and attitudes. In bellwether fashion the basic beliefs of the founding members—termed in the early *Confession*, "a living faith,"—have endured and produced fruit. The church, rooted in two distinct heritages, has wedded them with other nourishing truths to form a unique identity.

At its beginning the denomination showed amazing balance between the two traditions. When one considers the Pietist tenet on "conversion of the believer" was decisive to starting the group the "center of gravity" tends toward Pietism. Except for moderating its pronounced Anabaptist stance on "separation from the world," the Brethren in Christ have historically given no hint of compromising basic truths that emanated from founding traditions. Even though there has been an ebb and flow in maintaining the church's commitment to its respective heritages, there has been a steadfastness and seemingly unalterable adherence to the dual streams.

During the "River Brethren years," there may have been a denominational shift toward Anabaptism.[93] From 1865 to 1910 the denomination became occupied with external concerns that were Pietist in character.[94] The transition period of 1910 to 1950 was marked by internal and "separation" issues that indicate a shift toward Anabaptism.[95] During the "Engagement in the World" period, 1950 to 1980, the church turned toward Pietist matters.[96] Since 1980, during post-modern times, both traditions have been perpetuated by the denomination.

The denomination has demonstrated an enduring faithfulness to its two theological traditions. The mind-set theories advanced by Owen Alderfer were dominantly Pietist in nature. The mindset theory set forth by David Weaver-Zercher was thoroughly Pietist in character. Additionally, the dispositional theory proposed in this work drew Pietist conclusions. Add to this that Brethren in Christ have historically shown minimal allegiance to tradition (a Pietist characteristic). One may further reflect that the two chief transitional periods of the denomination were bounded by significant decisions to move in a Pietist direction,[97] a confirmation of the chapter 3 conclusion affirming that the most essential truths of the church body have first been Pietist. It seems clear that the Brethren in Christ throughout their history have been most defined by their Pietist convictions.

If one concedes that the Brethren in Christ denomination is in essence a Pietist body, and at the same time is judged to be a "mainstream" Anabaptist group,[98] the question arises—how well does the denomination represent Pietism? To answer that question the meaning of Pietism needs clarification,[99] especially since Pietism is often simplistically defined.[100]

Early Pietists perpetuated a religious self-understanding which Ernest F. Stoeffler characterized as experiential, biblical, perfectionistic, and oppositive.[101] If Brethren in Christ were tested on these four criteria they would probably pass to the head of the Pietistic class. While other denominations may equal them in their emphasis on the Bible and conversion, the unremitting Brethren in Christ commitment to these beliefs, has probably not been exceeded by other fellowships. Regarding perfectionism, Brethren in Christ acquired the holiness supplement of entire sanctification which accentuated their early pursuit of the pure and holy life ideal that true Pietists sought. As to the oppositive characteristic, the denomination's separation belief, upheld in its Anabaptist commitments served to accentuate and even outdo the world-negating stance typically taken by Pietist believers. Few, if any, denominations would be able to correspond with Stoeffler's Pietist criteria to the degree that the Brethren in Christ have exemplified.

There is one dimension where Brethren in Christ may have fallen short in measuring up to the highest classical ideal of Pietism. It is in an area often overlooked by scholars, a "hope for the world" consideration, which calls the church to assist with meeting human needs.[102] While this element could be subsumed within Pietist perfectionism, it is an aspect where Brethren in Christ, especially during times of their pronounced separation from the world, could have been charged with failing to attain the classical Pietist standard.

While it is well known that Pietism has significantly influenced Protestant Christianity through more than three centuries, there are only a few denominations who consider their roots to be solely Pietist. This is because the movement's fathers, Arendt, Spener, and Francke were intent on reforming the territorial churches. They had no design to form new church bodies. Nevertheless, some radical groups did break away from the established churches to begin independent bodies.

The Pietist-oriented Moravian Brethren (today called The Moravian Church) and the German Baptist Brethren (the main body of which today is the Church of the Brethren) started on the European continent. Many of these adherents then migrated to the colonies in the new world. Pietist values were critical to the formation of several religious groups indigenous to America, including Brethren in Christ and United Brethren in Christ.

From an historical perspective, the Brethren in Christ denomination appears to be first and foremost classically Pietist.[103] This writer has not performed out a detailed historical analysis of denominations clearly distinguished by their Pietist roots and their continuing Pietist emphases. However, a general assessment of current emphases within these denominations leads me to preliminarily surmise there may be no better model today of classical Pietist features than the Brethren in Christ denomination.

At the same time the Brethren in Christ body is considered to be within the mainstream of Anabaptism. In spite of modifying their long-held Anabaptist doctrine on "separation," Brethren in Christ continue to acknowledge their Anabaptist connectedness—as do other major Anabaptist denominations that have altered their "nonconformity" stands. Even though the question as to whether Brethren in Christ are classically Anabaptist is not covered in this study, this writer suspects that Brethren in Christ may have closer classical ties with the writings of Menno Simons and Michael Sattler than do those who endorse the essence of Anabaptism as outlined in the mid-twentieth century "Anabaptist Vision" authored by Harold S. Bender. In sum, the Brethren in Christ denomination continues to be a blend of its two founding traditions. This is who the Brethren in Christ are.

---

[1] This new church growth thrust was actually initiated in 1967 and led by Roy Sider, Donald Shafer, and Henry Ginder.

[2] The postmodern movement appeared to be spawned in the field of literary criticism.

[3] Brian D. McClaren writes that broadly speaking, modernity was an age of the *machine,* an age of *secular science,* an age of *analysis*, an age aspiring to absolute *objectivity*, and a *critical age*. *A New Kind of Christian*, Josey Bass, 2001. pp. 16 and 17.

[4] Postmodernism has brought positives such as countering the positivist domination of the academic realm. Crystal Downing, a literature scholar at Messiah College, has written an excellent book favoring dynamic spiritualities, entitled *How Postmodernism Serves (My) Faith*, Intervarsity Press, (2006). On the down side of postmodernism, truth too often tends to be defined according to ones situation, and it often destabilizes traditional systems of thought, logic,

and action.

5 Glidden, *The Consequences of Modernity*, Stanford, Calif., Stanford University Press, 1990, p. 2, and *Brethren in Christ History and Life*, Oct. 1997, pp. 140-144.

6 The revival of religion and spiritual life during this period is borne out in the strength of the New Age movement—a product of post-modernity. Lars Johansson described "New Age" as a synthesis of pre-modern, modern, and post-modernism. *Faith and Modernity*, Regnum Books, Oxford, 1994, pp. 208-210.

7 *Religion in the Secular City: Toward a Postmodern Theology*, New York, Simon and Shuster, 1984.

8 The Pentecostal movement has shown robust growth in the West, and has witnessed unprecedented worldwide growth, especially among the poor in the lesser-developed countries. One estimate is that 450 million people throughout the world worship Christ as Pentecostals. (From Karen R. Long, of the Religious News Service, as reported in the *Mennonite Weekly Review*, March, 26, 1998, p. 3.)

9 In spite of these apparent strengths within the current Pentecostal movement the Brethren in Christ would presumably view Pentecostalism as mistaken when it assumes that certain and discreet spiritual gifts are indicative of possession of the Holy Spirit. It also perceives the movement as being somewhat "consumerist" in orientation–especially when it stresses a "prosperity gospel," or centers attention on good feelings and entertainment values, at the expense of service and ministry values.

10 There is a prominent view that when broad evangelicalism rose to new heights of recognition on the public scene the cause of true evangelicalism lost ground as segments of the movement became unduly aligned to partisan political ends which, in turn, often co-opted spiritual ends. Evangelicals see spiritual ends as being paramount. The image that the media and the general public hold about evangelicals is often confused. They perceive them as being immersed in political ends and typically espousing political ideas and religious ideas as one and the same. It has not helped matters that fundamentalists often became lumped by the media into the evangelical camp. David F. Wells in *No Place for Truth: Whatever Happened to Evangelical Theology*, speaks of an evangelical decline, and lays the blame for it on the failure of evangelicals to adequately articulate the evangelical movement and the world theologically. Regardless of the causes, it seems that the influence of the evangelical movement as a spiritual force became somewhat clouded. (Eerdmans, Grand Rapids, 1992).

11 The tradition that the NAE avoid partisan politics goes back to Clyde Taylor, known as "Mr. NAE." As Dwight Eisenhower took office in 1953, Taylor stated, "We are rejoicing that NAE has never allowed itself to become entangled with the political influences and parties of Washington, but has maintained itself as a service organization and a voice for our constituency, carefully avoiding all political implications." ("Report to the Board of Administration," April 14, 1953) While the NAE failed at times to follow this higher calling, they appear to have returned to the Clyde Taylor policy.

12 Understandably, the NAE is not able to provide the staffing and specialized programming that "specific purpose" groups can carry out. Organizations such as the National Religious Broadcasters, the Coalition (today called Council) of Christian Colleges and Universities, and the Evangelical Foreign Missions Association, somewhat preempted the programming previously carried by Commissions of the Association.

13 In 2004 the NAE represented 49 denominations and 300 para-church organizations and educational institutions.

14 The Evangelical Fellowship of Canada maintains considerable interest and effective programming. It is an association of nearly 30 denominations more than 100 Christian charitable organizations, academic institutions, missions, and relief organizations.

[15] The apparent decline of major interdenominational activity through the NAE Commissions and the discontinuance of the CHP organization, it appears, has not affected the basic identity of the Brethren in Christ. The denomination continues to be in full support of its long-standing evangelical and holy-living messages.

[16] Insights shared with the writer by Rich Stevens, a life-long Free Methodist and retired President of Greenville College.

[17] See chapter 3 for an analysis of the Wesleyan influence on the Brethren in Christ denomination.

[18] The leadership giants of the modern era in the Brethren in Christ would include Bishops E. J. Swalm, Charlie B. Byers, and Henry A. Ginder.

[19] Included in this group were leaders who moved out of key offices in the '70s such as A. C. Burkholder, bishop of the Midwest and the Pacific regions; C. N. Hostetter Jr., President of Messiah College and holder of several trans-denominational offices; J. N. Hostetter, editor of the *Evangelical Visitor* during a critical time in the life of the denomination; C. J. Ulery, Bishop of the Central region; and others.

[20] Five of the new church leaders—among others—included Rev. Roy Sider, elected Bishop of the Canadian Conference, later to become Executive Director of BIC World Missions; Dr. R. Donald Shafer as Bishop of the Midwest and Pacific Conferences, later to be elected the first six-year-term General Secretary of the denomination; Rev. Harvey Sider, former President of Niagara Christian College, to serve as Bishop of the Canadian Conference, later elected to be the first six-year-term Moderator of the denomination; Dr. John Byers, elected Bishop of Central Conference, later to serve a six-year-term in the office of Director of Bishops; and Dr. Warren Hoffman, elected to be Bishop of the Atlantic Conference, later to serve six years as the denomination's General Secretary, and then be elected to a six-year-term as its Moderator.

[21] The goal to recruit a nucleus of lay members to be part of the new church planting strategy proved to be a difficult task that consumed much time and effort on the part of church leaders. It probably never fully attained the ideal that was initially envisioned.

[22] In order to accomplish greater church theological unity each Regional Conference began to hold intermittent pastoral retreats (at least every four years).

[23] Quoted from the current General Conference Brethren in Christ *Manual of Doctrine and Government,* 2006, p. 5.

[24] From the early *Confession*, see Appendix of this work.

[25] Bishop Levi Luckenbach of West Milton, Ohio, who served 62 years as an ordained minister, died in 1899. The local *Record* praised his educational accomplishments and added, "he had an excellent command of language." Dr. W. O. Baker, a minister in northern Ohio during the 19th century, was also an exception in having advanced formal education.

[26] "Poor sinners" is a Pietist expression used at least five times in the original *Confession* of the Brethren in Christ. It was perhaps gained from the Moravian Brethren, a strongly Pietist group heavily concentrated in a neighboring area (Lititz, Lancaster County, Pennsylvania) to where the early River Brethren began.

[27] This writer recalls vital and spirited "testimony meetings" in the Grantham, Pennsylvania, congregation during the decades of the 1930s, '40s, and '50s and beyond. In addition to Christians testifying about personal spiritual experience(s) they might share how they were able to witness the faith to a non-Christian, or they could instead cite a request for prayer relating to personal spiritual encounters, or make other petitions.

[28] A service for "penitent seekers" was reminiscent of what some revivalist groups referred to as visiting the "mourner's bench." "Altar services" in the life of the Brethren in Christ are generally held in conjunction with an evangelistic effort in a congregation, at a denominational-sponsored Camp meeting, or in former years, at an area-sponsored tent meeting.

[29] Today the tenets of the church clearly acknowledge that man is by nature sinful and needs to have a work of God's saving grace. Also, to join the church a potential member is expected to give public testimony to a saving knowledge of Christ.

[30] See 2006 edition of *The Manual of Doctrine and Government* under "Life in the Spirit" p. 17.

[31] Except for a select group of Brethren in Christ preachers, the key resource people on the subject of the holy life at the Brethren in Christ sponsored Holiness Camp Meetings seem to be drawn from other holiness communions.

[32] Luke Keefer, Jr. in a presentation made to the Commission on Ministry and Doctrine and the Leadership Council of the denomination in May, 1997, said that "Between 1950 and 1960 the Wesleyan emphasis in the denomination reached its "high water" mark and began to decline."

[33] The denomination did not officially incorporate these specific provisions as part of their doctrine on "the holy life."

[34] Brethren in Christ have preached both.

[35] Admittedly, the sensibility stated here was not gained from a controlled study, but rather is the result of extended exposure to varied areas of the church and contact with church leaders and academic personnel within the denomination.

[36] Evangelical and Wesleyan emphases are joined with Pietism because they are rooted in Pietism, stress values that duplicate each other, and because the term Pietism is not generally used to describe contemporary religious values and doctrines. Within this combine, however, it appears the truths typically termed Wesleyan, are becoming increasingly diluted.

[37] This disposition within the academic realm particularly pertains to scholarship and writing in the fields of theology and history.

[38] The discord that was evidenced in the conference papers is perhaps indicative of post-modern times when pluralism and perspectivalism seem to rule the day. Beyond the conference, another sign of fragmentation is a growing tendency for individuals to identify themselves or the Brethren in Christ according to their own preference, be it holiness, evangelical, or as Anabaptist, to the exclusion of other traditions. Some are even known to express themselves as not personally identifying with one or another of the traditions.

[39] Keefer, *Brethren in Christ History and Life*, Vol. XIX, No. 1, pp. 26-63.

[40] Zercher, *Brethren in Christ History and Life*, Vol. XIX, No. 1, p. 173.

[41] Ibid. Harvey R Sider, p. 18.

[42] Ibid. Brubaker, p. 125. Speaking of acculturation by lumping together fundamentalists and evangelicals as holding common viewpoints is clearly different; Stambaugh, pp. 226, 234. Reflecting on Evangelicalism and Wesleyanism as being at odds with Anabaptism shows a lack of consensus.

[43] Ibid. Chamberlain, p. 256.

[44] Ibid. Keefer, pp. 48, 50. Implications are made that a changed life or a life of discipleship are not important to Evangelicals, and Evangelicalism was typecast as not being concerned with imparted righteousness; Brubaker, p. 127, The reflection is offered that Fundamentalists and Evangelicals are one and the same.

[45] Ibid. Chamberlain, pp. 253-258.

[46] Ibid. Brubaker, p. 127; Zercher, p. 176.

[47] Ibid. Keefer, pp. 39, 40. It is acknowledged that in the initial years of NAE the Association may have had an image of being somewhat Calvinistic because some of the most visible early leaders of the Association, Harold Ockenga and Carl Henry, had ties to the Calvinist tradition. However, it needs to be recognized that Arminians were strongly represented on the initial executive committee in the persons of Leslie Ray Marston, First vice pres. (a Free Methodist); Stephen Paine (a Wesleyan Methodist); and others. It is further acknowledged that those of the Reformed tradition, while not seeking to impose "election" or "security of the believer" posi-

tions as evangelical doctrines, had their primary influence in a non-doctrinal area—the intellectual, academic, and "Christian Mind" sides of biblical interpretation.

[48] Relating to the Calvinistic-leaning question, historian George Marsden, who was raised and worked within the Reformed tradition (prior to his appointments to the faculties of Duke University and University of Notre Dame he taught at Calvin College), and was distinguished as a scholar on the subjects of Fundamentalism and evangelicalism would surely include the "security of the believer" and "election" doctrines as critical truths if they were definitive of who evangelicals were and are today. But he does not include them. For Marsden's definition of "evangelical truths" see footnote in chapter 10, "Descriptive Designations to Identify Who the Brethren in Christ Are."

[49] In a letter dated September 25, 1996, Climenhaga noted the following: "My predecessor as Executive/General Director, Dr. George Ford, was a Free Methodist—thoroughly Wesleyan/Arminian. The interim director before I became Executive Director was Dr. Stan Mooneyham, a Free Will Baptist—thus basically Arminian. The man who became General Director just before I became Executive Director was Dr. Clyde Taylor. While he was Baptist (American/Southern), he was an Arminian theologically from his Christian and Missionary Alliance roots. Then I, of course, was thoroughly Wesleyan/Arminian as well as identified with the Anabaptists. My successor as Executive/Director, Dr. Billy Melvin, was Free Will Baptist—ergo Arminian. His successor, now known as 'President,' Dr. Don Argue, is an Assemblies of God minister, and thus within the Arminian theological camp." Dr. Climenhaga further observed, "more recently the Pentecostal element was introduced into the rotating Chairman position (This office had previously alternated between individuals representing 'Reformed and Arminian persuasions). Interestingly enough, a couple of presidents who were selected as representing the 'Reformed' position were respectively Evangelical Free Church and Baptist General Conference, both stated that they were basically Arminian in their theological understandings."

[50] Bill Winger, the Director of Administration and Finance of the EFC, is a Brethren in Christ.

[51] Ibid., Weaver-Zercher, p. 176.

[52] Ibid., Zercher, p. 176.

[53] Ibid., Brubaker, pp. 116-144.

[54] Ibid., Stambaugh, pp. 213-235.

[55] Ibid., Sider, p. 14.

[56] Ibid., Stambaugh, pp. 219-235.

[57] Ibid., John R. Yeatts and Ronald J. Burwell, pp. 69 and 113, A report on this study was given at the same conference where the "Anabaptist decline perceptions" were voiced. This may have been one of the most divergent interpretative conclusions of the study conference. There has been a more recent study of this nature, but because of the changes in participants see this writer's thoughts on the use of that study in a note of chapter 3.

[58] Since 1950 some of the main Mennonite bodies have also modified their understandings about "separation from the world." Therefore, it may be timely to study the views of other Anabaptist groups about their perceived strength of specific Anabaptist principles within their respective denominations. Is there an Anabaptist decline syndrome that reaches beyond the Brethren in Christ?

[59] Wilbert R. Shenk, *Write the Vision: The Church Renewed,* Trinity Press International, Valley Forge, Pa., 1995, p.73.

[60] The North American Brethren in Christ membership in 2006 was 26,957, and the membership in other nations was 77,558. From a study report issued from the Brethren in Christ Archives in January 2008.

[61] Within a decade of the denomination's founding, families of the group migrated to Canada

where they were called "Tunkers." The settlement to Canada which in that era was motivated by economic factors, surely indicated a church maintenance goal as well (colonies), and it appears by the church's growth that they eventually succeeded in enlarging their membership through such outreach.

[62] Jacob Eisenhower, the grandfather of Dwight Eisenhower, a minister in the Brethren in Christ church in the Upper Dauphin County area of Pennsylvania, with his family, was one the colonists to central Kansas in the latter half of the nineteenth century who demonstrated a religious-mission intent.

[63] *Evangelical Visitor*, May/June 2002, p. 3. As to progress made toward achieving these goals the BIC offices reported that as of December 2007 the church had attained 305 congregations (from 250 in 2002) and 80 missionary equivalents mobilized (from 50) with another 65 enrolled in the Missionary Development Program.

[64] The largest international Brethren in Christ churches are in Zimbabwe, Zambia, and India.

[65] In a 2002 issue of *Momentum*, an official release from the Brethren in Christ church Offices, it was reported that the church had spent $20 million over the past 25 years to start 166 congregations (a third in the past five years) with around 11,000 attendees.

[66] *Evangelical Visitor*, January/February 2001, p. 13.

[67] Jacob Engel was a weaver by trade and, as a church leader, traveled and ministered to extended parts of the church (indicating faithfulness as a leader). Since information about him is scant, and since there are no writings, theological or otherwise, that can be attributed to him, and since he affirmed the early *Confession* as one of a group of signers, and his name was toward the middle of the list (a highly democratic indication on the part of the chosen leader of the group), and since there is neither written record nor oral tradition about who baptized one another in the initial group, or the order in which they were baptized (added indication of a rather democratic setting), all factors that are atypical for high-profile religious leaders, this writer conjectures Jacob Engel was not a highly dominating type of person.

[68] As late as the 1840s when John Winebrenner published his work that described religious denominations in the United States, the account giving information on the River Brethren, instead of being written by a minister or official from the denomination, as was typical for other denominations, was authored by "a familiar friend." (Church of the Brethren historian, Donald Durnbaugh, surmises that "the familiar friend" who wrote the River Brethren account was Rev. Philip Boyle who also wrote the German Baptist Brethren account.) The account on the River Brethren was "friendly" to the denomination. The fact that the Brethren did not provide a writer for the account may indicate they held a reserved stance as a religious body, or that they placed little value on being listed with more "worldly" churches. This writer speculates that it may have been the former since the Brethren had displayed some trust for editor Winebrenner's brand of Christianity by using songs he had authored (Winebrenner founded a revivalist group called The Church of God and was noted for his evangelistic lyrics).

[69] This was borne out by the body from its beginning. The early *Confession* stated: "Where the teachings of our Lord are silent, there we will be silent."

[70] Harvey R. Sider, *Brethren in Christ History and Life,* Vol. XIX, No. 1, p. 7.

[71] There was a bowing to tradition in certain church forms, including patterns of separation. During the 1930s and 1940s, that is, the denomination sought to freeze certain dress patterns in time. Although they had spelled out these forms with biblical intent in mind, the church came to recognize that their expression of traditions in attire extended beyond mere biblical precepts. These short-lived actions regarding uniform dress were rescinded in 1950.

[72] The adoption of the American Holiness Movement's perspective on "entire sanctification," and the implicit acceptance of new interpretations about "truth and the world" (Reformed in terms of theological thought and perspective), indicate that the Brethren in Christ were ready

to follow "biblical truth" rather than tradition for its own sake. For further analysis on these new insights see essay entitled "Theses Concerning Essential Truths of the Brethren in Christ" (chapter 3).

[73] *Brethren in Christ History and Life*, April, 1998, p. 226.

[74] Historical reference is made (on the next page) to church leaders being concerned about the denomination being legalistic. While some may interpret their reaction as image conscious-ness, the editorials and articles of the *Evangelical Visitor* during this time, along with the an-nual conference sermon, and the sponsorship from the Church Review and Study Committee, indicate that the church leaders' reactions to "legalistic" standards centered on the issue of ef-fectiveness in ministry rather than image. For additional information on the leader's reactions see C. O. Wittlinger, op. cit., pp. 479-481, and Jeffrey Garis, *Brethren in Christ History and Life*, Vol. XIX, No. 1, pp. 184, 185.

[75] C. O. Wittlinger, op. cit., p. 475, and Samuel M. Brubaker, *Brethren in Christ History and Life*, Vol. XIX, No. 1, p. 116.

[76] Owen H. Alderfer, "Anabaptism as a 'Burden' for the Brethren in Christ," *Within the Perfec-tion of Christ: Essays on Peace and the Nature of the Church*, edited by Terry Brensinger and E. Morris Sider, Evangel Press, 1990, pp. 250-264. It should be noted that most of the points of Brethren in Christ modification to which Alderfer hinged his "Anabaptist burden" thesis, the other main Anabaptist groups have also adjusted. Regarding the peace issue most all of the larger Mennonite groups have evidenced difficulty in attaining a high degree of unanimity (thus making it a "burden")—especially during conscription times (when the military option is most measurable).

[77] The fact that substantial change in individual dress patterns followed the General Conference's actions indicated that such patterns ceased to be highly meaningful to a vast majority of church members. Kent Byer, from his paper entitled: "Brethren in Christ Images," *Brethren in Christ History and Life*, Vol. XIX, No. 1, 148.

[78] An editorial printed in the April 23,1949, issue of the *Evangelical Visitor*, entitled "The NAE Convention," began a procession of concerns that would follow in future issues. (This NAE meeting preceded by a year the one held in Indianapolis when a group of Brethren in Christ leaders gathered in a hotel room for prayer and sharing reputed to be the "catalyst formative time" that was to lead to significant change in the denomination). A June 6, 1949, editorial on "The Lord's Work" pointed out that "We must remember the Church is an institution of Grace and not of Law." In an October 3, 1949, editorial, "Let's Go" J. N. Hostetter wrote of carrying on "a church program in a bit of a recluse manner . . . while keeping ourselves from entangle-ments," a clear message that the church may be too isolated from the world. In the May 1, 1949, issue the editorial subject was titled, "At the Crossroads." It suggested that the denomi-nation needed to reevaluate and face some important decisions. In the October 16, 1949, issue, an editorial, "The Fields—White Unto Harvest," continued the "reaching out" theme.

[79] C. O. Wittlinger, *Quest for Piety and Obedience*. Evangel Press, Nappanee, Ind., 1978, p. 480.

[80] For analysis of the two mind-set views see David L. Zercher, *Brethren in Christ History and Life*, Vol. XIX, No. 1, pp. 154-183, and Owen R Alderfer, Ibid., (December 1984), pp. 125-134, and Ibid., (April 1985), pp. 3-12.

[81] Alderfer implies that the early Brethren in Christ absorbed the German Baptist Brethren mind-set and, therefore, related it to The Brethren Church, the body that sponsored Ashland Theo-logical Seminary where Dr. Alderfer taught for many years.

[82] One of the four points in Alderfer's "Brethren Church matching" mind-set theory seems ill-fit-ted to the Brethren in Christ. It is that they "view truth as open-ended." While the Brethren in Christ may view secondary truths as "open-ended," they do not appear inclined to be tentative regarding primary doctrinal views that relate directly to the faith.

[83] The Pietist view as expressed by the Moravian, Count Zinzendorf, was to preserve the values of diversity in unity according to the motto: "In essentials unity, in non-essentials diversity, and in all things charity."

[84] While certain Pietist-type values would not be considered foreign to Anabaptism, this evaluation is made between the two traditions according to their comparative degree of emphasis on the respective factors.

[85] David Weaver-Zercher, op. cit., p.165.

[86] Keefer's support of Pietist, Wesleyan, and Anabaptist truths are unabashed, but it was certain dispositional values that seemed to be highly determinative of his basic presuppositions.

[87] Keefer, *Brethren in Christ History and Life,* Vol., XIX, No. 1, p. 53.

[88] 198 Ibid., Keefer, p. 45.

[89] Kent Byer, Ibid., p. 146.

[90] Jeffrey Garis, Ibid., p. 207.

[91] Doneen Dourte, Ibid., p. 216

[92] Ibid., p. 214.

[93] cf. Martin H. Schrag, op. cit., pp. 77, 299.

[94] The instituting of protracted evangelistic meetings was approved, a missionary fund was started that supported newly instituted home and foreign mission efforts, and the denomination exhibited a broadened social conscience as a benevolent home, a number of orphanages, and a Bible school and missionary training home were established.

[95] Group issues that were somewhat introspective in nature seemed to attract particular attention during this period as the church spelled out codes of dress for both men and women, decided that ministers should not be granted remuneration for their services, and reaffirmed that it is inconsistent for church members to take out insurance.

[96] Interdenominational associations were entered, strict separatist standards were relaxed, and church growth was given special emphasis by instituting trained and paid clergy and encouraging full-time pastorates.

[97] The decisions were to approve the concept of "entire sanctification" (1910), and to join the National Association of Evangelicals (1949), and the National Holiness Association (1950).

[98] The conclusions of two different studies on Anabaptist identity and values place the Brethren in Christ denomination in the mainstream of Anabaptism when compared to other Anabaptist denominations. One study was carried out by Mennonites Kauffman, Harder, and Dreidger, and the other, authored by Yeatts and Burwell, Brethren in Christ scholars, *Brethren in Christ History and Life*, Vol. XIX, No. 1, pp. 69, 113.

[99] For a definition of Pietism see chapter 2 entitled, "Traditions and Concepts Linked to the Brethren in Christ."

[100] It is assumed that a theological tradition is best defined according to its original manifestations and must be seen with reference to its center, not its circumference.

[101] Stoeffler, *Continental Pietism and American Christianity*, Eerdmans, Grand Rapids, 1976, p. 9.

[102] Pietists were regularly occupied with issues related to transforming the church, but they were also concerned about transforming social conditions around them. Stoeffler alludes to the fact that Pietists exercised social responsibility when he considers their idealism and their pursuit of perfectionism, but he did not include social concern as a discreet emphasis of Pietists. For a more complete analysis of Pietist characteristics of exhibiting a social conscience and carrying out social services see Dale Brown, *Understanding Pietism*, Eerdmans, p. 131.

[103] The term classic is defined as being of a high standard.

Chapter VIII

Three Meaningful Qualities
of the Brethren in Christ

Stories about the origin of denominations or religious movements often center on a theme set forth in reaction to adverse conditions in either a broad or more limited religious context. A common desire to correct circumstances perceived to be deficient is what triggers the start of something new. One course toward such correction has been to stress or emphasize a particular doctrine or set of beliefs—perhaps even to the neglect of other important truths. Numerous denominations have come to be identified with historic movements or traditions. Martin Luther's theme of "justification by faith" was central to the Protestant movement. Calvinism was marked by an emphasis on the "sovereignty of God." For Anabaptists, "believers baptism," and the church as community were key doctrines. The touchstone of distinction for Pietists was the doctrine of conversion-regeneration.

As denominations were spawned from broader movements, they became distinguished according to more distinct doctrinal formulations. The Quakers' distinctive emphases were peace and personal illumination from God. The Methodists, whose origins were affected by Pietism, gave special attention to the Holy Spirit and its empowerment. German Baptist Brethren, rather than underscoring one truth, featured a new combination of tenets originating in Pietism and Anabaptism. Mennonites became typed for their nonresistance and separation distinctives (Their European mark of believers baptism was less distinct in America where it was practiced by other groups). In these modern times of ecumenism theological differences are often perceived as being historic, with current interpretations often becoming quite obscure.

The Brethren in Christ also possessed a vision of their own. Their commitments, rooted in Pietism and Anabaptism, were not unique, as noted above regarding German Baptist Brethren. The Pietist doctrine of conversion-regeneration was significant for both groups. That is also where they differed. Distinctions between the two were in areas of timing and process of the conversion-regeneration experience. The Brethren in Christ interpretation leaned toward a faith-oriented position, with the changed life to be demonstrated. The German Baptist Brethren interpretation had a works component within the process of the salvation experience. Although both groups followed the same duality, the Brethren in Christ leaned toward a Pietist interpretation, while the Church of the Brethren tended to follow a route described by some Anabaptists as the salvation process.[1]

Religious denominations differ in many ways beyond the mix or blends of doctrines they hold. They vary in the polity that guides them, the forms they follow, the traditions they revere, the values they uphold, and the practices they carry out. The total of such characteristics produces varied qualities in denominations. Three qualities that Brethren in Christ, when compared to other religious groups, seem to exhibit with consistency are: wholeness, balance, and being relational (connecting with other Christians).

Quality One: Wholeness
The Brethren in Christ Demonstrate a Holistic Faith

Most denominations profess being holistic in their theology and are concerned about the full range of faith. But there are indications to the contrary. The church at times fails to demonstrate a full understanding of the human condition (that sin is a root problem) and that God's truths have a unity that can meet the man's varied issues and problems. Also, denominations are frequently foiled by post-modern society's emphasis on individualism (from modern times) and its increased degree of relativism—in that the church tends to become unduly influenced by these factors.[2] As a result, when society searches for answers to questions of meaning about the world, the church often falls short in providing a helpful response. Failing to find whole answers our communities become atomized—a condition evidenced by narrow special interests, single-issue politics, and truncated worldviews.

Regrettably, many forms of Christianity are often perceived as inadequate to meet the diverse needs confronting society today. It appears, however, the Brethren in Christ expression of Christian faith manifests a high measure of wholeness. John Zercher, the late *Visitor* editor, told of the time he was asked to characterize the Brethren in Christ denomination in one word. He stated, "the occasion did not allow much time for reflection. The word I chose was somewhat spontaneous. I selected the word wholeness. I have had more time, since our conversation, to reflect on the question of my friend and on my response. I have not yet come up with a better word." Zercher then explained, "There is a wholeness to the denomination's understanding of salvation, the human situation, and the church's mission."[3]

There are additional areas which can help us see the quality of wholeness in the denomination:

1. A Holistic Concept of the Church Is Recognized by the Brethren in Christ.

Of course, the Brethren in Christ are not unique in emphasizing a multi-faceted church ministry, but their interpretation of the church seems broader than it is for many denominations. The new group was born in a cradle-area of various sect-like groups that lived the visible church idea. Presumably, many of its initial members came from families that had been part of such a heritage. Therefore, the initial concept of the church was grounded in the Anabaptist view of the visible church.

For one and a half centuries the denomination maintained a degree of communal exclusiveness and religious separation. Not until the mid-twentieth century did the Brethren in Christ begin to formally invite outside believers to the Lord's Table (open communion). Yet the universal church, it appears, was always perceived by Brethren in Christ to be inclusive of other Christians. From early times the church used hymns written by Christians from other communions and referred to members of other groups as brother or sister (reserved for those who acknowledged being spiritually converted).[4]

Within their church-community setting, the individual believer was accountable to other members of the body. This meant that believers should work together and be dependent on one another instead of being entirely self-reliant. These communal principles were not limited to the period when the denomination was somewhat sectarian. They continued to be important as the denomination revised its understandings to allow for more direct engagement in the world.

From the church's beginning, its separatist community practices were supplemented by outreach characteristics. The beginning group envisioned the ministry of the church to include that of spiritual edification (in private gatherings), evangelism (in public gatherings), and service. In spite of sectarian forms, they seemed to recognize no single group in time or place fully represented the church. The church body understood the Christian church to be universal.

Through the centuries Brethren in Christ have supported a holistic doctrine of the church that envisions its ministry to include community, discipline, edification, service, and evangelism. Most mainline denominations vigorously pursue the edification and service dimensions and may do less well in other areas. In contrast, many smaller denominations or groups carry out a broader ministry.

Commitments of the Brethren in Christ indicate they have a full-orbed church understanding, and seriously endeavor to carry out its varied dimensions.

2. There Is Recognition That Both Individual and Corporate Dimensions of the Faith Are Vital to the Church.[5]

George Buttrick described the holistic nature of Christianity in this manner,

"If religion does not begin with the individual, it does not begin; but if it ends with the individual, it ends." Buttrick's depiction portrays both the order and scope of the Brethren in Christ approach to faith. Yet, the denomination is aware that either individual or group aspects of the faith can be carried too far. Undue emphasis on the individual believer can lead to self-centeredness. By the same token, when a church manifests an excessive tendency toward group self-centeredness, it can disintegrate into sub-cultural Christianity.

Even though the denomination's first emphasis is on personal conversion, Brethren in Christ seeks to balance individual and group emphases. Following a person's spiritual encounter the believer is encouraged to become part of the church—Christ's church. It is as a body of believers that the church becomes whole. Both the individual and corporate aspects of the faith are important to Brethren in Christ. God calls the believer (singularly) into relationship, first with Himself, and then with brothers and sisters in Christ. The denomination sees believers called to work together to accomplish what God has set before them.

3. The Brethren in Christ View Discipleship as Being All Encompassing.

During the past half century, the term discipleship has increased in use in the brotherhood. It has displaced previous references to the regenerated life or the transformed life. Discipleship is frequently considered the process of following Christ and the Scriptures in both religious practice and general conduct. However, Brethren in Christ would first of all see discipleship as a relationship. John D. Roth describes well the Brethren in Christ position, "Discipleship is first and foremost about a relationship with Jesus, both as transcendent Savior and as Lord . . . . Discipleship . . . is about abiding in Christ."[6] Richard Halverson also stressed how a relationship with Christ is the key element of discipleship when he observed that the most effective strategy for attaining discipleship is to be with the person or people one wants to disciple. A disciple is a learner as well as a follower of Christ. This relationship principle was Jesus' strategy as it took three years to train His disciples who went on to change the world. The Gospels were written by Jesus' closest companions—the men who lived and worked with Him. They were His disciples, not just because they believed in His teachings, but, because of their love for Him and His love for them. This rapport, however, is a master-servant relationship wherein the Christian manifests he is no longer his own. The disciple gives up his right to himself in a relationship to Christ.

Beyond discipleship being first viewed as a relationship, Brethren in Christ would interpret discipleship also to mean right living—according to the teachings of Jesus—wherein both personal ethics and morality, as well as right acts and attitudes regarding social needs and issues, come into play.

An additional facet to discipleship going beyond right acts and a vital relationship is the concept of discipline. The word discipline, closely associated with disciple, means to train the mind and character. Christ was a model for us in exercising the spiritual disciplines of prayer, meditation, and study of the Word. The holistic ideal of Christian discipleship encompasses all three—a personal relationship with Christ, living according to His example, and maintaining strength through the spiritual disciplines—this seems to be the Brethren in Christ interpretation of true discipleship.

4. The Brethren in Christ Recognize That an Omnipotent God Rules History, but That Concurrently Man Is Causal and Free to Exercise Choice.

Within Christian traditions, there are differences about the will of God and the freedom of mankind. A hard Calvinist view of the elect gives minimal room to human choice. The Brethren in Christ view is more holistic. Martin Schrag, in an article entitled, "The Genius of the Founding Fathers," points out an aspect of wholeness demonstrated in the early *Confession* as follows:

> The Confession emphasizes both God's initiative and the importance of man's response. It is God through Christ who has acted in history to make provision for man's salvation, and it is the grace of God which convicts the sinner of his wayward nature, resulting in sorrowfulness of heart. It is Christ who enters the sinner's open heart. Only then is faith borne ("We have not this faith according to Nature."). In the conversion experience man is relatively passive. The accent is closer to surrender. Man is responsible to follow Christ. . . . There is no evidence that the founding fathers were trying to avoid the pitfalls of the extremes within Calvinism and Arminianism, but such they did.[7]

To Brethren in Christ the choice of faith is for all since Christ died for all. Human freedom and divine will are joined within providence. An interaction exists between divine will and human will since a person needs freedom of choice to be morally responsible. Ultimately, God's will prevails and we mortals serve it.

5. The Brethren in Christ Reach Beyond a Single Tradition.

Martin Schrag further observed that "American denominationalism is not noted for fresh understandings. Much of it is an over-emphasis on one aspect of the faith at the expense of other aspects." In comparison, he wrote: "The

Brethren in Christ original vision sought to bring together the strong points of several traditions, and the uniting of these traditions resulted in a balanced perspective of unique creativity."[8] The Brethren in Christ are a synthesis of a number of Christian traditions. Marlin Jeschke, a committed Anabaptist, in a book review of *Reflections on a Heritage*, was impressed by what he termed "one of the bolder chapters"—David Weaver-Zercher's analysis and critique of Owen Alderfer's thesis, "The Brethren Mindset." Jeschke noted that "Alderfer's thesis (an openness to new light) offered the BIC a rationale to come to terms with, and even to justify, the radical changes that occurred during and after World War II." Commenting that "it is an openness that risks leaving historic BIC values behind," Jeschke continued:

> At its best the BIC mindset I find appealing. It is "openness to new ways of thought, doctrinal formulation by synthesis and allowance for differences within trusting relationships" rather than harboring an abrasive spirit. Trusting relationships is a mindset the Mennonite church needs very much today. . . . The BIC are to be commended not just for discussing the question of identity but also for trying to shape an identity that preserves the best from their past.[9]

At times the question arises as to whether the Brethren in Christ may be too much of an amalgam to portray a clear identity?[10] A retort to such a query is— a denomination that is discerningly open to insights that cross theological interpretive lines can avoid becoming narrowly entrenched in perspective—a condition that often accompanies a tradition-restricted mandate. Again, single-tradition denominations were often created to meet given problems at a specific time in church and social history,[11] and therein may fail to have the breadth of insight exhibited by those representing multi-heritage perspectives. Biblical truths extending across traditions tend to be more enriching and are surely more holistic. Multi-heritage denominations' impulses tend to be biblically driven rather than tradition-restricted. Because the Brethren in Christ have borrowed from a variety of traditions, they have not been a tradition-conscious body.[12]

6. The Brethren in Christ Understand That Both Success and Failure Accompany the Gospel.

Joy and sorrow, success and failure, exhilaration and pain, all of these come to the Christian. A breadth of life experiences can be expected for the believer as well as the unbeliever. The Brethren in Christ have not been adherents of the "prosperity gospel" wherein the Christian expects to enter a "charmed circle" to receive mundane advantages or benefits.[13] By the same token, they have not given credence to the opposite view that Christians should expect a fate of "suffering for the Gospel," although it is acknowledged that persecution may come to the Christian. On the other hand, Harold Bender, who authored, "The Anabaptist Vision," along with other Mennonites, saw separation from the world, which he termed "nonconformity," and argued that the logical outcome of nonconformity was a suffering church.[14]

In a similar vein, Martin Schrag in his work, *The Brethren in Christ Attitude Toward the World*, alluded to an expectation of suffering when he said that personal conversion was an intense experience because it meant becoming part of "the despised people."[15] Perhaps this is a reason some recent Brethren have described the conversion to God process as a "crisis experience." The word "despised" is very negative—especially since in most countries where Brethren in Christ churches are located significant freedoms have been extended to religion.[16] "Crossing the threshold of faith" will surely continue to be identified with repentance, confession, perhaps emotional upheaval, and possibly estrangement from family. However, making a serious decision to follow God would presumably entail less today in the way of detailed conformity to be separate from the "world."

Brethren in Christ would say that a Christian's destiny is not ordered by either prosperity or suffering and neither of these fates should necessarily be the expectations of Christians. Brethren in Christ do not anticipate either the good life or persecution as a norm—they are guided by the Scriptural admonition that "the rain falls on the just as well as the unjust."[17]

7. The Denomination Is Diverse in Its Worship Experiences.

Today there is more diversity in group worship experiences than some Christians care to be a part of. A breadth of worship opportunities in varied forms is found in most denominations. Diversity in worship is deep within the heritage of the Brethren in Christ. The Pietist tradition had its "conventicles" which modified the constancy of worship patterns. The Brethren in Christ counterpart to these small-group religious meetings consisted of "private gatherings,"[18] experience meetings, later termed testimony meetings, and today frequently referenced as cell-groups.[19] Worship experiences today run the gamut from thought-provoking, to challenging, to nurturing, to inspiring, to ecstasy in the Lord.

Worship is an intensely personal experience.[20] Worship is also an activity, an orientation of life, and an expression of love to God that is not dependent on place or set time. It can take place in the church, in private devotions, at work, in the school, or in the home. Worship is attained as there is holy expectancy, and it ideally ends in holy obedience—which turns into a holistic experience.

8. Christianity Needs to Impact the Whole of Life.

As a preamble to this subject of "Christianity needing to impact all of life," the values guiding the Brethren in Christ denomination are cited as printed in the March/April 2000 issue of *Visitor*, (p. 4). They are:

Experiencing God's Love and Grace—We value the free gift of salvation in Christ Jesus and the transforming power of the Holy Spirit; *Believing the Bible*—We value the Bible as God's authoritative Word, study it together and build our lives on its truth; *Worshiping God*—We value heartfelt worship that is God-honoring, Spirit directed, and life-changing; *Following Jesus*—We value wholehearted obedience to Christ Jesus through the empowering presence of the Holy Spirit; *Belonging to the Community of Faith*—We value integrity in relationships and mutual accountability in an atmosphere of grace, love, and acceptance; *Witnessing to the World*—We value an active and loving witness for Christ to all people; *Serving Compassionately*—We value serving others at their point of need, following the example of our Lord Jesus; *Pursuing Peace*—We value all human life and promote forgiveness, understanding, reconciliation, and non-violent resolution of conflict; *Living Simply*—We value uncluttered lives, which free us to love boldly, give generously, and serve joyfully; *Relying on God*—We confess our dependence upon God for everything, and seek to deepen our intimacy with Him by living prayerfully. Surely, as one honors these values, all of life will be impacted.

The Brethren in Christ vision sets forth the ideal that every part of human activity should be consistent with Christianity. To carry this out one's faith needs to pervade one's thoughts, one's will, and one's conduct. Such an ideal is supportive of a world and life view that is holistic. This wholeness is borne out in its concept of truth; its perception that God's call is relevant to a wide span of vocations; and its view that Christianity should not be privatized or compartmentalized. These holistic characteristics are reviewed as follows:

A. Consistent With Wholeness, There Is a Unity to Truth.

Brethren in Christ appear to be increasingly acknowledging that all truth is God's. For more than a century the founding church tended to give scant attention to the relationship between knowledge and piety or between culture and the Christian faith. While early Brethren in Christ recognized the necessity for a degree of involvement in the general culture, the spiritual side of the Gospel was their primary focus.

As the church ventured into education, and especially higher education, it began to recognize that God's creation, which He called "good," is part of His truth, just as the truths of revelation are His. Also the church came to see that God created man with mind powers and the mind should be exercised and developed. Added to these understandings was a dawning awareness that the love of beauty is not evil, and it should not be stifled. Indeed, as the church began to recognize its responsibility to be God's stewards in the world (since all truth centers in Jesus Christ) it gained a new awareness that Christians should be active in every branch of knowledge.

While the Brethren in Christ do not specifically clarify in the denomination's *Manual*[21] that all truth is God's, this realization is increasingly manifested in individual members by their approaches to training, their choices of vocation, and their growing diversity of service to society.[22]

B. God's Call Is Perceived to Be Relevant to a Wide Span of Vocations.

For nearly one and a half centuries, the primary occupation for early Brethren in Christ members was agriculture. Therefore, the "call of God" for a person to enter a non-traditional vocation, in service to the Master, was not a persistent issue. The "call of God" for those in church leadership came from the church body through congregational or district votes by the members. E. Morris Sider observed that the congregation's call to ministry "was life-long unless terminated by grave spiritual or moral error, or sometimes by financial failure."[23]

Early exceptions to what was considered the traditional call of God, as initiated by the church body, came when individuals started to report independent personal calls to serve in international missions. These calls to mission services abroad began to surface in the brotherhood during the late nineteenth century. A person witnessing to a personal call from God became the conventional way of informing the church of one's interest and potential availability for missionary service. Indeed, anyone who could not openly acknowledge a personal call from God would presumably be viewed as being ill-prepared for such service. The consummation of each individual call, however, was subject to the approval of the Home or Foreign Mission Board of the church. These respective boards either affirmed one's call or counseled otherwise regarding potential service.

As individual work roles began to diversify for Brethren in Christ, the church broadened its personal-call-of-God pattern beyond mission assignments to other church roles. Carlton Wittlinger showed that the call to missionary work, a full-time commitment, "decidedly helped to promote the idea of the 'personal call' to the congregational ministry."[24]

The shift occurred because of values deeply imbedded in the denomination from its roots. First, a personal call from God fits squarely with the Pietist tradition wherein the Holy Spirit deals with, and illumines the believer. Also, while early Brethren in Christ probably had scant knowledge of Martin Luther's concept of the priesthood of all believers, from their own biblical insight they resonated with such practice.[25]

There was a significant change regarding vocation from 1950 onward. In order to enhance its witness and service the church was now ready to be increasingly engaged in the general culture. This gave fresh alternatives for members to serve the Lord in secular vocations and callings. The concept of a personal call became appropriate for those entering educational service, medicine, and other professions for their value to society and indirect benefits to the church. *Vocatio* (Latin for calling), "a divine summons to service of God," became applicable to fields other than church and missions roles.

C. Christianity Should Not Be Compartmentalized or Privatized.

This section's title is intentionally cast in a negative form to show that the church, by its actions in the 1950s, adopted a new worldview. Paul Hiebert pointed out at the Brethren in Christ and Culture Conference, in February 1998, a worldview underlies how a denomination acts and thinks.[26] All denominations represent a worldview regardless of whether it is specifically stated or acknowledged.[27] After 1950 the church's views changed as it discarded restrictive and internally-focused church tenets that were "compartmentalizing" to the life and services of the church. Non-compartmentalization, stated in the positive, means that all spheres of activity belong to God, and distinct boundary lines between the sacred and the secular are removed.

Consistent with the non-compartmentalized faith idea, when one's faith becomes whole it will not be privatized. A non-privatized Christian is under divine orders and will be concerned with both personal holiness and social holiness—individual morality and wholeness will not be emphasized to the exclusion of collective morality or well being of the general culture and society.

The evolution of the denomination to more holistic, non-privatized positions has been a transitional process. The Brethren in Christ history reveals that the faith of the early body, to 1950, was somewhat compartmentalized and privatized. Before 1950 the dichotomies of church-world, spirit-body, and evangelism-social ethics were strongly present in the church's sense of reality. Life was sharply divided into secular and sacred realms.[28]

The church taught separation from the world. Their separation was based on a two- kingdom doctrine—Christ's and the world's—and the belief that membership in one ought to preclude serious involvement in the other.[29] Social, political, and cultural involvement belonged to the worldly kingdom. Prior to 1950 most Brethren in Christ refrained from becoming politically and culturally involved—even when society contradicted their Christian and ethical values.[30]

Brethren in Christ have always exerted their most direct and primary efforts toward meeting the vast spiritual needs of humanity. With eternal ends in view, the denomination, prior to the mid-twentieth century, had participated in caring for human needs through international relief, and by establishing social-service institutions in North America and abroad. The church also made contributions to the broader culture by sponsoring educational institutions in America and in other nations where their mission work grew.

As to the political sphere, the denomination and its people did not become seriously involved.[31] During the nineteenth century one political exception that drew special attention from the church, as recorded in the *Evangelical Visitor*, was a call for legislation to stop trafficking of intoxicating beverages.[32] In 1894 there was increased attention to the social and political order by the church allowing members to serve in public office.[33]

But a vivid reversion to the 1894 action, which condoned political service at the discretion of the local district, came a generation later. The 1924 General Conference, in response to a request for direction made from a Canadian district, acted to suspend "from full fellowship . . . until he retires from such position," anyone who accepted a seat in the Canadian Parliament. However, Archie C. Carmichael, a minister, did not heed the General Conference prohibitions against political activity was elected to Parliament, and forthwith was "suspended from communion privileges" at the next meeting of the Canada Joint Council of the denomination.[34]

By 1950 the church began to see that rather than the two kingdoms being in contradiction, they overlapped. The culture-denying tendencies were breaking down as the body sensed that God's Word had relevance to all of life. The church was coming to perceive some parts of culture were good and that Christians need to be engaged in the culture and society.

This denominational worldview shift should not be construed as a sudden turn wherein the denomination instituted major new programs. The church's primary programmatic thrust continued to be in international missions, but a new interest was forming toward the planting of new churches in North America. Clear changes were particularly evident in the denomination's higher educational institutions and their curricula.[35]

While this broadened view of Christian reality should not be read as a decision by the church to exert its corporate influence strongly in the direction of redeeming the culture and meeting social needs, there were clear changes of orientation and how individual church members perceived reality. Without compromising their distinctives, Brethren in Christ sharply increased their cooperation with other Christians and extended their interaction to non-Christians and secular society. There was a new attitude—the church should not be marginalized from society except where that caused one to surrender one's Christian values. The members wanted to be accessible so as to better serve both believers and nonbelievers. The church's underlying goal in this new orientation was to be increasingly effective in their faith witness.

The new understandings that became critical to the church's on-going ministry consisted of: First, that God's truths should not to be compartmentalized. Second, there are implications of faith that reach beyond the individual Christian. One's faith needs to extend beyond personal morality. The Christian who possesses a vital faith should not overlook the possibility a being of positive impact on society and the culture. A private religion contributes little to the holistic functioning of today's late-modern society.

Even though a new and somewhat different attitude toward the culture and its potential change now appears to prevail, there are surely areas of life where some Brethren in Christ withhold their participation. The acceptance of a more integrated worldview by the church does not mean there is full involvement of its people in the broadest of sectors. For example, one can be assured that Brethren in Christ, as a corporate body, do not rest their basic hope on political solutions as the primary means for improving adverse societal or world conditions. Clearly the Gospel is considered much more important than a political agenda.

Brethren in Christ who are firm in their Pietist moorings would agree with Don Eberly's observation that "for a nation's public life to be regenerated, the spirit and mind of its citizens must be renewed first."[36] The agenda of the church vividly discloses its belief that the most effective influence for cultural and social restoration lies in spiritual renewal. It has refrained as a corporate body from making judgments or official pronouncements about public policy. It has also not encouraged its members to affiliate with political groupings of any particular stripe, including those that loudly herald their Christian intent.

Brethren in Christ members in North America have filled public offices at local levels, but not in the broader public square. This fact probably should not be interpreted as a prohibition from public service, including major elective office.[37] With the expanding role of the public sector, and ways in which government is involved in every aspect of peoples' lives, many Christians in an effort to be holistic about their faith give consideration to what the political order ought to be. In turn, some sense the need, under the lordship of Jesus, to be involved in the process.

In spite of the denomination's apolitical views, the church is aware that Christians must live responsibly within their social settings by helping solve problems and thwart monstrous evil within society. Therefore, the Brethren in Christ are not counter-cultural, *per se*.[38] The church is also not prescriptive about cultural issues deemed to be in the realm of Christian liberty. They want to follow the Apostle Paul: "I have made myself a slave to all, that I might win the more. To the Jew I became as a Jew . . . To those outside the law I became as one outside the law. To the weak I became weak, that I might win the weak. I have become all things to all men, that I might by all means save some." (1 Cor. 9:19-22)

As mentioned, the Brethren in Christ voice for enunciating the theory of the Christian worldview has been Messiah College.[39] An example of the church and the college abandoning earlier tendencies to marginalize the faith is given in the area of political science. Several decades ago Messiah College moved beyond offering basic courses in political science toward instituting a full major in the field. The purpose of the major was to integrate the Christian faith with this academic field and help prepare students for service in public life, whether elected or appointed. Adding this major was consistent with a Christian worldview and counteracted the marginalization of civic and political affairs from the faith.[40]

Messiah College and other Christian colleges, by integrating the field of political science with the Christian faith, seek to accomplish two critical objectives:

1. To relate political science and the faith to some of the shattering moral questions that face society as a whole including racism, injustice, exploitation, world hunger, and nuclear arms.
2. To prepare students who are to be salt and light to the world to become political scientists, teachers, and governmental servants who are guided by faith.

The removal of church policies that tended to squeeze religious life into a compartment of private experience does not mean that all Brethren in Christ members incorporated the broader worldview into their lives. Some members simply have not considered the scope of the Christian worldview, while others knowingly disagree with the principle that faith should be integrated into every aspect of life. Some church members, for example, out of personal compunction, refrain from voting.

Nevertheless, the denomination in its actions, and through the lives of its members, has sanctioned the more holistic view that Christianity should impact all of life. It has increasingly shown that a divided persona and a dualistic worldview are not God's ideal for the Christian. The view is based on the principle that the basic ingredients of the culture are neutral to religion, and that Christians should contribute to the culture, but as loyalists to the cause of Christ. These understandings help validate the quality of wholeness as a characteristic of the denomination.

Quality Two: Balance
The Brethren in Christ Pursue a Balanced Faith

Many groups within the Protestant tradition profess fidelity to the basic doctrines of the Christian faith as composed in the Apostles Creed; yet, in reality, they often are divided in their emphasis on and interpretations of specific beliefs.

Denominations also vary with regard to the attention they give to living out the faith, and they are quite disparate about their emphasis on Christian perfection. A specific belief in one denomination may receive significant attention and for another be totally ignored. One denomination may be active and another comparatively lifeless. One may display a high degree of balance in their interpretation of historic beliefs and the next denomination may be more extreme.

Regarding the issue of balance in the denomination, the article by Martin H. Schrag, long-time Brethren in Christ historian and theologian, entitled "The Genius of the Founding Fathers" is again referenced. In this article he acknowledged the brilliance and originality of the church fathers as they set forth an "emphasis on the individual balanced by an emphasis on the church as the body of Christ." He contended that "Christian groups have often been tempted to relieve the tension between the individual and corporate aspersions of Christianity by over-emphasizing one or the other." [41]

Another rather obvious balancing factor for the Brethren in Christ that tends to keep the denomination from extremism is the fact that the denomination crosses theological-tradition lines. [42] Vernard Eller stressed this point about the Church of the Brethren, who like the Brethren in Christ, stand within two traditions. Eller wrote about his denomination this way:

> When the radical Pietist tendency would slide off into subjectivism, private inspiration, mysticism, enthusiasm, or vaporous spiritualism, it is pulled up short by the demand for concrete, outward obedience to an objective Scriptural norm. Conversely, when the Anabaptist tendency would slide off into formalism, Biblical literalism or works-righteousness, it is checked by the reminder that faith is essentially a work of God within the heart of the individual believer, an intensely personal relationship rather than a legal one. Thus . . . Anabaptist influences discipline Pietism as the same Pietist influences inspire Anabaptism, [43]

Portraying Brethren in Christ as balanced in their beliefs and actions is at times best expressed by the church steering clear of or not dwelling on controversial issues deemed to be secondary in nature. [44] It is also shown by portraying openness to differing views when Christian liberty is considered appropriate. These items alone indicate an evenness of faith and an avoidance of extreme stands in the denomination.

Balance is achieved by substantially more than steering clear of secondary or extraneous issues. The Brethren in Christ equilibrium is more strikingly illustrated as it brings into union seemingly opposing truths. Just as the Gospel is somewhat paradoxical in many of its key themes such as, "the first shall be last," "the weak are the strong," and "to find life one needs to lose it;" and just as the Good News holds in harmonious tension such concepts as the heart and the mind, the law and grace, this life and the heavenly life, personal piety and corporate responsibility, freedom and accountability, certainty and mystery, so the Brethren in Christ seem to emphasize values that are frequently viewed as being polarities in the Christian faith. Some of these values create dissonance within the Christian church. On the other hand, "seeming polarities" may come together in amiable balance. The Brethren in Christ story not only depicts the concept of wholeness, it illustrates the quality of balance as it joins precepts that appear to be contrary.

The Brethren in Christ merging of "seeming polarities" includes: the wedding of faith and works, the joining of separation from and engagement with the world and the bringing together of declaring truth and ministering reconciliation. These combinations which require proper balancing are reviewed as follows:

1. Are Both Faith and "Fruits" (Works) Essential to Being a Balanced Church?

Some Christian believers who profess God's saving grace have been contentious about the value of good works.[45] Brethren in Christ are clearly within the Protestant tradition since they emphasize salvation through God's grace. Salvation is viewed as an unearned gift from God.

While works are not considered the first step to faith for Brethren in Christ, the words of James admonishing that "faith without works is dead" (James 2:26) is taken seriously. While faith is prior, works provide completion to the faith-works equation. The denomination's theology (Arminian) joins faith and the fruits of faith into a satisfying balance. Truth perceived needs to be truth practiced in order to validate one's belief. Holy living is an indication of one's genuine faith in Christ. It is faith and works in living unity.

2. Can There Be Non-Conformity with the World and Engagement with the World at the Same Time?

Equilibrium between two potential polarities is also shown in the denomination's non-conformity vs. engagement doctrine regarding the world—"Being in the world, but not of the world." While at times it is difficult to interpret the non-conformity doctrine, it has been basic to Brethren in Christ since their founding. Separation from the world is a doctrine from its Anabaptist roots.[46]

In Western society, a Christian is part of a general culture that exhibits both virtues and vices. Choosing to be nonconformist in certain cultural values and at the same time seek to be part of improving the culture can create tensions. It may be both ambiguous to understand and untidy to carry out. However, it is a holy untidiness. The Brethren in Christ perceive that being cut off from the general culture is a retreat from Christian responsibility. The church loses opportunities to counter evil and to extend the Gospel when it withdraws.[47]

When Brethren in Christ present themselves as God's new people in the world, and no longer depend on insularity from the community or unique attire to indicate their non-conformity,[48] their separation principles are portrayed by upright values and habits, by right use of time and resources, and by wholesome social practices. Spiritual values that clearly signify the church is not of the world include: love, discipline, self-restraint, and purity. Concurrently, values such as being mindful, attentive, and interactive with others show the church is truly in the world.

The tensions of living both "in the world" and not being "of the world" are real. But a key to Christian discipleship is a balanced interaction with the general culture and society.

3. Both Contemplative and Action Realms Are Considered Vital to the Faith.

Denominations born in Pietism, if true to their original vision, expect their members to exhibit personal piety. The focal point of Pietistic belief is the conversion-regeneration experience that brings a person into relationship with God through the Holy Spirit. This personal relationship to the Divine is then nourished through regular Bible reading, prayer, and contemplative communion with God. Pietists noted that in the midst of an exceedingly busy ministry Jesus made a habit of withdrawing to a lonely place apart. He did this not just to be away from people but so He could be with God.

The Brethren in Christ are among numerous denominations that place high importance on a devotional life. Christians are expected to use certain spiritual disciplines in communing with God, not because they are righteous, but because man has a tendency to be self-centered and needs direction and power from the Divine. The person who understands the importance of contemplation with God is not guided alone by personal needs, but by responsibilities as well approaching God with a sense of expectancy.

True contemplation and communion with God for the Brethren in Christ is not a psychological technique, it is a Christian grace. Contemplative prayer is a way of life. The Christian is to "pray without ceasing" (1 Thess. 5:17). It is in contemplation with God that the Scriptures can be internalized and personalized. In contemplation the Christian can also recall and exalt God. The psalmists did this often.

Denominations that stress the contemplative or illuminative side of faith are often classified as being subjective. It is true that denominations that emphasize spiritual reflection and communion, at times, take it for granted that the active side of the faith will follow. They tend to give less attention to social implications of the faith. On the other hand, some denominations fail to give adequate consideration to the devotional and spiritual empowerment dimensions. For Brethren in Christ it is not an either-or situation.

While Brethren in Christ give prior attention to personal relationships on to the divine side of the balance, in true Anabaptist and Pietist fashion,[49] the church is heedful of the need for Christian action and conduct. Both moral behavior and ethical acts are recognized as important dimensions of the faith. The church expects its members to portray the fruits of the Gospel. Both passive and active dimensions of the faith are viewed by the Brethren in Christ as combined in the Gospel, and in union they signify balance as well as wholeness.

4. Truth Is Singled Out (Dividing), but It Is Balanced by a Commitment to Reconciliation (Connecting).

Searching for both peace and truth is evident in the Brethren in Christ. The church brings dissonant concepts of the faith into refreshing accord as they declare truth, which entails dividing, correcting, disciplining, and at times excluding. On the other hand the church ministers reconciliation, which involves forgiving, reaching out, mediation, love, and inclusiveness.

Some churches today, in order to be reconciling, settle for a form of Christianity that denies the very things that are distinctive to Christianity. Such churches lean unduly toward rapprochement, and do so at the expense of truth itself.

As an historic peace church, the Brethren in Christ have always considered non-resistance and concord to be the Christian way to solve conflict. The good-in-return-for-evil response is part of a pervading spirit of reconciliation. Christianity is viewed as first a right relationship with God, whereby the sinner is reconciled, followed by the Christian living out a reconciling relationship to others. Within the church particular, a brotherly kinship characterized by humility, kindness, compassion, forgiveness, and cooperation is expected. A sense of oneness is anticipated toward each member of the body.

While reconciling relationships are keenly important to Brethren in Christ they are not all encompassing. Unity is not pursued for its own sake and faith is not reduced to the lowest common denominator. The Brethren in Christ have a limit to cooperation. That limit arises when the purity of the church is threatened. The content of the Gospel is critical and obedience is expected of the true believer. The church gives initial attention to the reliability of truth which they discover by experiencing the power of the Gospel, by ascertaining the teachings of the Bible, and by learning from the saints. These truths provide a theological framework within which the church gains meaning and finds structure to maintain its basic character.[50]

The church does not condone delinquency within the body in either doctrine or life, and the body of Christ can only be fruitful when there is unity. Any fellowship without purity of faith and life is perceived to be flawed at the core. Unity and purity are viewed as being interdependent church elements. It is only as both prevail together, in proper balance, that the Brethren in Christ are truly the church.

5. The Brethren in Christ Exhibit Balance by Avoiding Extreme Positions on Political and Social Issues.

For a major part of Brethren in Christ history, there existed a prevailing attitude that society's social and political structures were strongly colored by demonic and sinful influences. The church refrained from political involvement and kept away from extended social involvement. After 1950, when the denomination moved to greater interaction with the world, there was significant change in cultural engagement as its members sensed God's call to penetrate and minister to society. In seeking to impact varied areas, and to improve the human condition, many members became more involved in the political processes in the United States and Canada.

In spite of increased political and social involvement, Brethren in Christ, within their deepest being, do not view political, social, and cultural means as the best avenues for changing society. They recognize that altering laws alone will not change aimless and self-centered individuals. While adjusting education and social and economic structures have their place for offering humaneness and justice, these still cannot change the hearts of people.

For many Brethren in Christ responding to these cautionary concerns fails to remove their sense of responsibility to fulfill the biblical call for Christians to do justice and show mercy in ways that reach beyond their individual acts and their own private sphere. They realize that the ballot's power needs to be exercised with responsibility for both leadership selection and policy formulation. Jesus had something to say about the Christian's sense of responsibility to government and to others (Jesus did not pray that we be taken out of this world, John 17:1). Some see government, at times, as being the final arbiter of the citizen's moral responsibility and therein sense a duty to help set the direction of that moral compass. There is also the positive realization that the church, consisting of citizens from many nations who are all citizens of God's spiritual kingdom, may engender a revival of righteousness that will "exalt a nation,"— and therefore many nations.

The biblical call for Christians to be salt and light has also influenced the degree of social and political involvement of Brethren in Christ. Since secularism cannot provide an adequate sense of meaning and purpose, a Christian who exercises power through the vote, discourse, and public service can be both a witness and of service to the world.

The Brethren in Christ, however, do not appear to concentrate on a narrow agenda of public issues. Under the Christian banner, two prevalent issues have recently been advanced in single-issue fashion. They are abortion and prayer in the public schools. The Brethren in Christ denomination stands in opposition to abortion, but it generally does not use aggressive means to make it known, and individuals are slow to rally behind abortion as a single-issue contention. On the matter of prayer and religion curricula in the public schools, most Brethren in Christ have avoided getting on that bandwagon as well. It is generally considered that religious exercises formulated to satisfy a broad diversity of citizens and also be politically palatable must be sufficiently compromised so as to represent little more than sentimentality. Also, the advancement of such issues is fraught with danger because for Christians the "separation of church and state" idea serves as a safeguard to religious plurality and liberty.

Ideally, the Brethren in Christ seem to be interested in approaching the needs of society in a more balanced and less dogmatic manner. They appear to resonate, more closely, with a Christian perspective that portrays broad historical, social, and biblical awareness. Since single- issue politics tends to be rather arbitrary and exceedingly partisan, there is apt to be inconsistency when one or two issues dominate an agenda that is intended for the public good. For example, many who are immersed in the issue of "killings through abortion," fail to consider the "killing-by-hand-guns issue," or to even give second thoughts to the "death-penalty issue." And vice-versa, those concerned about "killing through the military" are too often voiceless about "killing by abortion." Brethren in Christ appear to display a reasonable measure of balance regarding the broad content of evil and the emphasis they give to political issues. Political issues are deemed important but not ultimate, and they ideally need to be considered in full context, along-side companion issues.

6. Extra-Church Affiliations for Brethren in Christ Members Seem to Portray Balance in That Such Attachments Seem to Be Loosely Held.

Both left and the right religious groups have seriously sought to be a major influence on society through government legislation. Some mainline liberal churches have shown periods of strong political effort. They have displayed commitment to the idea that the world can be saved through the political process.[51] In recent decades it has been some of the more conservative churches that have resorted to the political process to try to achieve their "saving ends" through political legislation.

The Brethren in Christ seem to understand that immorality and injustice are serious problems in our society and that the church has a responsibility to promote righteousness. The corporate church has shown little inclination to influence public policy, and it refrains from politicizing religious and moral issues. The church seems to sense that a dependence on political power would be dampening to its spiritual power—corporate religion becomes neutralized when it is politicized.

The relation of an individual Christian to the state, since 1950, has never been clearly spelled out in the Brethren in Christ church. The church, in not being specific, seems to say by default that the public dialogue on crucial moral questions should be done by individual believers rather than the corporate body. Therefore, a Brethren in Christ member's responsibilities, actions, and services in the political arena are in the realm of Christian liberty, to be determined according to each Christian's sense of duty in rendering "unto Caesar the things that are Caesars, and to God the things that are God's" (Matt. 22:21).[52]

Some conservative religious groups have identified God and country together. The Brethren in Christ, although essentially conservative in their theology, have not fallen into the civil religion fallacy whereby the nation is viewed as God's specially chosen kingdom.[53] They are also quite circumspect and reserved in legislating morality.

Again, some members of the Brethren in Christ refrain from political involvement of any kind.[54] Since the denomination would contend that statutes and laws are not the ultimate solution for meeting man's deepest need, and that government policy is not the lone instrument for social change, it appears that the denomination informally supports a less-government philosophy. This less-government stance may account in part for the Brethren in Christ individuals being heavily Republican in their political activities.[55] Members of the church body seem to carry any political affiliations rather quietly. The public-policy-type organizations of the 1980s and '90s that brandished Christian intent (the Call to Renewal and the Christian Coalition) did not appear to generate a strong attraction for them.[56] Also, the "religious right" leaders who have sought to broker a religiously-political influence on the evolving scene do not appear to have stirred much interest from the Brethren in Christ. While a segment of Brethren in Christ have identified with prophetic-type declarations that came from Jerry Falwell, Pat Robertson, and James Dobson on the right it would appear they are listeners rather than joiners of any concerted political efforts.

In the pursuit of justice and righteousness Brethren in Christ presently seem to recognize they cannot retreat from or escape a secular society to safeguard their faith. Even though one dare not ignore the fact that means need to be consistent with ends, it should be recognized that good public policy can be enacted by individuals who make no transcendent claims. Although Brethren in Christ members surely become associated with organizations and parties that have platforms which can only be partially endorsed, they presumably advocate public policies that are congruent with Christian values. And moreover, their ties to political and social-action causes appear to be largely in line with denominational values—they are secondary allegiances loosely held.

7. The Brethren in Christ Appear to Be Balanced in Their Interaction with the General Culture.

In the fourth century when the Roman emperor, Constantine, became part of the church, the independence of the Christian church was surrendered. This started a gradual merging of state and church providing an early model that continued to influence many parts of the church throughout the Middle Ages. Following the Reformation, the subjection pattern was then extended to the territorial churches. The Christian church was often dominated by the state.

A different expression of accommodation entered the church in modern times. Instead of compromise with the state, its new tendency was to surrender to values of the general culture, even though not forced to do so. In the process of undue cultural accommodation, the church started to echo the voices of society. This Constantinian model of the church being somewhat subservient to the state or to the general culture continues to persist today.

When the church's integrity becomes compromised to the values and attitudes of the general culture, the church tends to lose its sense of mission. One way Brethren in Christ avoid bowing to the culture is by steering clear of political or social-interest groups, including those that use the term Christian to sanction their efforts. The church, according to precedent (rather than stated norms), has not become involved in pseudo-political efforts, nor does it broker its influence in political ways.

At the other pole are "counter-cultural Christians" and "separatist Christians," ranging from reactionary to radical in intent, who are highly antagonistic to the general culture or see it as sweepingly hazardous or demonic. Such views conclude that little good exists within the structures and life of society today; but this view is not congruent with Brethren in Christ patterns of reaction to the culture.

The Brethren in Christ seem to avoid both extremes. They neither advocate one specific cultural form, nor are they anarchical about forms. Their cross-cultural relations demonstrate a belief that there is no single Christian culture. As a missions-minded church they learned, despite earlier nonconformist tendencies, that neither "cultural Fundamentalism" nor causing cultural upheaval is the Christian way.

Jesus depicted to the varied cultures he moved among (as they suffered under Roman occupation) a model of transcending culture. He did not question the culture. He lived above it. Wilbert R. Shenk said, "the stance of Jesus was not that of rejecting the culture; rather, he started where people were and pointed them to life renewed through God's loving redemptive power."[57] The Brethren in Christ ideal seems to be just that—to transcend culture.

Living in transcendence is not easy to do. It means engaging culture in light of the gospel. Shenk further points out that "the church that is no longer anchored by a convictional center that transcends culture, and which, therefore, is dependent on culture for definition, is headed for a crisis of identity."[58] Living out convictions of the church will involve tensions. It may mean questioning the culture, sitting on the sidelines in noninvolvement, or sometimes getting behind and pushing, depending on the issue. The Brethren in Christ believe their making Christian truth visible and understandable will lead to changed lives and a renewed church—but it will also serve as light to the culture.

Quality Three: Relational
The Brethren in Christ Demonstrate Kinship and Fellowship with Other Believers (and Open Conversation with Non-Believers)

The church is "the bride of Christ." It is not owned or controlled by denominations or combinations of them. From their early founding, the Brethren in Christ believed that Jesus established a universal church of which they are a part.[59] By definition, the church consists of one and all who are born anew and follow Him. The particular churches and the church universal are animated by the Spirit, and stamped in the image of Christ. This means that members of the broader Christian church partake of a common faith and are drawn together in a common bond of love. The Brethren in Christ have always sensed the broad dimensions of the church, but the denomination's most vivid displays of that understanding have been during the last six decades.

In John 17:20-23, Jesus prays "for them who believe in me" that "they may be made perfect in one; and that the world may know that thou hast sent me, and hast loved them, as thou hast loved me." The Lord's message is clear—His church needs to demonstrate complete unity so that the world might believe on Him. Christians, in general, often fall short in defining themselves by who they experience relationship with. Instead they tend to retreat into their own corners so as to identify themselves more by what they do or don't believe—their relationships with other Christians become quite secondary.

The Brethren in Christ denomination seems to be unusual in the many ways it affirms the unity of Christian believers. Brethren in Christ have erected numerous bridges to other Christians. A brief review of some ways the church connects with other believers, and how it has seized opportunities to reduce barriers or divisions follows:

1. The Denomination in Its Early History Displayed Pietist Values That Were Bridging to Other Christians.

The principles and objectives around which the Pietist movement began were formulated within the established church. The founders of early Pietism, Arndt, Spener, and Francke, sought to reform the spiritual and action dimensions of the church. They envisioned themselves as a renewing force to transform churches that had become dead in creedalism and were failing to live out the faith. These leaders had no intention of causing division within the church. Their reformational objectives spread to other territorial churches and eventually affected dissenting groups as well. Pietism from the start was trans-denominational in character, and the basic goal of the movement was unifying rather than dividing.[60] Early Brethren in Christ recognition of outside believers paralleled values of these roots and served to moderate the separatist and sectarian tendencies consistent with their Anabaptist background.

The Brethren in Christ, while supportive of the "visible church" concept (Anabaptist), appear to have accepted an entire "Pietist package," including the "invisible church" idea—that of spiritual kinship with all redeemed followers of Christ.[61] This Pietist insight reached across the lines of different communions, as Brethren in Christ addressed regenerated Christians from other communions—"brother" or "sister"—just as if they were part of their own group.[62]

Early Pietists considered certain faith doctrines of the faith as primary and others as secondary. Their emphasis was on "a living faith" rather than on theology *per se*. To them, exacting formulae and finer points of doctrine were not the emphasis of the New Testament. This facilitated their fellowship with Christians across denominational and territorial lines. Pietists understood the doctrines of conversion-regeneration ("new birth"), and holy living (a transformed life) as central to the faith.

Although not often acknowledged, it appears the Brethren in Christ had a certain doctrinal sophistication. For one and a half centuries the church was specific about certain Christian practices that were well established. There were other life practices, however, in which resolutions of the church's General Conference actions were introduced with the qualifying phrase "it is not consistent to . . . ," followed by the specific action or practice that was not condoned. This qualifying preamble was far less judgmental than declaring the specific inconsistency an outright sin. Undoubtedly, the church was serious regarding such actions,[63] but one wonders whether assigning items such as lightning rods, participating in parades, etc., as not consistent, provided the needed space, as true Pietists, to address Christian believers from outside the brotherhood, as brother or sister in the faith.[64] It is speculation, but since most of the items prefaced by "it is not consistent" were eventually abandoned by the church, even though they were never officially abrogated by legislation, the qualifier, *it is not consistent,* for practical purposes may have meant they were legislating for the group rather than judging other Christians. Just as early Pietists saw a difference between primary and secondary doctrines, the Brethren in Christ, on the basis of their inconsistency proviso, had their own set of penultimate matters.

Along with recognizing closely known Christians from outside bodies within their neighboring area as brother and sister, the earliest issues of the *Evangelical Visitor*, at times granted believers from outside the brotherhood the same close relationship terms even though they likely were not well-known to the editor. Supposedly this was because of the orthodox views of their writings. Apparently, a similar fraternal-type spirit could be said for the Christian hymn writers they used from outside the brotherhood, such as John Winebrenner "(founder of the Church of God), John Wesley, Charles Wesley, and others.

One should not conclude the early Brethren in Christ were taking unbiblical liberties by interpreting potential error as being primary and secondary. There are cases for tolerance on lesser matters in the Scriptures. A flexible standard was set forth by the Apostle Paul. His message was that absolute uniformity is not required of the believer who demonstrates a sincere faith in the centralities of the Gospel. As Paul states (Romans 14:13-18) there are many matters of belief and behavior that the Scriptures leave unsettled, and for those whose faith may be weak, they need to be accepted without passing judgment on them. Paul's example "to be all things to all men that I might win some" presents a rather open position on disputable matters.

Related to building bridges to other Christians, a Lutheran churchman, who had close awareness of the early River Brethren offered candid views in 1814 regarding the development of several new religious bodies and their relations toward other Christians—particularly the River Brethren and the United Brethren in Christ. He was highly critical of the early United Brethren in Christ denomination's outreach tactics—characterizing them as "a wild seed . . . and self-righteous . . . a Christian name but heathen's heart." However, he praised the early River Brethren in this way: "Engel's (the founding bishop) Pietistic group was the only one to avoid the failings of other sectarian and revivalist groups.[65]

A further descriptive statement regarding early Brethren in Christ, written and signed by "A Familiar Friend," was part of an extensive work compiled by

John Winebrenner wherein all religious denominations in the United States in 1848 were reviewed. In summary form, the statement characterized them this way:

> The River Brethren are simple plain and unassuming . . . zealous in maintaining what they believe to be truth, they manifest an unusual degree of kindness and forbearance toward those who differ from them in matters of faith. They reduce to practice, at least in respect to diversity of sentiment on minor points, what the doctrines of Christ enjoined upon all his disciples—forbearance. They avoid what appears to have been forgotten by many; harshness and denunciation towards fellow Christians—for harshness instead of closing the breach—widens it. They show a spirit of moderation and love for their fellow Christians.[66]

This description made two generations after the denomination's founding, seems to reveal several points regarding the early denomination. For the body to be identified as a group that "manifest(s) an unusual degree of kindness and forbearance toward those who differ . . . on minor points" and show "a spirit of moderation and love for their fellow Christians" indicates both a clear perception that some differences were viewed as being secondary,[67] and that other Christians were considered part of the universal church.

The Brethren in Christ over the course of many years perpetuated practices and traits that some perceived as somewhat sectarian. Such would include: their plain attire, their pure life style, and closed communion. At the same time they revealed signs of following the divine injunction to foster unity among Christian believers. While there were surely pockets of the brotherhood that displayed lesser forbearance with Christians who differed on minor matters of faith, overall they seemed to exhibit attitudes of acceptance.

2. During Their Periods of Marked Separation from the World, the Brethren in Christ Denomination's High Regard for Spiritual Vitality Served as a Bridge to Other Christians.

Brethren in Christ have always manifested strong spiritual idealism. They show a yearning for spiritual vitality and place a heavy emphasis on being engaged in the spiritual disciplines of Bible study and prayer. Theirs has been a strong commitment to the priesthood of all believers and an abiding disquiet about the dangers of becoming spiritually lukewarm. In view of the historic demonstration of a thirst for the things of God and His Spirit, this question pertains: What differences have come to the denomination in light of its concern for spiritual growth? There are a number of possible outcomes. It has surely meant increased spiritual empowerment, new levels of discernment and understanding, greater clarity of mission and calling (collectively and individually), more effective ministry, strengthened faith, and perhaps new levels of spiritual enthusiasm. On the negative side, there may be some who "seek God" for self-oriented reasons.

But there is another probable attainment for those genuinely seeking the Spirit's action in their lives—improved relationships with God and with others (Christians and non-Christians). Like relationships that connect the believer with God and with others, one's soul cannot be nourished apart from Christ. To be authentically spiritual requires that one be in touch with God, with the realities of life, and with other Christians—including a unity with the broader household of God (Eph. 2:19).

In sum, a heightened spiritual thirst by Brethren in Christ has contributed to nourishing relationships within the denomination as well as created an increased sense of union and enhanced fellowship with Christians outside the denomination.

3. The Denomination's Relationships with Likeminded Evangelicals (Since 1950) Opened the Door to Fellowship with the Broader "Household of Faith."

The Protestant church gained a spiritual awakening and right-living dimensions from Pietists. Pietism also added a uniting impact to Christians across territorial, national, cultural, and eventually denominational lines. But Pietism as a German movement was succeeded by a movement that was English in its leadership and complexion. The new movement consisted of proponents named Evangelicals, who having been affected by Pietism continued to emphasize the messages and doctrines that were promulgated in early Pietism.[68] Like the Pietists, the Evangelicals were trans-denominational in character and gave priority concern to communicating the Gospel through word and deed.[69]

Evangelicals comprised a movement that had special impact on English and American Protestantism throughout the eighteenth and nineteenth centuries.[70]

A number of Brethren in Christ individuals were named to leadership positions in NEA. C. N. Hostetter, Jr., served as chairman of the association's World Relief Commission for the better part of two decades (1950s and 1960s). Arthur M. Climenhaga served as the chief executive officer for four years in the 1960s and served on its Resolutions Committee for twenty-five years. Henry Ginder, Donald Shafer, and Warren Hoffman were closely involved in a variety of association offices or commissions.

The collaboration and fellowship with other evangelicals was of greatest affect on the denomination by affirming the church's Pietist side of its vision and assisted the church in interpreting that vision into the modern context.[71] A side benefit of the affiliation has been its impetus to the denomination as it responds to the biblical call for church unity. Becoming part of the evangelical movement helped to facilitate and give honor to Jesus' admonition that His church be united.

4. Other Cross-Denominational Alliances Provide Additional Means for Relating to and Fellowshipping with Christians.

The common bond of Brethren in Christ with other Christian believers was not just Pietist/Evangelical, it was also in an Anabaptist direction. The denomination, prior to joining the National Association of Evangelicals, entered into direct cooperation with Mennonites for administration of the Civilian Public Service program (alternate service during World War II) and in International Relief efforts. Other associations included affiliation with the Mennonite Central Committee, the Council of Mennonite and Affiliated Colleges (later named the Council of Mennonite Colleges), the Mennonite World Conference, Mennonite Disaster Service, and Mennonite Mental Health Services. These Anabaptist associations opened new horizons of service and facilitated the church's witness of peace, reconciliation, and service. They also gave many new opportunities for unity and fellowship with those of like faith.

The Brethren in Christ also joined the National Holiness Association (1950), which later changed its name to the Christian Holiness Partnership. This new connection recognized the importance that the doctrine of holiness holds in the denomination's vision. It also offered the church an additional opportunity to affirm common cause with other believers. While the Christian Holiness Partnership recently ceased to exist, the denomination continues to be part of the Canadian Holiness Federation and the Wesleyan/Holiness Women Clergy organization.

It should also be noted that during the 1960s the denomination's college, Messiah, became part of the founding group, the Christian College Consortium. This initial group of thirteen and later twelve evangelical colleges cooperated in sponsoring key educational programs. During the 1970s it was instrumental in forming the Christian College Coalition, later to become the Council of Christian Colleges and Universities. The president of Messiah College was one of the participants in the founding of both of these Christian educational bodies, which continue today.[72]

John Wesley said to those with whom he was embroiled in a serious theological dispute: "If thy heart be as my heart, give me thy hand." These cross-denominational cooperatives have been Brethren in Christ acts extending a hand of fellowship and oneness to other Christians.

5. By Being Open to Light That Is Integral to Other Theological Traditions the Denomination Erects Bridges to Other Christians.

Many denominations point to their origins as emanating out of a single theological tradition. However, some groups claiming singular-tradition beginnings may have been influenced by additional theological traditions or movements. The Brethren in Christ have no reservation about acknowledging that their ongoing theological vision is a synthesis of varied traditions and movements. While the Pietist and Anabaptist traditions were primary, other traditions that have also contributed to defining Brethren in Christ.[73]

The fact that the denomination has been vulnerable enough at times to alter its direction, and has been open to incorporating new biblical insights that are integral to other theological traditions, widens the door of respect for other believers. It also helps break down walls of division. Perhaps the greatest indirect benefit from the approval of new light is a derived sense of common identity with other believers.

David J. Bosch in his work, *Believing in the Future: Toward A Missiology of Western Culture*,[74] concludes that the future mission of the church in the West will need to be increasingly ecumenical. This implies that a rather critical attitude toward traditionalism and denominationalism may be necessary for effective future ministry. The Brethren in Christ characteristic of being highly relational to other Christians helps break down the barriers that divide the church at large, and in so doing it promotes both spiritual fellowship and unity.

6. The Denomination's Institutions and Ministries Are Highly Relational and Their Services Promote Non-Sectarianism.

From their inception to the present, institutions founded by Brethren in Christ have exhibited a ready openness to serve people within the broader spans of society and the church. They have displayed a genuine commitment to help Christians, and others, regardless of their background, denomination, or culture. In the first half of the twentieth century the denomination's numerous orphanages ministered to a broad spectrum of the society.[75] The institutions to serve the elderly, along with other social services, demonstrated an openness to assist individuals from a variety of church preferences. The mutual relationship of Christians to each other is acknowledged through services to other believers.

The denomination's schools and colleges, although in earlier years their image was somewhat sectarian because of the plain attire of the Brethren in Christ, collectively demonstrated from the start, both attitudinally and by actions (admitting and serving enrollees from many different denominations), that they really were not sectarian. Today, both Brethren in Christ educational institutions, Niagara Christian Collegiate and Messiah College, seek to maintain close connections with the denomination. At the same time enrollments at both institutions are composed of only a significant minority (in numbers) of Brethren in Christ students. Their faculties consist of Christians representing a wide variety of groups and traditions. The composition of the governing boards at these institutions, although significantly Brethren in Christ, are also diverse in makeup.

The programs at denominationally sponsored camp meetings as well are non-sectarian. Such meetings tend to present a diversity of speakers from varied denominations. In this way connections are built and walls of division fall as Christians from other groups are featured in lead ministry roles and audiences are composed of cross-denominational Christians. The interchange and fellowship that accrues from such meetings are matched only by the nourishment of attendee's souls—Brethren in Christ and other believers alike.

The Importance of Christians Being Relational

Christians from many denominations and groups partake of a common faith and are part of His universal church. Owen H. Alderfer emphasized in the centennial General Conference sermon—from the Apostle Paul—that Christians need to be relational. He said, "Paul's word is clear: good works arise out of relationship." In projecting the denomination's future, he continued: "We must engage our best, most creative people and our most outgoing, loving people to show us the way and to lead us in contact and in witness . . ."[76]

A distinct relational quality, abetted by bonds of authentic spirituality, appears to be embodied in the denomination and its members. The attitudes and behaviors of the Brethren in Christ demonstrate that they are in unity with the church universal. This relational quality is enhanced by core doctrinal emphases that cross theological traditions, by the denomination participating in several trans-denominational associations, and by non-sectarianism being modeled in the denomination's institutions and programs.

Three Distinct Qualities of Brethren in Christ

At a denominational Study Conference on the Nature and Function of the Church, the Findings Committee at the close of the conference posed an interesting question: Could it be that denominations are gifted with distinct attributes for special tasks? The report stated:

> We recognize a wide range of functions and ministries of the church of Jesus Christ. Is it possible that Christ gives gifts to a denomination for a particular type of ministry just as he calls individuals to a special task. If this would be a valid assump-

tion could it be that the Brethren in Christ by virtue of our heritage is called to a special type of witness and ministry and if so what form could this take?[77]

While this writer is not aware of any individual or group stepping forward to respond to the Findings Committee's query, the Brethren in Christ appear blessed with a number of distinct gifts: among them are the qualities of wholeness, balance, and being relational to other Christians.

---

[1] The Brethren in Christ interpretation of conversion-regeneration is seated in Divine grace, with the new birth generated by faith and transpiring at repentance, then to be followed by an obedient life. They see the work of salvation by grace actualized and appropriated at conversion prior to water baptism. In contrast, the German Baptist Brethren interpret conversion-regeneration in terms of obedience (right deeds and works) to be manifested prior to the new birth, an experience directly tied to the ordinance of water baptism. In water "baptismal regeneration" the Holy Spirit is disclosed to the believer in the third "dip" of "trine-immersion," as the name "of the Holy Spirit" is invoked (particulars pointed out to the writer by Dale Brown, Church of the Brethren theologian, in a conversation on Jan. 5, 1998).

[2] While post-modern times brought with it the dimension of being strongly communitarian in one's attitudes and commitments, the modernist characteristics of individualism and relativism continued—with both becoming increasingly difficult due to special-interest communities becoming more pronounced and narrowed in the concerns they addressed.

[3] E. Morris Sider and Paul Hostetler, eds., *Lantern in the Dawn*, Evangel Press, Nappanee, Ind., pp. 62, 63.

[4] In the first issue of the denomination's periodical, *Evangelical Visitor*, (Vol. 1, No. 1, Aug. 1, 1887) an article was published written by evangelist Charles Finney, who at the time was President of Oberlin College, indicating the church's openness to outside believers (and thus affirming its belief in the invisible church—the mystical body of Christ). The *Evangelical Visitor* repeatedly disclosed a willingness to relate to other Christians by publishing articles from sources outside the Brethren in Christ; announcing deaths of other Christians (e.g., Elder James Quinter who was an editor of the *Gospel Messenger,* a German Baptist Brethren paper—cited in the June 1, 1888, issue p.160); and they promoted institutions of other denominations, e.g., McPherson College, a German Baptist College in Kansas, which was cited by the Brethren in Christ editor, Henry Davidson (whose daughter, Francis, attended McPherson and later was called to the mission fields of Africa) referred to it as "destined to be the best school in the denomination." From the Feb.1, 1890 issue of the *Evangelical Visitor*, p. 42.

[5] Most denominations would claim this perspective regarding individual and corporate dimensions of the faith. However, they don't always fulfill it. This account expands on how the Brethren in Christ demonstrate it.

[6] *Refocusing A Vision,* Mennonite Historical Society, Goshen, Ind., 1995, p. 62.

[7] Schrag, "The Genius of the Founding Fathers," *Notes and Queries*, Vol. 1, (January, 1964), p. 7.

[8] Ibid.

[9] From "On my Desk," p. 4 of the January 27, 2000, issue of the *Mennonite Weekly Review*.

[10] The Brethren in Christ have historically been oriented toward biblical theology rather than systematic theology, and their beliefs are viewed as a biblical synthesis, rather than a representation of multi-traditions.

[11] Dan Chamberlain has noted the interpretation of "truth is more dependent than we realize on circumstances and surroundings." *Brethren in Christ Life and Thought*, Vol. XIX, No. 1, April 1996, p. 251.

[12] For expansion on the Brethren in Christ not being a tradition-conscious denomination see Section entitled "Followers of the Bible, not Tradition; and of Purpose, not Image," in chapter 7.

[13] At least three times Paul asked the Lord to remove his "thorn in the flesh" or a weakness. God's response was: "My grace is sufficient for thee; for my strength is made perfect in weakness."

[14] The redeemed ones will experience both joys and despair of life. This condition is shown in the Psalms where the feelings articulated demonstrate both praise and anguish.

[15] Schrag, Ph. D. Dissertation, Temple University, 1967, pp. 89, 90.

[16] The word for "crisis" in Chinese culture can be interpreted as conveying a double meaning— it presents danger as well as opportunity. In like fashion, Christian joy does not deny the reality of pain and suffering. Indeed, we are told to "count it all joy" when we endure various trials (James 1:2), but the teaching of verses 3 and 4 of James 1 is not that our pain by itself makes us joyful; but rather that trials help to make the Christian mature and complete.

[17] A "prosperity perspective" has been promulgated by "charismatic" Christians who at times have given immoderate attention to the "feeling good" part of Christianity. The "suffering destiny" has roots in the Anabaptists who during their history suffered martyrdom. James Juhnke, for example, observes that the sixteenth century Mennonite martyr tradition is "alive and meaningful to American Mennonites." *Mennonite Weekly Review*, April 17, 1997.

[18] "Private gatherings" is the term used for spiritual sharing meetings as cited in the original Confession of the Church.

[19] The Pietists were noted for their emphasis on private devotions, and small-group worship.

[20] It is recognized that many congregations work hard at making worship a group experience, and accomplish it.

[21] The Brethren in Christ college, Messiah College, is quite clear in clarifying the wholeness of God's truth and a Christian world and life view.

[22] For more information regarding the "unity of truth" concept see chapter 3, "Theses Concerning Essential Truths of the Brethren in Christ."

[23] Sider, "History of Ministry in the Brethren in Christ," *Brethren in Christ History and Life*, XV, 1, (April 1992), p. 82.

[24] Ibid., p. 85.

[25] Martin Luther's view that the works of monks or priests was in no way superior to the works of a farmer laboring in the field, or a woman looking after her home, surely coincided with the church's lay-ministry pattern, which continued to the mid-twentieth century.

[26] "An Anthropologist Looks at World Views," *Brethren in Christ History and Life*, April 1998, pp. 151, 152.

[27] The Christian worldview has been more carefully articulated by the church's institution, Messiah College, and its respective academic departments. The college, which is covenanted to the church, perceives itself to be in vital service as an arm of the Brethren in Christ when it teaches principles regarding a Christian world and life view.

[28] For information about the denomination's revision of its worldview see chapter 3, "Theses Concerning Essential Truths of the Brethren in Christ."

[29] There are various versions of the two-kingdom doctrine.

[30] Martin Schrag described the Brethren in Christ as a separated church body in this way: "The redeemed community stood in opposition to the un-regenerated structures of society, namely, the ecclesiastical, social, economic, educational, political, and military establishments . . . (they were) the people of God characterized in the New Testament as "strangers," "exiles," "aliens," and "pilgrims." From paper entitled, "The Brethren in Christ Concept of Separation and Involvement," *Brethren in Christ Church Archives*, Grantham, Pennsylvania.

[31] The denomination has seldom been proactive on political issues. However, it has exerted its corporate influence through correspondence and/or meetings with government officials on war and peace related issues during the American Civil War, World War I, and World War II.

[32] Between March 1889 and July 1891, at least eight major letters or articles appeared in the church's periodical, the *Evangelical Visitor*, on the need for legislation to stop the manufacture and sale of alcoholic beverages. These releases included a January 1, 1889, article (p. 64) that cited the resolution being considered by the congress. In a later article (dated June 1, 1889, p.139) a number of instances were recounted of local option ballots on the sale of liquor, wherein it "called to task" certain Mennonites who lived in an Ohio township where a local option vote was lost. Regret was expressed that "these brethren for conscience sake abstained from voting, and prohibition was defeated by just two votes." The article continued, "had these brethren cast their votes for the cause of temperance . . . there would now be no liquor sold there." The General Conference ruling was that voting was permitted on moral issues (by which was especially meant intoxicating beverages).

[33] The early *Confession* of the denomination prohibited any members from holding public office. A century later, in 1894, at the General Conference convened in Dickinson County, Kansas, May 16-18, it was decided that subject to the "careful and discriminate consideration" of one's local District, it is allowable for members to hold public office.

[34] Mark W. Charlton, "Trends in Political Participation Among Brethren in Christ Ministers," *Brethren in Christ History and Life*, Vol. IV, No. 2, pp. 142, 143.

[35] Broadened philosophical changes had already started in the denomination's colleges. In the case of Upland College, in the late 1940s, they were the first to offer liberal arts concentrations and the granting of baccalaureate degrees. Messiah College soon followed them in the 1950s.

[36] *Restoring the Good Society*, Baker Books, Grand Rapids, Mich., 1994, p. 36.

[37] See a later note of this chapter for the latest denominational action on the question of serving in public office. Even though the action to allow service in public roles was made more than a century ago, its essence was not altered by General Conference except for the case in Canada (in 1924) mentioned above.

[38] It is no longer a matter of choosing culture or Christ for the Brethren in Christ.

[39] Messiah College seeks to serve the denomination by intelligibly articulating for the church and the college the Christian worldview; just as the denomination's camp-meeting institutions, including Roxbury, Memorial Holiness, Camp Freedom, etc., represent the denomination by expressing and making more understandable the denomination's doctrine of holiness.

[40] Since all of the academic disciplines are viewed as being part of general revelation, and therefore God's truth, it seemed inconsistent for Messiah College not to offer a major concentration in the field of political science when other social science areas such as history, social welfare, sociology, and economics were being offered or projected to be offered in the future. It also appeared arbitrary to say that students may choose to serve God and the good of society in the major academic disciplines, save one area. But most of all it would seem to be an anomaly for the church to challenge Christians to find their place in service to God, including the prospect of being involved in social action, and rule out the alternative of the political process, or formal preparation for possible public service.

[41] *Evangelical Visitor*, May 11, 1965, p. 4.

⁴² For a review of the effect of multiple traditions on the Brethren in Christ see chapter 3, "Theses Concerning Essential Truths of the Brethren in Christ."

⁴³ *Brethren Life and Thought*, Autumn 1961, pp. 50, 51.

⁴⁴ The Brethren in Christ are conservative to moderate theologically, yet they have not become embroiled in some issues such as "inerrancy" and "creationism-evolution" as some groups have addressed themselves. See a later footnote in this chapter for expansion on these issues.

⁴⁵ The proponents who strongly emphasize "security of the believer" may, at times, be the most fractious on this issue. While the Bible gives lots of evidence about the security of salvation in Christ, it calls Christians to balance that with good works (Col. 1:22, 23 is a pattern here).

⁴⁶ The concept of being separated also correlates with being holy or being sanctified, both of which are represented in the Pietist, and what has been termed *Wesleyan*, emphases that have been perceived as being part of the denomination.

⁴⁷ Richard Niehbuhr, in his work *Christ and Culture,* indicates by his classifications that denominations need to determine the relationship of the church to the culture. Accordingly, it seems that most Brethren in Christ would be aligned with the "Christ over Culture" classification rather than with the "Christ and Culture" or "Christ against Culture" categories.

⁴⁸ The denomination abandoned its guidelines for uniform dress around 1950. This is not to infer that within the Brethren in Christ church today there are no elements preferring the interpretation that God's "new people," be withdrawn from culture; however, the church's standards and its interaction trends appear to value a more balanced ideal.

⁴⁹ Anabaptists have been known throughout their history as those who integrate the faith into their lives. The early Pietists introduced the idea of social action to the Protestant church. They were noted as persons who practiced their faith. F. Ernest Stoeffler, *Continental Pietism and Early American Christianity*, Eerdmans, Grand Rapids, Mich., 1976, p. 15.

⁵⁰ The Brethren in Christ have not been afraid to take important stands regarding truth; yet in line with historic Pietists, they are not doctrinaire about matters considered secondary. Issues regarding Christian practice appear to be more important than lesser theoretical issues. They refrain from getting involved in heated theological controversy. For example, the "evolution of species" concept has not been an issue that has come before the body. The church has seemingly been satisfied with the foundational belief that God was the creator of all, including all of life.

As to the matter of "inerrancy," the denomination considers the Scriptures to be fully reliable and inspired by God. The denomination has not developed a more detailed view of that question. A statement by Luke Keefer, Jr., seems to satisfy the group. It reads: "Terms like 'inerrant' and 'infallible' are negative terms. They declare what the Bible is not . . . (Since the Brethren in Christ do not attack the trustworthiness of Scripture) . . . words like 'inerrant' and 'infallible' cannot be construed as necessary words they need addressed to themselves." "Inerrancy and the Brethren in Christ View of Scripture," *Brethren in Christ History and Life*, IV, 1, April 1992, pp. 4, 5.

⁵¹ During the early and middle parts of the twentieth century mainline churches, especially those influenced by the liberal views of the social-gospel movement, often sought to influence public policy as part of their religious mission. But the political dynamic for the liberal wing of the church late in this century has withered. It is not actively engaged in presenting fresh views for political consideration. In recent decades, however, the conservative side of the Christian divide has moved into political discussions by way of political organizations.

⁵² Robert Ives tells of sitting under the teaching of David Hubbard who asked, "What does it mean to render unto Caesar when we are Caesar?" (In a democracy we vote and so choose the leader.) Would it not mean that in a democratic society the Christian has a greater responsibility regarding crucial moral questions faced by the civil authority—because the citizen is part

of the civil authority? The Brethren in Christ have shown considerably more concern about "rendering unto God what is God's."

[53] Sometimes the Evangelical Movement is simplistically caricatured as endorsing "Civil Religion," but such a generalization is in gross error. The National Association of Evangelicals, for example, does not support such a view. At one point a speaker at the N.A.E. Convention in the 1950s presented an address that had "God save the country" militaristic and civil-religious implications. At the behest of the Brethren in Christ, and surely others, a special session was called to give opportunity for an address that declared counter views.

[54] Ron Burwell reported from the "Tradition and Mission" study that the most "politically involved people" of the denomination were those in "near complete agreement" with Brethren in Christ teachings, most frequent church attenders, and prayers. *Evangelical Visitor*, June 1989, p.11. In the same vein (which may on the surface seem surprising, it is often thought that the Anabaptist leaning members of the Brethren in Christ would be those prone to refrain from political involvement. John K. Stoner, however, a writer and former Brethren in Christ pastor, noted for his firm Anabaptist views, was quoted in a letter submitted to the editor of the *Evangelical Visitor* dated March, 1995, (p. 27) as follows: "Three cheers for Sam Brubaker's (whose topic, though in opposition, was titled) 'Restoring Prayer to the Public Schools'" (February 1995 *Visitor*). Stoner continued (in this surprising manner from a staunch Anabaptist), "Dr. Brubaker reminds us that discipleship is political, and that discipleship involves taking a stand on questions debated in courts and palaces, legislatures, and executive mansions. This is the way it was in Bible times. Jesus announced his mission in political language when he announced the 'Kingdom of God' . . ."

[55] Yeatts and Burwell, in "Tradition and Mission," *Brethren in Christ History and Life*, p.111, found preference in the denomination for the Republican Party to be very strong. There was no reporting of Canadian party preferences.

[56] These are two political groups that attempted to represent Christian-oriented views on public issues: "Call to Renewal" from a more liberal perspective, and the "Christian Coalition" tended toward offering a conservative perspective on issues.

[57] Shenk, *Write the Vision: The Church Renewed*, Trinity Press, Valley Forge, Pa., 1995, p.46.

[58] Ibid., p. 28.

[59] For further analysis of the Brethren in Christ understanding of the church universal see chapter 3 entitled, "Theses Concerning Essential Truths of the Brethren in Christ," and chapter 10 entitled "Descriptive Designations to Identify Who the Brethren in Christ Are."

[60] Isolated elements of the movement were sufficiently radical to start new groups such as the Moravian Brethren, the German Baptist Brethren, and the Lutheran Brethren; but in the main the movement sought to reform the established churches.

[61] Many reformers contended that the body, referring to God's invisible church, was made up of all Christian believers past and present.

[62] The Pietist understanding of life, which regards every fellow believer as sister or brother tended to break down the rigid barriers between denominations.

[63] The General Conference of the Brethren in Christ declared such things as photographs, mustaches, lightning rods, bride servants, etc., to be inconsistent. For a more complete listing of these items and the initial year the church declared them to be inconsistent, see note in chapter 2, "Theses Concerning Essential Truths of the Brethren in Christ."

[64] The most important qualifications for affirming that one from another denomination was a Christian brother or sister appears to have been an affirmation regarding a personal experience of the new birth and the demonstration of a transformed life.

[65] *Gestalt des Reichs*, (1814), quoted from *Plain Women*, op. cit. p. 27.

[66] *History of All the Religious Denominations in the United States*, Published by John Winebrenner, Harrisburg, Pa., 1848, p. 552.

[67] Faith matters and doctrines considered by the early Pietists and the later Brethren in Christ to be primary were those clearly detailed in the Bible. It was the varied understandings, religious practices, and particularities tied to biblical-sourced traditions that they would have viewed as being secondary. The Brethren in Christ historically acknowledged that they themselves may have been too attentive to certain secondary matters—and upon gaining new light proceeded to adjust such understandings.

[68] For further analysis of evangelicalism as an extension of Pietism see essay ten, "Descriptive Designations to Tell Who the Brethren in Christ Are."

[69] Early evangelicals fostered missions and evangelism as well as social action (opposing slavery, assisting the needy, and fostering basic education). In these respects, the evangelical movement was a successor to the Pietist movement.

[70] In considering God's call that His church be united there were several potential groupings for the Brethren in Christ to choose from—on the conservative theological side—there was either the National Association of Evangelicals (which they joined), or several fundamentalist organizations which appeared to be atomizing rather than uniting. On the more liberal end was the National Council of Churches where most of the mainline denominations were affiliated.

[71] For more than one-hundred-sixty years this small denomination had been somewhat sectarian and separated from the world and had not become part of a standing interchurch group. It was now reaching for new insights to become more effective in outreach and service to the world. In terms of Anabaptist church bodies becoming part of NAE— from the Mennonites, consisting of more than a score of possible denominations—the Mennonite Brethren were the only group other than the Brethren in Christ who chose to join the group at its beginning.

[72] The Council of Christian Colleges and Universities currently has more than one hundred members.

[73] For more analysis regarding the varied theological traditions that have contributed to the Brethren in Christ vision see chapter 3, "Theses Concerning Essential Truths of the Brethren in Christ," and chapter 10, "Descriptive Designations to Identify Who the Brethren in Christ Are."

[74] David J. Bosch, *Believing in the Future: Toward A Missiology of Western Culture*, Trinity Press International, Valley Forge, Pa., 1995, p. 57.

[75] Due to societal changes, including legal modifications and welfare transitions (the government made significant alterations to welfare delivery systems), the denomination no longer sponsors institutionalized homes for children.

[76] From "Living Doctrine," the 1970 General Conference Sermon, *Evangelical Visitor*, July 10, 1970, pp. 4, 5, 22, 23.

[77] From the report of the Findings Committee, *Study Conference on the Brethren in Christ Concept of the Church*, 1968, p. 4, (Brethren in Christ Archives box VIII, 12, 1.1)

Chapter IX

Four Priorities of the Brethren in Christ
and Their Order

Throughout the history of Christianity numerous avenues have been followed in the name of fidelity to the church. Scores of denominations and countless individuals express their Christianity in many varied manners. Faithfulness to Christ and the church is expressed as Christians participate in the sacraments, affirm a set of doctrines, acknowledge spiritual experiences, observe rituals, recite prayers, participate in spiritual reflection, live according to biblical tenets, give alms, support social action, or by combinations of these elements. Christian fidelity is witnessed in many different ways and according to varying magnitudes.

The growth of Islam in its most radical form during this late-modern era, and its opposition to religious pluralism, indicates that some individuals and groups take their religion quite seriously, while others are less passionately inclined. There seems to be a lack of strong conviction for many who designate Christianity as their religion. The Gallup Organization recently found that while more than ninety percent of the American public believe in a God, less than half of the population attend church on a given Sunday morning, and only six to ten percent of all Americans are what Gallup terms "highly spiritually committed."[1] Gallup also found that among evangelicals (a group considered to be more committed and holding stronger spiritual propensities) only twenty-five percent tithe.

Along with vast differences within Christianity regarding spiritual intensity, there is also much doctrinal disparity. But doctrinal disagreements have always been part of Christianity. Disputes over tenets of the faith were the source for many of the epistles that became part of the New Testament canon. In light of differences in spiritual commitment and doctrinal interpretations, the more orthodox brands of Christianity make a distinction between "professors" and "believers." The former are thought to be less fully committed Christians. The Brethren in Christ, as a Pietist/Evangelical group, concur with such distinctions. They would view a Christian who fails to affirm a new life in Christ as being a "cultural," "generic," or "nominal" Christian.

Approaches to the faith that separate the Brethren in Christ from other denominations: they stand committed to historic Christian beliefs, and are considered doctrinally orthodox. However, the Christian faith is more than doctrinal statements, and numerous denominations would claim to be orthodox. A simpler, yet reasonable, set of assessment criteria is necessary to distinguish them from other groups that might also be termed classically Christian. Therefore, a portrait of the Brethren in Christ faith, as contrasted with other denominations, is drawn according to the priorities they tend to follow and the order given those priorities.

There are varied ways one might evaluate a denomination's priorities. It could be done according to giving patterns as they garner and allocate resources of personal service and monetary contributions, or by the published beliefs internalized in the lives of a cross-section of the members. However, such approaches would require use of highly sophisticated instruments of measurement. It, therefore, seems more feasible to determine a denomination's priorities by reviewing what is required to become a member and to maintain favorable standing.

The priorities or standards by which a potential denominational member crosses the threshold into the church (the church particular and the church universal) and then remains engaged as part of the church, for evaluation purposes, are divided into four clusters of similar belief and practice. These clusters could also be called "contours of faith" since they show distinct lines of difference between denominations. Contours of faith can be aligned according to the priority they receive in a given denomination. From the four contours which signify Christian fidelity and allegiance to the church, the denominational profile can be drawn. The religious contours to be ordered according to priorities of a given denomination are:

1. Matters of the heart (the place of spiritual experience).
2. Matters of the mind (the importance of beliefs and understandings).
3. Matters of behavior and action.
4. Matters of church form and practice.

Matters of the Heart

A kind of experiential tradition has run through the Christian church beginning with the apostles. It was manifested in individuals and clearly demonstrated in group settings, especially at Pentecost. During the Middle Ages it expressed itself in a mystical approach to Christian life. The concept of Christian experience was renewed in the turbulent times of the Reformation, as Martin Luther, influenced by mysticism, testified of the power of God's forgiveness and justification by faith.[2] But experiential manifestations in the church became evident in new waves of magnitude in the Pietist movement that affected all of Protestantism in Europe and North America during the seventeenth and eighteenth centuries.

The Scriptures are full of accounts concerned about the deepest recesses of our lives — an inward spiritual reality. Through the centuries Christian writing and singing is filled with sentiments about sacred experiences of peace, joy, and penitence. For the Psalmist the heart is that deep inner place of a person where one feels true things about oneself and about God. Psalms 73:1 says, "God is good to those who are pure in heart." Blaise Pascal wrote in *Pensees*, "The heart has its reasons of which reason knows nothing. . . . It is the heart which perceives God and not the reason. That is what faith is: God is perceived by the heart, not by reason."

For denominations that stress Christianity as being heart-felt and heart changing, the faith consists of more than pondering a new philosophy of life, or embracing a benevolent ideology. It involves a "new birth," wherein the believer receives salvation through divine grace. As a "new creature" the Christian can seek for and receive divine assistance to live a "new life." This conversion-regeneration experience is disclosed to the believer through the Holy Spirit. The concept of conversion-regeneration represents a new sense of reality. To the true believer there is a transcendent, morally binding relationship to God that is enriched by one's newly formed spiritual ties to His body, the church.

The church, a diverse body composed of His redeemed ones, exceeds a social club united for pleasure and convenience, and it supersedes a political body for the furtherance of social action. It is a spiritual body that is held together by charity, love, and by the possession of His Spirit.

Accepting Jesus into your heart is considered a transformative experience. Jesus gives new life. Paul in Galatians 2:20 says: "It is no longer I who live, but Christ who lives in me." There are a number of requisites and consequences that accompany a "heart-changing" faith experience. Brethren in Christ would consider these elements as validation of one's membership in the universal church. For many denominations, a saving knowledge of the faith is the foundational requirement for a given believer to be accepted into membership of the church particular, as well as the key to being part of His universal church. A personal consciousness of divine heart change follows one's repentance of sin and a decision to turn from sin. Other heart matters can include a fellowship and communion with God and special anointing by the Holy Spirit. The following "heart matters" are briefly reviewed: repentance, decision, fellowship, anointing, calling, and purity.

1. Repentance of Sin Is a Prerequisite to Conversion.

A denomination's concern for heart matters is most visibly demonstrated by placing the issue of personal salvation at the forefront of ministry. The Pietist legacy emphasizes that we are born in sin, and we as individuals need to acknowledge our sins before God. But repentance has fallen on hard times in many sectors of Christianity. Between Rome's mischaracterization of it as penance and some Dispensationalists' denial of its place in Gospel preaching, it is currently possible for some to attend church regularly and never hear a repentance message.

Beyond this acknowledgment of one's sins and the need for repentance that leads to life, it is also understood that a vital faith is not produced by outer conformity, the right genes, or by good works. Although true faith involves amending one's life, conversion is attained through a depth of repentance that in turn affects a divine act of change within the believer. The Protestant principle of justification by faith is joined to the Pietist belief that the God who is good enough to save a sinful person is powerful enough to change that person. The change brings them into a spiritual sonship or daughtership.[3] The natural world cannot claim this status. It is reserved for the believer. They become a child of God. This is the believer's crowning glory.

2. A Personal Decision to Turn From Sin Is Involved in Regeneration.

The regenerative power of the divine (a matter of the heart) was not a teaching to which Pietists merely assented; it became a reality in their lives. Salvation meant more than repentance and the forgiveness of sins; it involved a turning from the way of sin. Although regeneration did not assure a sinless future, it did signify the believer's commitment to live scripturally. When an encounter with the living Lord transpired, the newly born person had decided on a new focus and a new goal.

3. An Intimate Fellowship with God Accompanies The Miracle Of Regeneration.

When God acts in saving power to regenerate a person it brings into effect a new relationship as well as a new purpose. Purpose is not about doing. It is about being who we are — not what we do. We determine who we really are as Christians by our relationship with God. Fellowship and interaction with God become possible through the Holy Spirit. The relationship is maintained through private prayer, Bible study, and meditation. A nurturing of that relationship demands that the Christian becomes intimate with God. This tie is best carried out by daily renewal and fellowship with God. Otherwise, spiritual degeneration can occur.

A Christian can have a close personal relationship with God the Father. Thomas á Kempis refers to the relationship as "a familiar friend with Jesus."

4. An Anointing from God Is Available to the Surrendered Believer.

When Jesus was about ready to leave His followers He said, "Anyone who has faith in me will do what I have been doing." (John 14:12). This was a tall order and bewildering to the disciples who had witnessed His wondrous miracles. However, to carry on His work the Lord promised to provide empowerment to them through the Holy Spirit (John 14:15-18). His assurance that the Holy Spirit would help them to carry the Good News to the ends of the earth became fulfilled (Acts 1:4-8).

Those who confess Christ in a saving relationship receive the Spirit of God. The Holy Spirit in turn becomes the driving force behind the church. It is not the quality of its organization, the status of its clergy, or the power of its intellectual life that generates its spiritual energy. Without the infusion of power and guidance from the Holy Spirit the church becomes a mere formality and degenerates to a lifeless state. When ministry of the Spirit is absent it is due to lukewarm and nominal Christians populating the particular church.

Divine empowerment is conferred on Christians who are wholly surrendered to Him. From a theological perspective, when one is anointed by God it signifies that an uncommon enablement is bestowed on the person. Spiritual gifts from God go beyond the natural God-given talents of the individual. The presence of the Holy Spirit within the church is an authentication of true Christianity.

5. The Calling of God to the Believer Is Expected.

Each person wants to know how they fit into the world. Who am I, and where should I be? The Christian believer can receive divine answers to these questions. God's anointed ones are more than divinely gifted, they are divinely placed. Anointed persons have a special mission in God's economy, and His economy is not confined to work within the church itself. Under a sense of calling from God the Christian relinquishes ownership of his/her life. This revolutionary teaching does not ask all craftsmen, farmers, or those in other occupations to be pastors or church workers, but that they respond to God's call as Christian's at work in varied roles.

Living life as a call is witnessed when God permeates the Christian's entire life— including work, demeanor, allegiances, and relationships. One's life is no longer a search for self-fulfillment. Instead, an ultimate purpose for life is discovered. When the culture says "seek your place in the world," God reveals "seek first the kingdom of God." And when the culture bids "find yourself," the church responds "lose yourself and so find life."

6. A Quest for Spiritual Vitality and Purity Is Pursued.

Denominations that demonstrate "matters of the heart" do so by their efforts to win new Christians and by showing a hunger for gaining spiritual strength and for attaining Christian perfection. The hunger for goodness is manifested in deepened spirituality through a divine work of holiness in the life of the believer.[4]

Denominations that preach the need for a personal heart experience generally recognize that Christian experience cannot be confined to a rigid mold. There is no set pattern for coming to the faith or for maturing in the faith. A believer's conversion may be dramatic as it was with Saul who was struck down and became Paul. Or, on the other hand, transformation may be more serene as it was for those who conversed with Jesus on the way to Emmaus. Within the Pietist/Evangelical tradition differing patterns of heart experience evidence the attainment of holy living.

How Important Are "Matters of the Heart" to Protestants Today?

Matters of the heart are not of highest priority to a substantial segment of those who consider themselves part of the broad Christian church. In fact, there are segments of Christianity that would view matters of the heart in a pejorative fashion. The sin factor is diminished by some, and the idea of Christian experience is frequently viewed with distrust. Some who claim Christianity tend to hold heart matters at arms length. They view heart matters as highly subjective, overly emotional, and perhaps insufficiently cerebral. There are many within Christianity today who are suspicious of Jesus' miracles, including a Christian's super-naturally changed heart—which is the heart of the gospel. Matters of the heart, the experiential and empowerment dimensions of the faith, are found of highest priority in denominations that are evangelical in character.

How Important are "Matters of the Heart" to the Brethren in Christ?

The Brethren in Christ church was founded in the aftermath of the First Great Awakening in America, a time when the Christian church was focused on matters of the heart. The new fellowship of believers came together to satisfy an emphasis on conversion-regeneration, as a conscious experience of faith.[5] The new body apparently felt their "heart matters" could not be met by becoming part of other groups that stressed the Anabaptist views to which they were strongly committed.

Throughout the history of the denomination the personal conversion of individuals to the faith has been the Church's paramount concern, and "matters of the heart" have been their primary theme.[6] The Brethren in Christ measure the authenticity of one's Christianity by their testimony to assurance of the faith (relationship to God), and showing evidences of a transformed life (relationship to man). They also exhibit concern that members of the body seek God for cleansing, and for the anointing of His Spirit so as to be enabled for ministry.[7]

The Brethren in Christ have demonstrated throughout their history that they want to be spiritually awake. A thirst for attaining Christian perfection and purity has been persistent with them. Excerpts from a paper entitled "Context for Renewal," prepared by a 13-member Task Force on Renewal and presented to the 1996 General Conference Board cite spiritual values that the denomination has held high and urged the church to give them continuing priority. The paper observes:

> Historically the Brethren in Christ have . . . standing expecta-
> tion for a life-changing relationship with the living God woven
> into the fabric of what is understood as the normal Christian
> life. . . . There is genuine desire to see and experience spiritual
> renewal, evangelism, and God's miraculous, life-changing
> power. . . . Historically, several disciplines have helped the
> church become more attuned and susceptible to the Lord's
> working in the world. These disciplines are repentance, redis-
> covery of the Holy Spirit, renewed interest in God's word, the
> reestablishment of genuine community, and the role of mis-
> sion and service.[8]

Matters of the Mind

At the core of a person's being is one's heart. This is where one's faith commences. But the heart is inevitably tied to the mind. One's heart is dependent on the mind for knowing and believing. Since Christianity not only offers a world view, but also a way to think and feel, it is important that there be a marvelous union between the heart and head. While the heart pertains to matters of grace and a new state of being for the believer, "matters of the mind" deal with Spirit-directed understandings, transformed values, and right attitudes and beliefs. There are numerous biblical references to the importance of possessing a Christian mind. Isaiah, the prophet of the eighth century B.C., entreated, "Come let us reason together." (Isa. 1:18). The followers of Christ were frequently enjoined to have the "mind of Christ." They were counseled: "let this mind be in you." Christ also related a rational task (theology study) when he said: "If you hold to my teaching, you are really my disciples" (John 8:31 NIV). In the first century Paul described unbelieving Jews of his day in this way: "I bear them witness that they have a zeal for God but it is not enlightened" (Rom. 10:2).

In each and every century since the time of Christ, the mission of the church has included caring for matters of the mind. It was not until late modern times

that the public sector surpassed the church in its magnitude of effort for culti-
vating the mind and supporting learning. Despite public education now exceeding that of ecclesiastical-sponsored learning, the importance of the mind
continues to receive priority attention by most denominations. There are a number of reasons why the broader church tends to pursue matters of the mind as
part of its mission. They include: (1) to ascertain truth, (2) to aid in transforming culture, (3) to understand and deal with change, and (4) to communicate
truth and support evangelism.

1. The Christian Mind Is Needed to Ascertain Truth.

We live in a world dominated by science and technology. The culture is
immersed in scientific premises and has been both blessed and cursed by scientific discoveries. Even religious truths are often analyzed with a scientific
bias. Yet truth precepts and ultimate reality cannot be determined by the scientific method alone. While Christians understand the usefulness of science in
dealing with truths of God's natural revelation, they are also committed to low
probability events such as the incarnation and resurrection, which are truths of
God's special revelation. What are the analytical bounds for determining truth?
Seeking to ascertain the span of God's truths is an area fraught with error.
Therefore, the mind and the heart of the Christian dare not be divided.

The economy of today, although continuing to be driven by scientific assumptions, is part of a general culture that seems to be shifting its basic premises. It has transitioned to a time and culture described as the Post-Modern Age.
A key characteristic of it is an increasing uncertainty regarding the merits of science. Along with the transpiring pre-suppositional changes, many people are
looking to experience God. Peter Berger has observed that even though modern culture is somewhat antagonistic to Christianity, today's society seems to
be irrepressibly religious. In a highly pluralistic fashion there has been a turning to multi-religions and combinations of them. There is also a turning to cultic groupings wherein unusual twists of belief are added to traditional religious
concepts. He explains such religious phenomena in this way: "The occult wave
(including a devil component) is to be understood as resulting from the re-
pression of transcendence in modern consciousness."[9]

The many cults in today's Western society range from satanic to scientific.
As one reflects on this religious landscape, one is apt to feel that the human
will to believe and to rely on astronomical and unbelievable things, is strong.[10]
Evil beliefs tend to start from a basic truth (fairly typical religious belief) and
work some subtle change to the truth. Therefore, Christians and others must be
careful and act responsibly regarding cultic claims.

Christians also need to be responsible about their own religious claims. The charge of delusional beliefs is not just directed at cults. At times heart-change Christians are justifiably accused of not giving a proper place to matters of the mind. Christianity can be easily dismissed as simply another mystery cult when mind matters are given short shrift. Consequently, the Christian mind is needed to separate doctrinal truth from doctrinal falsehood. When one, for example, considers the core Christian truth of the resurrection the delusional idea can be clearly dismissed because there are sound reasons to believe it.[11] It is a truth that is both spiritual and rational. Matters of the heart and matters of the mind should be considered together.

When our lives and our theology are examined for spiritual answers, the faith must be understandable. If anti-intellectualism is tied to the faith it runs counter to the biblical precept to "love God with our minds Matt. 22:37)." The lure of simplistic answers can be an intoxicating kind of message. Any ideologies and beliefs that Christians support need to be tested by the mind as well as the heart. Matters of the heart and matters of the mind need to be considered together.

2. The Christian Mind Contributes to Reforming the Culture.

God's children look with anticipation to an afterlife with God. As to this life, however, there are differences among Christians regarding the degree of engagement they should have with the culture. Some Christians interpret the faith to mean they should be highly separated from the society, while other Christians see their responsibility as interacting with the world so as to "occupy till He comes." They serve in the world and seek to influence it for good.[12]

Fulfilling a broad cultural mandate requires full use of the Christian mind. It involves intellectual labor. There is no intent to oppressively impose religious faith on others. The Christian is respectful of religious pluralism. Nor does it mean legislating away man's freedom to choose. It is instead the sharing of God-given understandings, through one's Christian life and verbal exchange, so as to persuade others to accept principles and values consistent with a Christian worldview.[13]

Paul Hiebert argues that Christians today must increasingly deal with Christian faith at the worldview level. He contends that for true Christianity to continue over the generations there must be a transformation in the worldviews of people.[14] Being protagonists for a worldview under-girded by biblical revelation is a formidable undertaking. It runs counter to relativistic and secular views permeating the culture.[15] Nancy Barcus observes, "there is no reason for the Christian to become the relativist's victim." She contends that the Christian mind enables one to analyze the most obvious assumptions of the relativist and relate them to the bedrock of Scripture.[16] The Christian worldview gives more than a coherent view of God and His creation, it is the light by which Christian's can evaluate society and react to culture.[17]

New religions, ideological crusades, and utopian schemes have penetrated western society to the point that today it is best described as a post-Christian culture. The society is both more secularized and pluralistic, and the shift in values has been characterized by some as a battle between religion and science. Others have referred to the philosophical struggle as a cultural war. Both characterizations seem misplaced because there is no inherent conflict between the scientific method and Christianity, and there are good and bad within all cultures.[18] Those who sense the need to work toward transforming the culture recognize that Christians, frail as they are, by meaningful interaction with and exceptions to the general culture, can shape it. On the other hand, Christians by their withdrawal, their compromise, or passivity toward the culture affect it as well, but in less positive ways.[19]

Christ confronted sin and error within the culture. The Apostle Paul used his rational and spiritual gifts to counter ungodly acts and mindsets in society. Many Christians today work toward a meaningful reversal of the present growth of secularism and relativism. With regard to establishing truth in the culture, Os Guiness observes that when Christians fail to fully use their minds they take on the role of "cultural imitators" and "adapters" rather than "originators."[20]

3. The Christian Mind Is Needed for the Church to Understand and Deal with Change.

It was estimated recently that the entire store of human knowledge doubles every five years.[21] Life is marked by continuous change, and the rate of new discovery seems to be accelerating. Simultaneously, the world is becoming more interconnected and increasingly interdependent. Unfortunately, going hand-in-hand with these waves of change are ever-arising dilemmas, and the long-term problems of man such as wars, poverty, and injustice continue. In kaleidoscopic forms new issues come to the foreground, such as genetic engineering, mass terrorism, computerized relationships, human cloning, etc. New ideas and solutions are proclaimed in profusion. While ideologies projected from mankind are new every day, there are certain things of a spiritual nature that are changeless and enduring—the truths from God are immutable.

Growing complexities of modern life, coupled with vast increases in knowledge, require the church to seek greater spiritual empowerment and discernment, but at the same time Christians must enhance their resources of knowledge and understanding. This can be done as the church follows the scriptural admonition to supplement (your) faith with virtue, virtue with knowledge, knowledge with self-control, and self-control with steadfastness, and steadfastness with godliness, and godliness with brotherly affection, and brotherly affection with love" (2 Peter 1:5-7). Only then are the Christian and the church ready to face bewildering problems and engage new opportunities.[22]

Matters of the mind are key elements to the faith and the effectiveness of Christians. Nancy Barcus points out that consistent with Scripture and the mission of the church, knowledge is not only a worldly endeavor when she says:

> (Knowledge) is part of the very fabric of what it means to be a Christian. It is not separate from such virtues as humility and love. We have the truth and yet we do not know everything. So we are humble. We speak the truth as Christ would speak, in love, because we are speaking to people. Enlarged understanding, humility, love—how we need them! In fact, they were to be the hallmarks of that first creature God created in His own image. The moment challenges us. It is time to reclaim, to exercise, the heritage of the Christian mind.[23]

God's people, the church, ever growing and maturing, need to be open to new conditions and new light from God. The transition from being "under the law" in Old Testament times to "under grace" in the New Testament era was a manifestation in new light. Christian believers gained additional new light in modern times as societal changes and inhumanities raised new questions, about the institution of slavery. As a result the Christian church advocated change wherein slavery was perceived as exploitive and sinful.[24]

The Brethren in Christ serve as an example of accepting new light from God that brought dramatic changes to the life, ministry, and understandings of an entire body. These new discernments came in the mid-twentieth century. The changes that evolved were striking and the degree of unity in instituting them so incredible that on the doctrine of "separation from the world" the body appears to have been in "God's waiting room" for 170 years.[25] The denomination's spiritual perceptions also underwent a transformation as the new light was followed regarding the Christian's interaction with the world.[26]

Owen H. Alderfer, in the 1970 Centennial General Conference sermon on "Living Doctrine," stressed that Church doctrine should represent new light and a growing faith as he quoted Titus 2:10, ". . .that they may adorn the doctrine of God our Savior in all things." Alderfer emphasized that living doctrine is ever fresh and had this to say about static truth:

> A misconception is that the shape of the doctrine of God is that of static truth which can be set down in neat statements, memorized, recited, and given out in parcels of truth. The doctrine of God is more than rigid orthodoxy.[27]

Dan Chamberlain commenting on new light coming to the Brethren in Christ offered these observations:

> It is not that truth changes, but that our capacity to understand truth is more dependent than we realize upon our circumstances and surroundings. It is for this reason we need to use a combination of caution and humility when we reach our conclusions. We need to be certain enough to act with the courage of our convictions; we need to be humble enough to realize that our understanding of truth is incomplete; and we need to be brothers and sisters enough to continue to respect and fellowship with those who differ from us.[28]

The shift among the Brethren in Christ by their flexibility with the general culture indicates that a denomination should not be highly dogmatic. As both Alderfer and Chamberlain contended, biblical doctrine is a "lively seed."[29] As new questions arise, the Spirit's leading will at times put His people on the cutting edge of change. Even if it involves pain the denomination has shown that it can remain consistent with biblical values and be open to new light when the mind and heart are joined.

4. The Use of the Christian Mind to Communicate Truth and to Support Evangelism.

Followers of Christ throughout the history of the Christian church have been aware of the command to preach salvation—they were called to specifically evangelize. Jesus made it clear that He was here for the purpose of evangelism. He said (Luke 19:10), "For the Son of Man has come to seek and to save that which was lost." After Jesus chose His twelve disciples, He sent them out to proclaim the message of salvation. In virtually every recorded personal encounter Jesus had with individuals, His goal was to bring them to a decision point about Him and about their sin. His admonition to His followers was, "Go therefore and make disciples of all nations" (Matt. 28:18-20). The church believes that man is lost and separated from God and can be reconciled to Him through faith in Jesus Christ.

Some people are specially gifted for evangelism (Eph. 4:11). Others seem to be less so. All Christians are called to the work of evangelism. There are varied ways to help in evangelism. All Christians can pray and most can give to the work of evangelism. In addition, Christians need to live a life that attracts others to the gospel (Matt. 5:16).

Paul said in order to take the message of Christ to those who had not heard he gladly endured being beaten, stoned, shipwrecked; in danger from rivers, robbers, the city, and the wilderness and enduring labor and hardship, sleepless nights, hunger and thirst, and cold and exposure (see 2 Cor. 11:25-27). Clearly Apostle Paul had the virtues required to surmount these many obstacles. He possessed zeal and understanding abundantly because he had experienced the power of the Gospel. He received understanding from God (the mind of Christ), but he was also a learned man (he possessed a Christian worldview). Paul was prepared for evangelism. He frequently testified that matters of the mind are important to the ministry of evangelism. Missionary Jay Smith, who has carried out an effective ministry to Muslims, including teaching Muslim/Christian apologetics at Operation Mobilization's Turning Point, states:

> We have raised a generation of young Christians ill-equipped
> to define what they believe, and even less equipped to defend
> it in public. We need to be able to show that our faith does not
> rest solely on personal experience. It is credible because it is
> backed by propositional truth.[30]

Christians are called to various roles of evangelism. Some believers are especially endowed to witness to matters of the mind. There needs to be respect for the mind in all areas of ministry. Regardless of calling, such matters of the mind have importance. D. Elton Trueblood, the Quaker theologian, observed that "if evangelicals are to maintain the vitality of the Christian faith, they must think and they must think with clarity and rigor." Trueblood continues, "we must out-think the world!"[31] His exhortation for evangelicals to "think with clarity and rigor" applies to all callings, including the ministry of evangelization.

The Christian, tempered by humility, reserved in judgment, and confident that God understands all truth even when the individual is baffled, will journey into the world of exploding knowledge and catapulting discovery to satisfy their curiosity. More importantly, they will do it for the sake of faith itself. In this vein the apostle Peter exhorted Christians to be ready to give reasons for their faith (1 Pet. 3:15). And Paul's letter to the Corinthian church indicates that Christians, no longer children, should be equipped with a Christian worldview (2 Cor. 10:3-5).

As Francis Schaeffer stated a generation ago, the need for Christians to articulate a Christian worldview is especially strong today because "America is living on the Christian memory." The secular mind does not understand how the Christian mind is changed by the gospel, and has little understanding of the gospel language and concepts. But more than that the Christian needs to understand other worldviews so as to meet secular people where they are in both thinking and commitment. To properly communicate with non-Christians, one must be in touch with the feelings of the times and should have a modicum of understanding about other worldviews, both secular and religious. Only then can true instruction and witness begin.[32]

Os Guinness points out that evangelical Christians display "a troubling ignorance and unease about apologetics."[33] He further states that most methods of witnessing assume that people are open and interested. However, we are stuck when we encounter people who are not open and interested. Rather than meeting them at their individual point of interest, there continues to be a heavy reliance on group proclamation.

In addition to proclamation, other means used by Christians to get their point across in society are protest and picketing. While these pressure-type means may call attention to truth concerns, they surely are not appropriate as methods of evangelism or for transmitting matters of the mind. The Brethren in Christ have generally not used these approaches. Instead, the Christian who takes seriously matters of the mind will ideally be an apologist for the faith in fresh, powerful, imaginative, compassionate, and persuasive ways. Mindful exchanges are mandatory if one is to discern points of personal contact and isolate points of disagreement with contemporary views. In using an open and mindful approach for communicating truth, Christians displays servant-hood, humility, self-control, and peace as they listen to the views of others and convey the gospel of Christ to the nonbeliever.

For the sake of effectively communicating Christian views and evangelizing new believers, the church will need to concentrate on the positive message of the gospel and find appropriate ways of getting it across. While tent meetings and revival campaigns were the hallmarks of previous American church awakenings, it may be that mediums such as the Internet or the ministry of a Christian university will become critical to stirring future awakenings.[34]

There will always be a need for powerful pulpiteers, but their message is often directed to insiders and according to Wilbert R. Shenk it is communicated in "church language."[35] Today's culture does not know church language. David J. Bosch feels that "a missionary encounter with the West will have to be, primarily, a ministry of the laity."[36] Clearly, such encounters need to emphasize listening, since we must seek to understand in order to be understood.

It also seems that for highest effectiveness in ministry, increasing attention must be given to matters of the mind.

5. How Important Are "Matters of the Mind" to Protestants Today?

Matters of the mind have always had a prominent place within the Christian church. The medieval church controlled education and explained the world to society. In modern times there has been a falling away from the church's supremacy in education. From the latter half of the nineteenth-century, Western culture, which was previously dominated by Judeo-Christian presuppositions, experienced an apostasy shift toward relativism and secularism.

With the coming of modernity it was not just the control of education and a shift in worldview that changed, the church itself changed. Instead of faith and reason being viewed as complementary, many leaders of mainline churches became skeptical and denied the very doctrines that for centuries were distinctive to Christianity. The faith-reason presuppositions that had been integral to Christian thought and belief frequently devolved into ideas and assumptions more closely akin to scientism and relativism than to a perspective of faith.

The strong modernist influence that moved to the forefront of Protestantism produced a reaction from the church's conservatives under the banner of Fundamentalism. Fundamentalists viewed the church at large as being insufficiently pure in both heart and mind. This group opposed the modernist postulations by which the faith was interpreted. But ill-fatedly many Fundamentalists came to an opposite polar position—that of anti-intellectualism. They viewed scholarly efforts as suspect. This conservative Protestantism condition was moderated in the mid-twentieth century when neo-evangelicals formed the National Association of Evangelicals, which supported matters of the mind as being essential to the faith.[37]

From 1945 through the 1960s Carl F. H. Henry, noted author and editor of *Christianity Today*, was highly critical of the modernist-humanist mindset that seemed to reign supreme in the academy. His writings contributed much to mind-and-reason themes as they related to the Christian faith. In 1963 an English scholar, Harry Blamires, wrote a landmark book entitled *The Christian Mind*[38] which set forth the idea that unless a Christian mind is possessed by the Christian one is not fully Christian. There were additional efforts to meet the challenge of developing a Christian mind and thinking Christianly. The Inter-Varsity Press released numerous noteworthy books that were mind-faith oriented. New study centers such as Regent College in Vancouver, British Columbia, New College in Berkeley, California, the London Institute for Contemporary Christianity, and the Zadok Center in Canberra, Australia, were started. The beginning of the Christian College Consortium in the late sixties was initially envisioned to move toward establishing a Christian University among twelve cooperating colleges. While that part of the vision failed, some of the pace-setting Christian colleges in the United States worked together assiduously, for a time, in serious efforts to integrate the Christian faith with the academic disciplines.[39]

These newly instituted efforts were deeply concerned about matters of the Christian mind and about modern cultural transformation. Despite significant efforts, the church's capacity to respond to the mind-related needs as they are tied to the gospel still seems inadequate from an evangelical perspective. The liberal Protestant academic community is also not meeting the Christian mind challenges in a faith-oriented way. Worst of all there is still no Christian university offering a broad range of graduate-level programs across academic disciplines that fully integrates the Christian faith with the varied disciplines. In assessing where the church is with respect to these matters, Os Guinness in *Fit Bodies, Fat Minds: Why Evangelicals Don't Think and What to Do About It* (1994), and Mark Noll in *The Scandal of the Evangelical Mind* (1994), contended that the mind of evangelicals appears to be in deep trouble.[40] However, the fact that negative signs are openly discussed gives hope that Christians will seek to become more engaged at the cognitive frontiers of today's culture.

6. How Important Are "Matters of the Mind" to the Brethren in Christ?

Early Brethren in Christ showed little regard for the benefits that might accrue from advanced learning of any sort, and they made little or no connection between matters of the mind and living out the faith. The church was largely composed of rural people with simple lifestyles. Although the initial body formulated a confession stating certain doctrinal positions, little attention was given to systematic Christian thought.

Brethren in Christ for the first 175 years showed little concern about impacting general culture, which in turn minimized the necessity to think through the broader societal and cultural issues. They did not feel the need for an educated ministry. They trusted the religious insights of untrained laymen. Their reliance was in spiritual things and obedient living which were understood according to Scriptures as interpreted by the common man. Explanations regarding the faith from educated professionals did not seem to be of high importance.[41]

In 1909 the Brethren in Christ opened a new door to matters of the mind when they founded Messiah Bible School and Missionary Training Home, later to become Messiah College. About a decade later Beulah College, later to be named Upland College, was founded.[42] At these institutions education was forcefully presented as being of significant help for understanding and disseminating the faith. The President of Upland College, Jesse F. Lady wrote:

It is my opinion that if evangelical Christianity is to keep the fellowship of a burning heart and to make its contribution to the kingdom of Christ here on the earth, it will depend largely upon the direction and effectiveness of Christian education in our church institutions of learning. That being true the very emergency of our times underscores the urgency for Christian training and for building of institutions which can arise to the occasion and meet the demands of this age.[43]

But by the mid 1950s an additional message that reached beyond caring for and enlarging His church was coming from the colleges. A broadened theme that Christians should be involved in shouldering social responsibility and impacting society for good was being disseminated. This proposition was basic to the two colleges becoming Christian arts and sciences institutions. It was now a matter of following the new light that all of life needs to be connected to the faith. The denomination moved away from the dualistic theology whereby goodness was concentrated in special revelation. Through its colleges the church was recognizing that all of creation is God's and His general revelation began to receive increased attention.

A two-fold reliance on the mind as well as the Spirit for finding the way became increasingly evident in the church. At a 1968 study conference on The Nature and Function of the Church, the Findings Committee Report stated:

It was suggested that in our stated concerns to minister to the world it is very likely we do not know very much about the world for which we are concerned. An effort needs to be made to inform the church of that world which we seek to minister to and for which we are training personnel and planning our program.[44]

The Brethren in Christ of today would surely affirm that faith is reasonable and rational as well as a heartfelt phenomenon. The Christian mind is to be sustained for helping to define right doctrine, for relating beliefs to life and ministry, for improving the culture, for determining the truth of God's created order, and for communicating to non-Christians. The denomination as a whole seems to interpret matters of the mind as an expression of Christian faithfulness. It seems equally clear that Brethren in Christ place human knowledge and reason secondary to the heart aspects of the faith. The church believes that only a heart changed by God's grace would properly understand God, His creation, and the full potential of human existence. Matters of the heart hold priority over matters of the mind.

Matters of Behavior and Action

The clusters of elements that comprise a committed heart and an understanding mind respectively are complemented by a third cluster that produces a contour of faith symbolized by the "serving hand." If Christians are in a right relationship with God, and they think right about God and the world, they should also conduct themselves rightly. This area consists of Christian acts, works, and deeds. For most all denominations the corporate endorsement of matters of behavior and action is a prime indicator that the body is rightly aligned to the Christian faith—and all members are encouraged to pursue moral and ethical lives. In many denominational situations, however, membership accountability regarding meeting such standards is missing, and corporate expectations regarding assistance from the Divine toward such attainments is wanting.

Ethical living and benevolent service have always been considered marks of Christians. The story of the good Samaritan as told by Jesus etched His humanitarian commands on the minds of the Christian church. Ministry and action to relieve stresses of the needy have been considered intrinsic to the Church. With Paul, who wrote about Christian action to the Ephesians, it is agreed, "For we are God's workmanship, created in Christ Jesus to do good works." (Eph. 2:10) And with James the broader church has affirmed that "faith without works is dead" (James 2:26).

The church, until late modern times when government became increasingly involved, was the strongest force for helping the poor and needy, for seeking to promote justice, and for struggling to undo injustice. Christians across the centuries have emphasized the precept from the Gospel of John, that those who fail to do "the will of the Father" cannot call Him Father. The question that man first hurled back into the face of God—Am I my brother's keeper?—the Christian church has answered in the affirmative, Yes!!

How Important Are Matters of Behavior and Action to Protestants Today?

Protestant churches, on the whole, strongly endorse matters of social action. In fact, support for social welfare and service is typically the major cluster-contour for groups that constitute the church's theologically liberal element. A minority of the broad Christian church, typically the theologically conservative-to-moderate churches, stress individual personal morality and tend to place emphasis on social needs as well.

There are differences between religious groups as they interpret what it means to live out the faith. Frequently the Christian groups more active in pursuing heart matters are the most involved in carrying out substantive social action. It is often the case that the more liberal churches, which theoretically stress an action faith, give little more than "lip service" to social-improvement causes.

From a per capita and potential resource standpoint, liberal churches contribute less liberally of themselves and their means to improve general conditions than do more conservative churches.[45] Churches that are evangelism-oriented typically contribute significantly more per capita toward missions, health, relief, and educational services, than do those who envision "doing the faith" as the primary indicator of Christian faithfulness.[46]

However, in modern times the church in general has come to depend on government to take the lead in providing a safety net for the poor and needy. Therefore, it seems that the Christian church at large is giving a declining portion of their resources to meet material and social needs of the world. It also seems clear that charitable programs operated by the church and the general society are more efficient than government programs, and religious charities have proven themselves more effective for turning around lives of people.[47]

How Important Are Matters of Behavior and Action to the Brethren in Christ?

Brethren in Christ have always considered the new birth, and a continuing personal relationship with God to be indicative of one's standing with God. But, consistent with their Pietist, Anabaptist, and Arminian heritages, they also have considered obedience to God and the Scriptures as critical to the faith and its most authenticating test. They believe, according to the Epistle of 1 John, "we know Him if we keep His commandments" (1 John 2:3) and that if "we say we have fellowship with Him, and walk in darkness, we lie, and do not live by the truth"[48] (1 John 1:6).

The Christian's relationship to God, for the Brethren in Christ, is best assessed according to one's daily conduct. Because of the denomination's long history of pronounced separation from the world, personal morality as compared to reforming social evils, were at the center of the denomination's behavioral attention. Participation in social and cultural discourse and service was minimal. Collectively and individually, however, the denomination became more involved in social and educational/cultural conditions around the beginning of the twentieth century. Such involvement increased considerably after the middle of the twentieth century.[49]

Brethren in Christ see God's truth and Christian fidelity as affecting varied aspects of life including: heart, mind, and hand matters. The Christian is called to pray, to think, and to serve. The service aspect of the faith and personal living according to God's commands, are not viewed with a works-righteousness mentality. They are viewed with a consciousness described by Dietrich Bonhoeffer when he said, "Only they who believe obey, and they who obey believe."

Matters of Church Form and Practice

The fourth cluster contour brings together ritual, form, and church practice as marks of the Christian faith. All denominations perpetuate conventions of some sort whether they are called ordinances, rites, rituals, liturgy, ceremony, creeds, confessions, or combinations of them. Such respective conventions spell out patterns viewed to be holy or have sacred implications. While churchly forms are the essence of the faith for a considerable segment of corporate Christianity, other parts of the broader church view them as being largely symbolic. The rite of baptism, for example, is interpreted as a cleansing and purging ordeal for some Christian adherents—for others it is merely a symbol of a divine cleansing or conversion. Baptism is sometimes viewed as a sign of entry into the visible church.

How Important Are Matters of Church Form and Practice to Protestants Today?

Some denominations tend to reduce the idea of faithfulness to Christ and fidelity to the church to participation in the sacraments. The marked increases in church attendance at commemorative times such as Christmas and Easter tend to indicate such inclinations.[50] Along with matters of the heart which in essence is to pray, matters of the mind which in essence is to think, matters of action which in essence is to do, this cluster, matters of form conveys the essence of being— to embrace. Those responding positively to churchly forms and ceremonies as the means of salvation, usually consider taking the sacraments and/or the instruction of the church (the catechism) as foreshadowing salvation.

Christian adherents who see churchly forms as paramount to the order of faith are often caricatured as being shallow regarding Christian accountability, as spiritually tepid, and as being rote in their worship patterns. It is true that this group tends to put less emphasis on a religion of the heart and at times can scorn serious piety; but there are segments of form-oriented denominations that show clear indications of spiritual depth, wherein the power of the gospel seems apparent.[51] In the main, however, churches noted for their formal nature generally interpret the gospel in a rather single dimensional way—primarily according to form.

On the other hand, many churches seek to avoid rigid form, and the trend toward informality in worship seems to be increasing, with ceremony appearing to be in decline. At the same time all religious groups perpetuate forms and ordinances that give a degree of structure to their worship and to other means of grace. While there are merits to informality, lack of form and tradition can also become undesirable if a church becomes captive to individualism or sentimentality.[52] A church cannot entirely dispense with the sacraments. Nor can the church fully abandon paraphernalia such as tradition and history, without being of detriment to the faith.

How Important Are Matters of Church Form and Practice to the Brethren in Christ?

There are numerous ways to define Christianity, and Brethren in Christ have always viewed defining the faith to be of high importance. They believe the Christian and the corporate church should be accountable for the faith. Although concerns regarding churchly form seem to be at the margin of their agenda, the denomination has not entirely overlooked that cluster of faith. They seek to observe ordinances and forms supported by the Scriptures. While the denomination is biblical rather than creedal in its values, Brethren in Christ are not without theological depth. The church body is highly democratic in its polity. Its churchly forms and doctrinal interpretations are approved by a General Conference that is strongly lay in its composition. At the local level the church programs are interpreted by a local church board composed largely of lay members.[53]

From their origin, the Brethren in Christ championed an inner heart religion rather than one of outward form that emphasized symbols, rituals, organization, and creeds. They perceived that the ministry of Jesus lacked anything that could be considered highly ritualistic. Their ordinances, from the start of the body, are in line with the instruction Jesus gave to His followers. The rite of baptism is understood as having no saving merit in itself. Its importance resides in being a symbol of renunciation of the old life, of confession of a new life in Christ, and of entrance into the visible church.

The Brethren in Christ Order of Priorities

All four clusters: matters of the heart, of the mind, of behavior and action, and of form and practice are deemed as essential to the faith and important to the Brethren in Christ. This indicates that the gospel is viewed as being holistic.[54] With the priorities of the gospel interpreted in four different ways the logical question follows: Which of these priority clusters take precedence within the denomination?

It seems clear that matters of the heart are considered to be prior by the Brethren in Christ. The church has shown that its basic impulses and beliefs are centered in a life-changing religious experience. It was matters of the heart that were the decisive factor in the origin as well as the two major historic transitions in the denomination. The first transition appeared in the late nineteenth century as new urban and international mission fields were entered, social institutions were started for outreach, educational institutions were started, and a new doctrine (entire sanctification) was germinating—all of which were heart matters. The second major transition in the mid-twentieth century was also closely tied to heart matters—a clear interest to become more effective in evangelism and outreach.[55] A clean heart is the first matter of concern the church has cared about, and it continues to be the key matter on its agenda today.

When matters of the heart are of highest priority within a denomination the ideal ordering of crucial faith elements seems to call for matters of the mind to closely follow. Therefore, a balance can be assured that extremes of subjectivism, mysticism, or even cultism are avoided. However, from a historical standpoint, the second priority of the Brethren in Christ seems to have been matters of behavior and action. In a world that has often had to wait for Christians to become Christian, and in the corporate church that at times has stressed the new birth while overlooking the new life, the denomination's concern has been about a faith that is patterned on how Jesus lived and taught His followers to live.

The third priority of the denomination today would appear to be matters of the mind. A clear recognition that there is no antagonism between the christian mind and the christian heart has become increasingly discernable during the denominations more recent history. Prior to the denominations establishing its schools (during the past century) the body was sheilded from doctrinal error because of their strong devotion to Scripture, their deep sensitivity to the leading of the Holy Spirit, and their belief in the simplicity of the gospel message.

The fourth cluster, matters of churchly form and practice, held considerable meaning for Brethren in Christ prior to 1950. In earlier times the denomination placed such matters ahead of matters of the mind in both sequence and priority—they were steeped in church forms of plain dress and other separation-from-the-world intentions. However, with an expanded view of God's world and of His truth in the latter part of the twentieth century, churchly form and practice were relegated to a lower position. These would be considered fourth in the church's priorities today.

Although today's Brethren in Christ priorities, stated in active terms, are to pray, think, do, and embrace, these elements can come to full reality through a spiritual vitality. When religion is seen merely as a process it becomes confused. When it is perceived as a set of ideals, it is reduced to a half-truth. The denomination seeks to witness to the secret of the Gospel wherein God gives the power to pray, to think, to do, and to embrace.

---

[1] The George Gallup Organization, from a study in 1992, Princeton Religious Research Center, Princeton, N.J.

[2] cf. Aeiko Oberman, ch. 6, *Luther: Man Between God and the Devil*, Yale, 1989.

[3] The finding of a "spiritual experience" is also professed by the New Age movement and other religions, such as Hinduism. However, none of the other religions have the key validation of super-naturalism that Christianity possesses in the historic resurrection of Jesus.

[4] In this divine work called sanctification, the Holy Spirit is manifested in fullness to the believer, and the power of sin over one's life becomes diminished.

[5] For further analysis of the reasons for starting a new group see chapter 3, "Theses Concerning Essential Truths of the Brethren in Christ," and chapter 4, "The Founding Vision of the River Brethren (1778-1865)."

[6] An example of how the church may have impacted one's "heart consciousness" is given in the case of two individuals who grew up in the heritage. Dwight D. Eisenhower is the most visible international figure to come out of a Brethren in Christ family. (In his boyhood years, he with his brothers and parents were regularly a part of the Sunday school and church in Abilene, Kansas—records of the regularity of Dwight's Sunday school attendance are in the Brethren in Christ archives at Messiah College in Grantham, Pennsyvania.) There are a number of items from Eisenhower's life that depict his "heart" heritage. In conversations with this writer in September 1965, Eisenhower recalled that when he enrolled at West Point "I almost broke my mother's heart." He continued, with affection (a tear welling in his eye), "my mother believed that the way to make change in the world was by changing men's hearts." He further reminisced how his grandfather, Jacob Eisenhower (a minister in the denomination), lived with his family in his boyhood home for some years and he learned to have great respect for his spiritual and moral values.

While Eisenhower's military career indicates that his religious upbringing did not transfer the church's peace and non-resistance position into his life, there are strong indications that he internalized the notion that matters of the heart were of high importance. In his inaugural address for the United States presidency he stated, "Whatever America hopes to bring to pass in the world must first come to pass in the heart of America." (Eisenhower's deepest heart tendencies were borne out when he successfully opposed calls for a preventive war against the Soviet Union and China. He said, "the only thing worse than losing a global war was winning one." He did not want the U.S. to become a "garrison state." He famously warned against the threat to America from its own "military-industrial complex.")

Another example of the church's possible impact regarding the importance of the heart dimension on one of its youth is Ernest Boyer, who after attending Messiah Academy and Messiah College, served for a year as pastor of a Brethren in Christ congregation in Orlando, Florida, and then went on to become one of America's leading educators. As such, he addressed many distinguished audiences and frequently spoke on a favorite theme that he termed, "The Educated Heart." The essence of the address stressed the importance of spiritual and moral dimensions in teaching.

[7] The anointing of the Divine has been of high significance to the denomination, as shown by its emphasis on sanctification. The importance of God's anointing was also demonstrated by each of the first three institutions to be formed in the brotherhood carrying the name Messiah (the anointed one). They were Messiah Rescue and Benevolent Home, Messiah Bible School and

Missionary Training Home, and Messiah Orphanage.

[8] *Evangelical Visitor*, April 1996, p. 6.

[9] Peter L. Berger, *Facing Up to Modernity*, Harmondsworth, Eng., Penguin Books, 1979, p. 255.

[10] The "doomsday cults" of Jonestown (Guiana), the Waco (Texas) Branch Davidian disaster, and the San Diego, California. (Heavens Gate) calamity are vivid examples of misplaced belief.

[11] The truth of the resurrection is intelligible because of the historicity of Jesus. There were many witnesses to the risen Jesus as He bodily came among them. In addition to being a historic reality Jesus the Christ is the fulfillment of Scripture, and His redeeming grace has been manifested in the changed lives of countless Christians who can affirm both His death and resurrection. Also, many of Jesus' miracles were verified by His contemporaries.

[12] Society is viewed as being in need of concerted help, because of its degenerated nature. (There are clear signs of degeneration in the general culture.)

[13] James H. Olthius defines a worldview as "an integrative and interpretative framework by which order and disorder are judged, they are the standards by which reality is managed and pursued, sets of hinges on which our everyday thinking and doing turns." *On Worldviews*, Reformed Ecumenical Synod Theological Forum, 19:3:2-14. Worldviews are also described as "the 'givens' about the way the world is put together. These are the basic assumptions people make about the nature of things, and the categories and logic they use to form a coherent understanding of reality." Paul Hiebert, op. cit., p.128.

[14] Hiebert, op. cit., 133.

[15] A growing, if not prevailing, societal view today denies the existence of absolute truth. Each person determines what is right or wrong in their own eyes.

[16] Barcus also contends that the notion that all truth is relative is "a rigid faith narrower than the narrowest Christianity . . . it is self-contradictory. For it falsifies itself, insisting that one believe in it absolutely," *Developing a Christian Mind*, op. cit., pp. 19, 20.

[17] "All of reason operates within a total worldview that is embodied in the language, the concepts, and the models that are the means by which those who share them can reason together." Leslie Newbigin, *Truth and Authority in Modernity*, Trinity Press, Valley Forge, 1996; p. 52.

[18] The Gospel is open to cultural pluralism. While it critiques culture, the gospel can be a part of any culture, and foundational to any culture. cf. Richard John Neuhaus, *The Naked Public Square* and Stephen L. Carter, *The Culture of Disbelief*, Harper Collins, 1993.

[19] The culture-reforming Christians sense that isolating from the culture, or retreating to a village sociology that no longer is, does little to improve a degenerating culture.

[20] *Fit Bodies, Fat Mind*, Baker Books, Grand Rapids, Mich., 1994, p. 14.

[21] This was stated as fact in the "State of the Union Address" by President Bill Clinton, Jan. 27, 1998.

[22] Peter was not the only apostle to exhort Christians to seek knowledge and to think Christianly. The Apostle Paul frequently referred to the faith as being both spiritual and rational. An example of that view is shown in Eph. 4:11-14. Another rather vivid example of Paul placing importance on the life of the mind is shown in Phil. 4:8 where he enjoins one to "think on these things."

[23] *Developing a Christian Mind*, InterVarsity Press, Downers Grove, Ill., pp. 10, 11.

[24] In the New Testament times biblical references are made to propertied individuals (slaves).

[25] Charlie B. Byers, a prominent bishop during the marked transition years of the church describes the changes this way: "I believe that God raised up the Brethren in Christ Church two hundred years ago, and that in all of this transition He has been preparing the church to be in a better position to go out into the streets and lanes of our cities and the world to "bring in hither the poor, the maimed, the halt, and the blind." *Brethren in Christ History and Life*, II, 1, June 1979, p. 26.

26 For analysis of this sharp change in relationship to the world and for elaboration on the biblical basis of being more closely involved in the general culture see chapter 3, "Theses Concerning Essential Truths of the Brethren in Christ."

27 *Evangelical Visitor*, July 10, 1970, p. 5. This centennial was of the General Conference rather than of the denomination's founding.

28 *Brethren in Christ History and Life*, Vol. XIX, No. 1, April 1996, p. 251.

29 A term used by Alderfer in his sermon.

30 *Yes*, winter, 2000. p. 2.

31 *Evangelicalism: Surviving its Success*, Eastern College, St. David's, Pa., 1986, p. 179.

32 In these post-modern times, with loss of structures and limits, and with extreme relativism, it may mean that for some individuals there is no discernable worldview. The only absolute they have left is their own critical consciousness.

33 *Fit Bodies, Fat Minds,* Baker Books, Grand Rapids, Mich., 1994, p. 89.

34 Many cults now have websites. Indeed the Internet offers a cheap, efficient, and secretive way for cult leaders to keep in touch with their members. The denominations that now stress the communal aspects of the faith via the Internet might well consider how the Internet could provide creative means of outreach.

35 *Write the Vision*, Trinity Press International, Valley Forge, Pa., 1995, p. 66.

36 Bosch, *Believing in the Future, Toward A Missiology of Western Culture*, Trinity Press, Valley Forge, 1995, p. 59.

37 For more analysis regarding the Brethren in Christ becoming associated with the National Association of Evangelicals see essay four, "The Unfolding of a Distinct Brethren in Christ Identity."

38 London: SPCK, 1963.

39 The Christian College Consortium in the late 1970s formed an additional group, the Coalition of Christian Colleges (later named the Council of Christian Colleges and Universities), both of which pursued association-type roles in promoting integration of the Christian faith with academic disciplines.

40 Guinness, Baker Books, Grand Rapids, Mich. and Noll, William B. Eerdmans Publishing, Grand Rapids, Mich.

41 A full century after the denomination's founding, when the church began publishing its periodical, the *Evangelical Visitor* (in the 1880s), the denomination began to open itself to outside religious views, including articles from educated clergy who belonged to other communions.

A sense of the shifting mood in the church toward the possible need for education, at the turn of the century, can be gained from an article entitled, "Education vs. Religion," that appeared in the Feb. 21, 1898, issue of the *Evangelical Visitor*, (pp. 54, 55). The article concluded with this question: "Are the true principles of education in opposition to the principles of the gospel? To this we say emphatically, No. Get God and then get education: and all of it within your reach. But remember first and last that all knowledge will not save you. The "cross and the crimson fountain" are the focus . . . Education is not salvation: but let us with no less—yea, rather with more—emphasis say that *ignorance is not salvation*, the opposite of which some would strongly vindicate."

42 In addition, two secondary schools were founded: Niagara Christian Collegiate and Jabbok Bible School.

43 Lady, "Scholarship on Fire," *Evangelical Visitor*, Nov. 28, 1949, p. 3.

44 Report dated July 1, 1968, Brethren in Christ Church Archives.

45 From studies of the George H. Gallup International Institute of Princeton, N.J., and a study entitled "The State of Church Giving through 1995," by John and Sylvia Ronsvalle of Empty Tomb, Inc., a Christian research organization that looked at the financial giving of 29 denom-

inations and compared the giving patterns of eight denominations in the National Association of Evangelicals and eight denominations belonging to the more liberal National Council of Churches.

46 World Relief, an agency founded by the National Association of Evangelicals (and now independent), had a budget for their overseas program totaling $24.7 million; received $9 million in private contributions and revenues with the remainder coming from the U. S. Agency for International Development and other federal or international organizations (*World*, March 28, 1998, p. 19). The Mennonite Central Committee follows a similar policy of accepting government funds. In 2005-06 they received $12.1 million in government grants, cash gifts of $28.9 million toward a total relief budget of $95.9 million—which included sales income of $28.2 million from Ten Thousand Villages, with sales expense subsumed into the various international programs (*Mennonite Central Committee Fact Sheet*, 2006).

47 Joseph Califano, an architect of Lyndon Johnson's Great Society and the Secretary of Health Education and Welfare under Jimmy Carter, more recently head of Columbia University's Center on Addiction and Substance Abuse, says he was surprised when, on a tour of center programs, nearly every ex-drug addict he met cited religious belief as a key to rehabilitation. *U. S. News and World Report*, Sept. 9, 1996, p. 47.

48 1 John, 2:3; 1 John 2:6; and in 1 John 3:4-10 "This is how we know who the children of God are: Anyone who does not do what is right is not a child of God; neither is anyone who does not love his brother."

49 The denomination's social concern was manifested in its numerous orphanages, founding of the Messiah Rescue and Benevolent Home, and the work of a Beneficiary Board, followed by Boards of Benevolence and a Board for Brotherhood Concerns, with varied social-service institutions amenable to them; the Peace Relief and Service committee; and efforts to improve cultural and social conditions through the Foreign Missions Board which later became the Board for World Missions; and efforts to contribute to the church, the culture, and the society by founding four educational institutions, two of which continue today as Messiah College and Niagara Christian Collegiate.

50 This might be termed the lowest common denominator.

51 This can be especially noted in formal groups that are charismatic in character—thus adding heart content to the forms.

52 A minority of churches appear to primarily serve the emotional needs of its members and spend much of their attention on apocalyptic speculation.

53 Even though the polity of the Brethren in Christ seems to be strongly democratic in both structure and goal there are hints that the movement is tending toward increasing centralization. However, the issue of participation in decision making should not become confused with the restructuring of the church's administrative arm in the 1980s and 1990s (of a "pyramidal" nature)—which seemed to be quite necessary and was intended to better serve the growth of the denomination and its efforts to minister to the shifting economic and social landscape that has accompanied our post-modern times.

54 For an elaboration of the quality of holism, as it relates to the Brethren in Christ, see chapter 8, "Three Meaningful Qualities of the Brethren in Christ."

55 For more information on matters of the heart being decisive to the origins of the denomination see chapter 3, "Theses Concerning Essential Truths of the Brethren in Christ," and for elaboration on their importance to historic transitions in the denomination see chapter 4, "The Founding Vision of the River Brethren (1778-1865)."

Chapter X

Descriptive Designations to Identify Who the Brethren in Christ Are

The initial Brethren in Christ congregation began near the banks of the Susquehanna River in Lancaster County, Pennsylvania. However, the soil was prepared by the first "Great Awakening" that swept across the colonies. The "Awakening" was evidenced by a dynamic spiritual restoration that affected most of the European-founded religious groups. These spiritual revivals also planted seeds for starting church groups committed to varying mixes of religious emphases and practices.

The leaders most visible to early America religious revivals were Jonathan Edwards, the prominent New England preacher, and Englishmen George Whitefield and John Wesley, who had ministry sojourns to the west. The spiritually regenerative efforts conveyed in English were correspondingly followed by pietistic-inclined German preachers possessing similar evangelistic zeal to the Anglo preachers. As a result, in the later decades of the eighteenth century, religious renewal penetrated the German-speaking settlements of southern and eastern Pennsylvania, where the Brethren in Christ church would be born.

Out of these religious stirrings the River Brethren, were conceived. They did not begin with an original set of theological assumptions. Their basic understandings crossed two theological thought systems—Pietism and Anabaptism. The nature and degree of synthesis of these traditions became the basis for what Martin Schrag, in an article published in the *Evangelical Visitor,* termed "The Genius of the Brethren in Christ."

The Brethren in Christ and Other Denominations Are Often Described in "Broad-Stroke" Ways That Tend to Convey Less Than Precise Understandings

Considering the melding of religious traditions and diverse interpretations regarding them, which in turn produces a unique theological synthesis, the question comes to the fore—What are the best ways to accurately describe the Brethren in Christ today?

Most contemporary people have little more than a shallow comprehension as to the differences between Pietist, Anabaptist, Wesleyan, Reformed, and other Christian church traditions. Christians, in general, do not think a lot about the unique aspects of their own religious denomination, let alone ferreting out the deepest meaning of other denominations and traditions. This absence of concern about distinguishing theological marks may partly be due to a lack of seriousness about the Christian faith. On the other hand, a reason for wide failure to understand finer theological differences is that denominations fall short in defining themselves. Additionally, the unique theology of denominations, while distinct in historical context, frequently have become homogenized or diluted into sterile understandings, one has compelling arguments that denominations should give careful attention to stating their identity.[1]

The Brethren in Christ denomination has formulated a statement of purpose that briefly outlines a mission for the church. This statement is clearly written and is readily available. However, the denomination has been less successful in providing an adequate identity statement that presents a clear picture of who the denomination is. There is no official statement formally and explicitly declaring the background and present nature of the church body. Some denominations are sufficiently diverse in their faith interpretations and commitments that it may be difficult to agree on a current distinguishing identity. As a result, denominational identities tend to be generalized or distinguished according to broad-strokes. An identity statement is most useful as it accurately states its historic connections, reflects on its current conditions, and affirms an intended direction for the denomination.

The Difficulty Accompanying the Use of Pietism and the Relative Ease of Using Anabaptism as Current Descriptors of the Denomination

Even though the Pietist legacy of the Brethren in Christ appears to continue to dominate its values, the term Pietism may be misleading if used to describe the Brethren in Christ. There are explanations for this lack of common understanding of Pietism. Historically Pietism was a trans-territorial-church renewal movement in central Europe that manifested a living faith both to the church and general society. The movement also crossed religious-group lines in America, but its focus was more narrowly reflected in revival-type settings known as the Great Awakenings of the eighteenth and nineteenth centuries. Therefore in America, even though Pietism impacted many religious groupings its affect was largely reflected in spiritual renewal. The more well-rounded Pietism from central Europe was formative to only a few smaller groups transplanted to America. Hence, Pietism can easily be misconstrued as strictly a cross-denominational movement, and described in a circumscribed manner— only emphasizing personal piety.

Smaller denominations founded in Europe and those newly founded in America in the late eighteenth and early nineteenth centuries initiated and exhibited more complete understandings and manifested the broader span of concerns lived by historic Pietists.[2] Present day understandings of the movement become even more complicated by the fact that some denominations founded in Pietism (but transplanted to America) put less stress today on spiritual-conversion than did early Pietists. Additionally, since the term *Pietism* today is rarely used to describe a denomination's contemporary state (the concept virtually always needs to be given an historic application), its communicative use is further curtailed.

There are few prototype Pietist denominations today that exhibit historic Pietist understandings. Pietism is not fully understood in either the general or the religious culture. Since the term may be misleading, the question arises: How does a denomination born in Pietism, that continues to be true to its founding vision, give a current and understandable account of its present self-image?

In contrast to Pietism, Anabaptism has a number of highly visible groups because of their strong separatist tendencies. The Amish and certain Mennonite groups often differ in appearance, convey clear understandings as to their identity in the religious community, especially regarding the doctrines of peace and non-resistance. When a religious tradition can be clearly referenced to the contemporary religious scene, it is more readily understood. Consequently, communication problems emerge with any effort to define the Brethren in Christ historically, through defining Anabaptism or Pietism.

A Succession from Pietism to Evangelicalism—Movements with Similar Messages and Characteristics

The basic beliefs and forms of the Brethren in Christ, as they enter the new millennium, continue to be Pietist and Anabaptist. In view of potential distortions or drawbacks in using the term *Pietism* to define the Brethren in Christ today, we might explore what term authentically and most clearly represents the key understandings of historical Pietists. There are clear parallels between the early Pietist tradition and the modern evangelical movement. Pietism, an antecedent to evangelicalism, served as its forerunner in significant ways. The substantive premises of evangelicals today correlate well with the basic views set forth by Arndt, Spener, and Francke. Most significant was their mutual emphasis on evangelical truths.[3]

One can readily see the high correlation of Pietism with the Great Awakening. The Pietist movement had penetrated a broad spectrum of religious groups on the continent and its stress on personal conversion became a part of Puritanism.[4] F. Ernest Stoeffler writes: "There can no longer be any doubt that the evangelicalism which became the dominant pattern for the individual and corporate religious self-understanding of American Protestants is heavily indebted to the Pietist tradition."[5] Mark Noll adds: "As historian Reginald Ward has demonstrated persuasively, a great range of connections—literary, personal, pastoral, hymnally—linked the spirituality of Continental Pietism to almost every phase of the British and American evangelical awakenings."[6] Pietism also had a critical effect on the experiential views of John Wesley. In turn, the "evangelical revivals" (a term used particularly in English circles) that spread across the United States and Canada were initially affected by Pietism (the term used in German circles). Both movements espoused the same essence (Pietism).

The term *Evangelical* came into broadened use following the "First Great Awakening" of the eighteenth century and during the "Second Great Awakening" of the nineteenth century.[7] The pivotal place that Brethren in Christ give to the new birth and a continuing personal relationship to God, allied with a commitment to the authority and reliability of the Scriptures, and their concern about winning new believers to Christ comprise cardinal elements of historic Pietism. More than this, they are also the very core of what it means to be evangelical. Pietism aligns well with evangelicalism. The beliefs and doctrinal order of the denomination are and have been both Pietist and evangelical in nature.

The "Pietist" Brethren in Christ and Their Relationship to Evangelicalism

As observed, the waves of spirituality expressed in the American religious awakenings (which are today characterized as evangelical) were critical to the origin of the Brethren in Christ. Even though the early church was in accord with the salvation/conversion emphases of the evangelical movement, they did not become a part of cross-denominational organizations fueling the movement. Even in the 1870s, after the denomination's stand against holding protracted meetings was abrogated, the denomination refrained from partnering with other evangelical groupings such as the Evangelical Alliance. However, the church body was provided intermittent information about inter-church evangelism and the Evangelical Alliance through the *Evangelical Visitor*.[8] The reticence of the body to become directly associated with more formalized or concerted efforts in promoting evangelism was perhaps connected with the "separation" issue. The broader evangelical movement, even if deemed faithful sotereologically may have been viewed as potentially compromising to the church's nonconformity-to-the-world principles.

Clearly, "evangelical truths" were intrinsic to the faith of the early body. While Brethren in Christ withheld full endorsement of generalized evangelical efforts and memberships, they did not shun the evangelical concept. Their longer-term vision for outreach was strengthened in the 1880s by naming the denomination's newly inaugurated periodical, The *Evangelical Visitor*. The initial masthead read: "Devoted to the spread of evangelical truth and the unity of the church." In the first issue's lead article, called "Salutatory," the editor defined the priorities of the church paper as follows: "But this we will say that the Bible, its doctrines and its evangelical truths shall constitute the basis of publication." The mere use of the term "evangelical truths" indicates that these "truths" were considered foundational or intrinsic to the faith of the Brethren in Christ.

Since 1950, when the denomination joined with like-minded evangelicals called neo- evangelicals, they have participated in cooperative evangelical efforts at a national level.[9] In addition, the Brethren in Christ have given lay and executive leadership to the evangelical cause, and at times within the National Association of Evangelicals body have been able to give special witness and leadership to social-conscience issues such as peace, non-resistance, and world relief.[10]

Arguments for and Responses to Questions Regarding Use of the Term "Evangelical" to Describe the Brethren in Christ

A denomination's identity should reference its heritage by describing its theological roots, should recognize other significant influences, should carefully define the major factors that have shaped the denomination, and then, most importantly, should describe in contemporary terms the denomination today.

The indicators cited above showing Pietist/Evangelical parallels include: (1) the term evangelical is congruent with the key elements of Pietism; (2) evangelical truths have been intrinsic to the Brethren in Christ, as demonstrated in the name and contents of the denomination's long-standing periodical; and (3) evangelical is the best term to communicate Pietism today. These alone would seem to be sufficient reasons for using the term evangelical to assist in describing the Brethren in Christ today.

John Yeatts and Ron Burwell, in a study entitled "Tradition and Mission,"[11] found that when a one-term self-designation was asked for from Brethren in Christ members, the strongest designation by a considerable margin was evangelical. This positive showing was made against contrasting terms that included: Fundamentalist, Anabaptist, Wesleyan, Conservative, Liberal, and Evangelical. The study asked how participants saw themselves. Hence, it seems the term *evangelical*, either with or without modifiers, should be freely used in describing the Brethren in Christ.

But there is an added dimension to this "grass roots" affirmation of using the term evangelical as the best one-word descriptor of the Brethren in Christ. At the 1997 Brethren in Christ Study Conference held on the subject "The Church and Culture," the Findings Committee Report, after acknowledging that a denomination's culture is largely shaped by its beliefs and values, prefaced their statement on Brethren in Christ Culture this way: "Our belief system by and large includes those beliefs common to the larger evangelical subculture as cited in Arlene Miller's reference to McGrath's 'cluster of six controlling convictions' of Evangelicals," which she called—"a distinctive ethos."[12] The critical point is that the committee, composed of a cross-section of church-leadership representatives, asserted that evangelical doctrines and values are at the crux of the Brethren in Christ as a Christian subculture.[13]

Brethren in Christ use evangelical to assist in describing themselves they assert a key distinction from other Anabaptist groups who, with the exception of the Mennonite Brethren denomination, have chosen not to be corporately identified with other professing evangelical bodies (members of the National Association of Evangelicals).[14] The term further provides a clear distinction with fellow denominations born in Pietism including: the Moravian Church, the Church of the Brethren, and the United Brethren in Christ church.

Denominations represent many different theological shades. They vary among each other and within themselves. Unless key words are used to indicate their location on the theological spectrum one must speculate about a denomination's theological orientation. The words "liberal' and "conservative" are quite definitive words. The words "right" and "left" are rather specific as to theological spectrum location. However, for most denominations, such terms are too confining, and these are not ideal terms to define the Brethren in Christ.

As with people, denominations are often both conservative and liberal in a variety of ways. While overall the Brethren in Christ could be classified as conservative, its position on pacifism, and its view on the Scriptures and "inerrancy," would in some circles be considered liberal.[15] The denomination's belief system is sufficiently distinct to be generally located on the theological spectrum and employment of the term evangelical helps to do that. Without definitive modifiers such as evangelical a denomination tacitly lumps itself with generic Christianity. When evangelical is used its theological perspective can be confidently placed in the conservative-to-moderate range.

It would be highly unusual to insert the word Pietist into a contemporary theological discussion. Because of this, there is need for language to indicate that the denomination is keeping faith with its founding vision. No concept brings the essence of Pietism into current theological discourse better than the truths that lie at the core of evangelicalism. The denomination would have difficulty defining its present state without using the term evangelical. Indeed, any description of the Brethren in Christ which fails to give an unequivocal place to the term *evangelical* will ignore present reality in the denomination and will neglect correlating its present to the past.

Even though evangelicalism, in this writer's analysis, does not merit an initial or primary-shaper classification for the Brethren in Christ denomination (it is a reinforcing theological stream),[16] as the modern extension of Pietist values, the term *evangelical* will provide both understanding and clarity in describing who the Brethren in Christ are today.

There are, however, legitimate questions to be considered about the use of evangelical to describe a denominational body during the current post-modern era. Questions that come to the fore about application of evangelical include: (1) Does the word describe the Brethren in Christ and its institutions? (2) Have the varied theological definitions regarding key beliefs that comprise evangelicalism, expressed differently by varied Christian traditions, including Arminian and Calvinist streams,[17] been sufficiently consistent to be a unifying factor that merits Christians working together? (3) Do Evangelicals exhibit a social conscience fitting the ideals of the Brethren in Christ? (4) Is evangelicalism a unique shaping tradition of the Brethren in Christ and, therefore, it can be ruled out as the contemporary equivalent of historic Pietism?

Question 1: Does evangelical describe the Brethren in Christ and its institutions?

Response: It does. This fact is affirmed by the church's long-held evangelical priorities, the importance that the denomination and its institutions have historically placed on evangelical truths, and the denomination's and her institution's close participation and membership in evangelical causes for more than two generations.[18]

Question 2: Are the key beliefs that define Evangelicalism (as expressed by theologians cited in this work) sufficiently unifying to merit the Brethren in Christ identifying with the term and joining with diverse Christians in its common message?

Response: This work references Pietism as a religious tradition or movement that has impacted the Brethren in Christ in very significant ways, including contributing certain basic theological understandings and doctrinal values at its beginning. Evangelicalism, as well, is referenced as a tradition or movement that, while not offering any new or basic doctrinal insights *per se* to the body's *Manual of Doctrine*, has contributed much in the way of helping the denomination reach out in new directions and more effectively extend its ministry. This broadened evangelical impact was initiated when the denomination joined the NAE. The denomination has been officially identified with the evangelical movement for more than two generations. Considering the length of such identity, which has included thirty years of service of this writer on one of the NAE commissions, it can be attested that the varied definitions of evangelicalism offered here are congruent with the finest evangelical tradition.

From an historical perspective there were many different shades of Pietism that were earlier expressed in Europe and then later in America, just as there have been numerous definitions of evangelicalism over the centuries. Reaching beyond the personal interpretation just offered, there seems to be a pleasing unity among scholarly theologians that come together in the varied definitions of evangelicalism cited in these pages—just as there is a pleasing continuity between historic Pietism and more modern Evangelicalism.

In earlier essays of this work the distortion of the term *evangelical* is discussed. The term is especially misused when political positions, either to the left or right are attached to it.[19] As with the early Pietists, the meaning of what Evangelicals are about has frequently been misrepresented. Pietists and Evangelicals have both been the object of mixed messages. Ironically this may be due to the broad influence of Evangelicals, who similar to the earlier Pietists, represent movements that have been strongly trans-denominational. This in itself can cause tension and antagonism within groups, which in turn can be a breeding ground for inaccurate stereotypes and misleading information.

Another problem is that the term *evangelical* is claimed, or more often is hastily (and at times inaccurately) assigned to a diverse group of professing Christians who represent a wide variance—including radio or television preachers who may be "skewed" in their messages toward fundamentalist-type positions. It is true that the meaning of a word, like evangelical, can become twisted by "bed-fellows" who profess the faith. However, any term can be misrepresented. The subversion of a term's true meaning is not a valid reason to refrain from using it—especially when it is highly descriptive of a body. If the extent of distortion is the cue as to whether terms should be employed, the church in general would likely lose many of its most meaningful words, including a true understanding of what it means to be Christian.[20]

In final response to this question, if one starts from the premise that the definitions of evangelicalism should pertain strictly to theological considerations and be separated from defining political concerns (excepting those with moral or religious implications), there appears to be strong unity as to what the basic evangelical beliefs are. There is also an evident sense of oneness about what such beliefs mandate Christians to be, and to do.

Question 3: Do Evangelicals exhibit a social conscience that corresponds with the ideals of the Brethren in Christ and therein make evangelical an appropriate clarifier of the denomination?

Response: Timothy Smith, the noted Wesleyan scholar, portrayed the diverse groups who claim the term evangelical as being an "artful mosaic." These varied groups are in complete agreement on the good news about a life-changing faith. In addition to conversion, Evangelicals seem to agree on other basic tenets of the faith including the authority of Scriptures and the call of the Christian to evangelism, missions, and service to others.[21]

It is acknowledged that there can be substantial differences among Evangelicals as to discipleship, the importance of holiness (Christian perfection), and the utter need to portray a transformed life with consistency. Evangelical believers should not be typed as those who overlook the social needs of the world. Some Evangelical groups are highly involved in social outreach. Evangelicals for Social Action and World Vision are examples of two evangelical-originated groups with social needs high on their agenda.[22] Another group sensitive to social needs and part of the National Association of Evangelicals is the Salvation Army—the former head of which was named to the NAE's top post of executive director in 2007. Intrinsically evangelical denominations that live out the faith to its broadest aspects would be unwise to abandon an evangelical identity simply because some groups that profess pursuing Evangelical truths may demonstrate a more restricted view regarding broad implications of the faith.

Question 4: Is Evangelicalism a unique shaping tradition of the Brethren in Christ, and therein should be ruled out as the "contemporary equivalent" of historic Pietism?

Response: Some writers have raised a question as to whether evangelicalism should be added as a unique shaping tradition of the Brethren in Christ. That question was considered in chapter 3 of this work where the contention is made that the Evangelical stream brought no new major theological insights *per se* to the Brethren in Christ. This study concurs with the historical-theological view that Evangelicalism essentially duplicates the key theological premises of early Pietism, and that Pietism is the direct antecedent to Evangelicalism.

It is acknowledged, however, that the growth of the denomination since 1950 was assisted greatly by the influence of twentieth century Evangelicalism, wherein it helped to facilitate theological continuity and offered a wide span of resources for ministry improvement. Both of these were welcomed by the Brethren in Christ as they were transitioning out of a "separatist" posture. The Evangelical world aided the denomination immeasurably as it sought to engage long-held Pietist-Evangelical principles to the current scene.

Carefully Chosen Modifiers Could be Employed to Communicate a Clearer Identity

It seems appropriate to restate that a theological tradition is best defined according to its original manifestations, and must be seen with reference to its center, not its circumference. Therefore, in order to bring greater lucidity and understanding to the denomination's identity statements, clarifying modifiers might be appropriately employed, especially when the term *evangelical* is used. An example of the process can be seen in the Evangelical movement itself. Evangelicals gained a new perspective during the 1940s. The movement had been strong in the nineteenth century, but became dormant in the early decades of the twentieth century, and then experienced a restoration in the 1940s. To denote the change in course the Evangelicals added the prefix "new" to their evangelical mission.[23]

There were substantial differences between the "new" evangelicals and their predecessors of the nineteenth century. The "new" evangelicals contended that Christianity should supersede the culture rather than be subsumed into the general culture—as was often the case for evangelicals in the nineteenth century.[24] They also distanced themselves from the combative spirit, the disregard for social needs, and the anti-academic posture that characterized Fundamentalists. The new group with new emphases and a new vision regarding the world about them, acquired the name "Neo-Evangelicals." The Neo-Evangelicals then organized the National Association of Evangelicals to help carry out their transdenominational efforts.

Soon after formation of this organization, the Brethren in Christ, who also were in the process of adopting something new—a renovated and more holistic worldview—joined the National Association of Evangelicals. The denomination has been closely identified with the NAE since 1949.

It may well be that if current evangelicals worked assiduously to return the movement to a fully religious vision, as was the case in the 1940s through 1970s (when the movement appeared to be at its greatest effectiveness), and would reclaim the "New" prefix to affirm renewal of a focused religious vision, it could possibly move to advanced heights of service. As a resolute and purposeful religious movement, corporate Evangelicalism would then largely confine itself to moral and spiritual issues—and thereby avoid being tarnished by political issues to either the left or right. Corporate Evangelicalism would then expect that individual Christians should deal with such matters on a personal level.[25]

Perhaps the high watermark of the Neo-Evangelical movement in the United States was when Jimmy Carter, a born again Christian, was elected President of the United States. Paradoxically this may have planted seeds for the potential decline of the movement (in the purist sense). This visibility brought new attention to theologically-conservative Christians and helped make the word evangelical a mainstream term. Following that time of increased religio-conservative visibility, the late Jerry Falwell, in the 1980s, helped found the Moral Majority, with a pronounced right-wing message. Soon thereafter, Pat Robertson sought to merge politics with conservative Christianity, including running for President of the United States under the distinction of being an Evangelical.[26] These efforts tended to taint the basic meanings of the term because prior to that time (and even more recently) both Falwell and Robertson would not be considered "new" evangelicals.[27] Prior to the two of them assuming the status or being Evangelical (assigned to them by the press, which in itself often presents problems and distortions[28]), Falwell, along with his programs and approaches to issues, would more accurately have been called a fundamentalist Christian; Robertson's religio-politico leanings would have been more manifestly rightist or rightwing-Christian.[29]

This opens the door to the real question: Who speaks for America's Evangelicals? The Brethren in Christ would respond—the organization of which we and some fifty other denominations are a part, the NAE. This organization is concerned about transmitting the Gospel; keeping the Evangelical label from becoming severely misunderstood; and assisting in maintaining the fact that Evangelicals stand in the mainstream of historic, orthodox, and biblical Christianity. In any event, regardless of the term "Christian" or "Evangelical," the basic values of Christians should not become hijacked by a small number of highly visible headliners, broadcasters, or political activists who skew their efforts in a particular direction.[30]

Modifying words added to the term evangelical could be used to give clearer insight as to who the Brethren in Christ were and are today. For example, David Zercher offers a fresh description when he refers to the Brethren in Christ as "irenic" Pietists.[31] They could also be described as "irenic" Evangelicals. The denomination's emphasis on nonresistance (Anabaptist) abetted by their ecumenical and conciliatory traits (Pietist) make them worthy of the modifier "irenic."[32] Another example of a critical modifier is that used by the Methodist theologian, Thomas Oden, who appreciatively speaks of "centrist Evangelicals"[33] to distinguish them from those who emphasize theological baggage not commonly associated with the term *evangelical*. Qualifying words like irenic, or centrist, or mere, along with other telling words, or prefixes such as new might be employed. In terms of modifiers it is noted that Jim Wallis, editor of *Sojourners* magazine, wanting to be spared being labeled "left-wing Evangelical," bills his position and that of the magazine his organization publishes as being "social-justice Evangelical."

In addition to modifier suggestions for enhancing clarity of identity, the dual-tradition modifiers such as "Pietism/evangelicalism" might be helpful to indicate an historic sense of continuity within the denomination. The denomination may consider it to be timely to adopt a rather concise identity statement. Such an assertion could be used to assist in translating, as well as affirming, the unique Brethren in Christ witness, and as the Lord tarries, could help to carry the denomination confidently into the future.

A potential statement of identity which, of course, could be reduced or expanded, is suggested as follows:

> The Brethren in Christ church is the first Protestant denomination to be formed in North America (*circa* 1778) that continues in ministry today. The church's original vision was grounded in the Anabaptist and Pietist traditions and its witness to that vision continues as evangelical truths are stressed, as holy living is espoused, and as service and reconciliation are demonstrated.[34]

Should the Brethren in Christ Consider a Revised Name?

For more than seventy-five years, the Brethren in Christ ministered without an official name. They were known as River Brethren in the United States and Tunkers, Canada. Their initial chosen name was Brethren (with nothing added). The name River Brethren was assigned to the group to distinguish them from other Brethren groups in their area.[35] This informal name was fitting since the initial body lived in the vicinity of the Susquehanna River and they baptized in the river.[36]

A denomination that is sensitive to portraying its identity in a precise and vivid manner will surely encounter the question as to how well its name fits the profile of the group. Since meanings can change over time, various organizations, including religious denominations, may sense a need to examine their respective names.[37]

The name "Brethren in Christ" was adopted in the United States during the Civil War. The Canadian part of the church officially adopted the same name later in the nineteenth century. These actions came nearly a century after the denomination began. Similarly, it may now be in order to again seriously review the denomination's name. There is a question: Does the name Brethren in Christ convey the same positive meanings today, to the church and to society, as it did when it was first adopted?

Except for classical Latin, language is living. Words acquire new associations and lose some of the old ones. Successive editions of *Webster's*

Unabridged Dictionary testify to this, as do our perceptive minds and our daily speech. The messages received from many of our words change with ever-evolving social conditions. Therefore, we have constructed words to fit new technologies, situations and events, new kinds of people, and attitudes.

A specific question regarding the denomination's name is whether the term *Brethren,* continues to be understood the same way as at the time of its founding (the brotherhood)?[38] During these post-modern times when linguistic meanings are closely examined for their potential exclusions,[39] one might predict that questioning about the name may increase.[40]

The name Brethren in Christ is strong in meaning and rich in its concepts. The name in its entirety is sourced in the Bible (King James Version). It is a salutation from Paul's writings to the church in Colosse.[41] Its special value extends beyond its biblical origin since the term Brethren is steeped in the tradition of Pietism and was highly indicative of Brethren in Christ at their founding. Pietist groups that were sufficiently radical to break away from the territorial churches typically used the name Brethren. Their common Pietist identity is signified in the names of the European founded Moravian Brethren (Moravians), the German Baptist Brethren (Church of the Brethren), and the Lutheran Brethren.[42] The River Brethren (Brethren in Christ) and United Brethren in Christ, in Pietist fashion, have retained the traditional brethren connotation. The designation also continues to be maintained by three denominations that profess an Anabaptist–Pietist dialectic. They are the Brethren in Christ, the Church of the Brethren, and the Mennonite Brethren.

The words—"in Christ"—contribute substantive meaning to the church's name. The "in Christ" idea is often stated in the New Testament as it conveys that believers have a vital relationship to the divine. It connotes a union with Christ as revealed in His startling farewell discourse to His disciples (John 14:20 NIV). His promise was, "You are in me and I am in you." And the concept is stated in an even more assuring manner when He involves the Father (John 17:21-23). In this statement Christ presents an analogy of the believer's union with Him—which parallels His own union with the Father.

Along with this heavenly union, an earthly analogy is developed (John 15:1-11) where Jesus is the vine and His followers are the branches. This picture language of what it means to be in Christ is affirmed when He says, "If you abide in Me and My words abide in you, you will ask what you will and it shall be done for you." In short, abiding in Christ means allowing the mediation of His Word and the power of the Spirit to fill the mind, direct the will, and transform one's affections. This is consistent with Brethren in Christ teaching and affirms the appropriateness of "in Christ" being part of the denomination's name.[43]

Brethren is a collective noun consistent with the original biblical texts. While the term can be interpreted as relating to the male gender only, its use in the Scriptures is fully inclusive of all believers and, without question, Brethren in Christ emphatically intend Brethren to include women believers.

When interpreted inclusively, the meaning of Brethren fosters favorable insights such as kinship, and close connection (especially when members address each other as brother and sister—which is with less and less frequency). *Brethren* is a word that upholds communitarian values. In this regard, the word *church* is generally added at the end of the denomination's name, i.e., Brethren in Christ church. When this is done the communitarian values provided by Brethren are reinforced by church.[44] When the term *church* is appended to the name it can also be considered duplicative to Brethren. In this sense, the word *Brethren* does not contribute nearly as significantly to the denomination's name as does its companion concept, in Christ.

Nothing is more forthright than a denomination's name. Accordingly, the name of a denomination should be consistent with messages it wishes to convey. However, it needs to be remembered that clarity of communication is not fully dependent on what is said or intended to be said. Good communication has more to do with what the receiver hears. A problem can arise when a name, like Brethren, is perceived as being partial, showing bias, or as being disingenuous.[45] The problem is accentuated if the connotation is perceived as portraying sect-like markings, (which is more apt to rise where the Brethren concept is new to those encountering it.

Repairing such perception errors involves careful instruction. A further difficulty comes when negative impressions are held, and the Brethren are unaware of them. Longer-term members may tend to take their denominational name for granted. They probably understand what the name Brethren is intended to portray, but a nonmember is not likely to encounter an occasion for examining its meaning since explanation of a denomination's name is generally not on the agenda.[46]

This discussion about the Brethren tag is not to suggest denomination pander to feminist pressures. It has to do with linguistic accuracy and understandably portraying the Brethren in Christ.[47] Also, since word meanings modify as perceptions change, a situation could develop where parts of the denomination may interpret Brethren to have controversial overtones deemed unnecessary for the denomination.

In view of the issues connected with using Brethren, which in today's increasingly complex and mobile society may become even more pronounced in the future, several questions come to the fore: Is the word *Brethren* so critical to the denomination's name that it merits the risk of being misunderstood? And, what word(s), other than Brethren, might be considered to replace the meaning that it represents?

An analysis of terms and new titles for a denomination, and then making a choice would not be easy. New terms would naturally seem quite strange to the ear and perhaps to the mind, as well. Therefore, several possibilities are given as suggestions. The "in Christ" part of Brethren in Christ represents a vertical relationship to God. Brethren shows a horizontal relationship with other believers. As mentioned, the term church which generally is appended to the denomination's name, depicts a community of believers, and reinforces the "horizontal" relationship represented by Brethren. But the "church," meaning the "bride of Christ," also supports the vertical relationship to God. Therefore, another way to emphasize the communitarian dimension in the denomination's name would be to give a more prominent place to the word *church* by making it the lead word as in "Church in Christ," or "The Church in Christ." This would parallel the names of present denominations such as "The Church of God," "United Church of Christ," "Church of the Nazarene," etc.

While church may be sufficient in itself to represent the horizontal dimension symbolized by "Brethren," other replacement words might also be considered. A more novel suggestion is the word *communion*. A communion is a group of God's people. The term has a deep tradition in the early church. A potential name of, "Communion in Christ" or "The Communion in Christ" might be another possibility.

The term *communion* was used in the early centuries as Christians gathered together. They were known as *communio sanctorum*, meaning "the communion of saints." It was not simply the Eucharist that signified communion. The ritual of receiving the bread and wine elements in remembrance of Christ was just one facet of their communion. It was a body united with Christ and with one another. They demonstrated that communion (the church) is a spiritual entity that made the mystery of God's salvation visible. Surrounded by a hostile world, they were indeed a communion bound together in oneness. Their very presence as a communion of saints invoked a power that even the most ruthless government could not repress.

Using "communion" in the name, until more accustomed to its broader meaning, might bring to one's mind the ordinance of communion. This would not necessarily be bad since the communion observance signifies all that is good within the term *brethren,* and then more (it adds the vertical relationship to God as well as the horizontal). It should be recognized that denominations are frequently referred to as communions. In its favor, the word *communion* carries no gender implications, is highly inclusive, and unites rather than divides. The question might be: Is the term *communion* so closely tied to receiving the Eucharist that it is hard to accept its broader meaning.

Another potential denominational name, which would permit retention of the BIC acronym, is "Believers in Christ." This suggestion was reported as being put forward by Dwight Thomas who at the time served on the staff of the Elizabethtown Brethren in Christ church and taught at Messiah College, and Dr. Donald Shaffer, former bishop and retired denominational General Secretary.

This writer will not expand further on potential names. Perhaps the reader may have expected that since true evangelicalism and historic Pietism closely correspond, that the term *evangelical* would have been suggested. While its inclusion surely could be considered, as the names for denominations and churches go, the word *Evangelical* has been used frequently in titles, making it a less appropriate option.

---

[1] The determination of a precise denominational identity may be a difficult undertaking. Nevertheless, the complexity of the task does not seem to be sufficient reason for it not to be done. It may well be that such an exercise could be highly beneficial to the denomination—leaders and members included.

[2] The several denominations include the German Baptist Brethren (known today as Church of the Brethren) which divided into the Old Order German Baptist and the Church of the Brethren. The larger of these two bodies, the Church of the Brethren, later experienced two splits—The Brethren Church and the Grace Brethren. Another group was the Moravian Brethren (known today as The Moravian Church).The two American denominations with basic Pietist beginnings were the Brethren in Christ and the United Brethren in Christ.

[3] For a definition of evangelical truths see the George Marsden citation in a later note of this chapter.

[4] cf. F. Ernest Stoeffler, *Continental Pietism and Early American Christianity*, Eerdmans, Grand Rapids, Mich., 1976, p. 268.

[5] Ibid. p. 267.

[6] Mark Noll, *The Rise of Evangelism*, InterVarsity Press, (2005) p. 60.

[7] The term evangelical comes from the Greek noun *euangelion* meaning "good news" or "gospel," and the verb *evangelizomai,* "to announce or proclaim or bear good news." The first popular usage began in the Protestant Reformation with the idea that the reformers were recovering the good news of the gospel. Further aspects of the term "evangelical" are reviewed in chapter 2 entitled, "Traditions and Concepts Linked to the Brethren in Christ."

[8] While the Brethren in Christ did not join the ranks of any trans-denominational evangelical group in the nineteenth century, as early as 1887 they showed enough openness to the evangelical cause to announce in the *Evangelical Visitor*, the church paper, a forthcoming Evangelical Alliance Conference to be held in Washington, DC. The announcement listed the questions to be considered at the conference, and named some of the individuals calling the meeting. This indicates a measure of interest in the broader cause of evangelicalism. *Evangelical Visitor*, Vol. 3. Nov. 1, 1887, p. 43. Also, there are indications that sections of the denomination including Lykens Valley had contact with the Evangelical Association of that area. See *Evangelical Visitor* Vol. 1, No. 2, Oct. 1, 1887, p. 24, which included a reference regarding the Evangelical Association.

[9] The Brethren in Christ denomination joined the National Association of Evangelicals, an inter-denominational United States body in 1950, and later the Canadian sector of the North American church became part of the Evangelical Fellowship of Canada, where presently (2007) a Brethren in Christ member fills one of its top leadership roles—William Winger serves as Director, Administration and Finance of the Fellowship.

[10] C. N. Hostetter Jr., of the Brethren in Christ, served on the executive committee of the World Relief Commission of the National Association of Evangelicals during the formative years of that commission, from 1953 to 1967, including eight years as chair of its relief agency. Today the agency, named World Relief, is perhaps the strongest adjunct of N.A.E. (no longer corporately connected to it). Also, Arthur M. Climenhaga, served for twenty-five years as a key member of the NAE Resolutions Committee (it considers world issues and formulates resolutions for the association). For examples of Brethren in Christ impact being brought to bear on peace, war, national, and international attitudes see *Messenger of Grace*, a biography of C.N. Hostetter Jr., pp. 211-221. E. Morris Sider, Evangel Press, Nappanee, Ind.

[11] *Brethren in Christ History and Life*, Vol. XIX, No. 1, April 1996, pp. 67-115.

[12] For a review of British theologian Alister McGrath's cluster of six doctrines or values see section of this work in chapter 2 entitled "Evangelicalism is Defined," or see Arlene B. Miller's paper submitted to the Church and Culture Conference entitled "The Brethren in Christ and Evangelical Culture," (*Brethren in Christ History and Life*, Vol. XXI, No.1, April 1998, p. 191.

[13] From *Brethren in Christ History and Life*, Vol. XXI, No.1, April 1998, pp. 224-226.

[14] Two of the largest Mennonite groups in the United States, the Mennonite Church and the General Conference Mennonites, historically it appears, have refrained from aligning themselves with denominational groupings of any sort (conservative or liberal theologically). However, since their merger to become "Mennonite Church USA," the united group evidently decided to become more identified ecumenically with the religious mainstream—as they became members of the recently formed (2006-2007) ecumenical group, "Christian Churches Together." (CCT when compared with other Christian denominational groupings is quite heterogeneous in its composition—including both theologically liberal and theologically conservative church bodies as members.)

[15] The denomination did not share the concern of inerrancy with "fundamentalists" in the twentieth century. Since Brethren in Christ believed the Bible was true, inspired, and authoritative they didn't get caught up in the arcane arguments of the character of Scripture. See Luke L. Keefer, Jr., "Inerrancy and the Brethren in Christ view of Scripture," *Brethren in Christ History and Life*, (April 1992), pp. 3-17.

[16] For a rationale on this statement see chapter 3, "Theses Concerning Essential Truths of the Brethren in Christ."

[17] There are varied definitions offered in this chapter and chapter 2 of this work.

[18] In a recently formulated official statement of identity for Messiah College (1996), the denomination's four year college of arts and sciences, the institution acknowledges that it is Pietist, Anabaptist, and Wesleyan in background and "embraces an evangelical spirit." For a definition of "evangelical truth" see the George Marsden citation located in a later footnote of this chapter.

[19] The meaning of evangelicalism is considered in chapter 2 entitled "Traditions and Concepts Linked to the Brethren in Christ."

[20] The term Christian has been abused to the point that it means not only different things but mutually exclusive things.

[21] George Marsden, the preeminent historian on Evangelicalism and Fundamentalism contends that Evangelicals emphasize (1) the Reformation doctrine of the final authority of Scripture; (2) the real, historical character of God's saving work recorded in Scripture; (3) eternal salvation

only through personal faith in Christ; (4) the importance of evangelism and missions; and (5) the importance of a spiritually transformed life. (George Marsden, *Piety and Politics*, Ed. John Neuhaus, Ethics and Public Policy Center, Washington, DC, p. 59.)

[22] The World Vision, formerly affiliated with the National Association of Evangelicals and now an adjunct organization denotes a strong concern for social outreach. In 1997 its overseas relief program totaled $24.7 million (*World*, March 28, 1998, p. 19).

[23] The prefix of "new" or "neo" also helped to clarify the 1940s evangelical movement difference between Reformation times, centuries earlier, when Protestants were often referenced as being "Evangelicals."

[24] The mission of the National Association of Evangelicals is to extend the kingdom of God through fellowship of member denominations, churches, organizations and individuals, demonstrating the unity of the body of Christ by standing for biblical truth, speaking with a representative voice, and serving the evangelical community through united action, cooperative ministry, and strategic planning.

[25] It is contended here that a group such as the National Association of Evangelicals settles for less than their highest mission if they corporately aim to be either a lobbying group or an advocacy group on finer points, and thus become unduly tied up in political issues and causes. The core commitments of such an association should primarily be focused on church, family, and evangelization-type issues. Since the political process often produces polarization that can thwart other important messages, it appears that religious-group politics should be avoided. However, this should not be interpreted to mean that individuals who claim to be Christian necessarily refrain from participating in civic and political matters. A gross error is clearly made when it is assumed, for example, that those who are conservative or moderate from a theological perspective should also be fully conservative or even right-wing on political issues. People of faith can, and often should, become involved in politics—but as reconciling forces for the good of society.

[26] Both Falwell and Robertson would have been more appropriately classified as Fundamentalist since they were never part of the National Association of Evangelicals membership.

[27] In addition to misplacing the efforts of certain conservative activists and their ideologies by defining them as evangelicals, there is a tendency on the part of press and pundits to exaggerate the influence highly visible, politically ultra-conservative leaders have on others who profess to be either conservative or moderate theologically. For further amplification regarding the meaning of "evangelicalism" see chapter 2.

[28] Misperceptions distort the meaning of the word *evangelical* when they are defined in the media largely by what they are against; when they become associated, in the public mind, with extreme Fundamentalism; and when they are linked by evangelicalism's critics with the secular political agenda of the hard-right.

[29] Their respective right-wing tendencies, and the political priorities that became evident in the conversation between Robertson and Falwell on Robertson's TV show, "The 700 Club," wherein two days after the 2001 terrorist attacks Falwell laid blame at the feet of "the pagans, and abortionists, and the feminists, and the gays and the lesbians," to which Robertson said "Well, I totally concur," in turn became interpreted by many as being both the belief of most Evangelicals, as well as an indication of their sweeping political priorities.

[30] Perhaps the term fundamentalist, an epithet more often used by liberals, should be revived for application to those who categorically preach reactionary views under the guise of evangelical Christianity.

[31] *Brethren in Christ History and Life*, Vol. XIX, No. 1, April 1996, pp. 169, 170.

[32] The Brethren in Christ ecumenical connections have more recently included the Mennonite World Conference, the Mennonite Central Committee, the Christian Holiness Partnership, the Evangelical Fellowship of Canada, and the National Association of Evangelicals.

[33] From an article entitled "Whither Christian Unity," *Christianity Today*, Aug. 8, 2002, p. 46. Oden, from Drew University, along with Canadian Anglican J.I. Packer authored *One Faith: The Evangelical Consensus*, InterVarsity Press, 2004.

[34] For a definition of "evangelical truths" see the George Marsden citation located in chapter 10 note 21.

[35] The fact that the group initially referred to themselves as Brethren was cited in a letter of E. Morris Sider to the writer dated Dec. 24, 1997.

[36] For new believers coming to the group from an Anabaptist background, and others, baptism and immersion in the river was a variant way to carry out the ordinance.

[37] Numerous denominations or groups have reviewed their names and altered them so as to communicate more clearly or to avoid confusion. An example of this is the Reorganized Church of Jesus Christ of Latter Day Saints, formed as a split from the Brigham Young led Mormon body on April 6, 1860, (which approximated the time the Brethren in Christ, who after 80 years of existence officially adopted their name). This group formed with Joseph Smith III (grandson of the Mormon founder named as president) was a split from the Brigham Young led Mormons. About 140 years later (May 2001) the "Reorganized Church," then numbering 250,000 members in 50 countries, acted to change the name of the body to Community of Christ, a name resembling that of the Brethren in Christ.

[38] Questions about the Brethren in Christ name have largely been raised informally, but in the July 1998 General Conference, among a series called "Workshops," one was held under the title, "What's in a Name?" At that workshop the name of the denomination was examined, first by way of two formal presentations, and then opening the meeting to general discussion. However, there has been no report submitted to the church at large on what transpired at that specific workshop. One presentation was made by Kathleen Leadley who outlined her remarks on such points as a good denominational name should communicate essential information, project the appropriate image to the intended audience, and convey a distinctive and inspired quality.

[39] "Man" is defined as the opposite of "woman," and "freedom" excludes "slavery." Every time we use the word "man" it is perceived by some that we are excluding women. A lack of inclusiveness in the term "brethren" may seem to be a minor concern to some, or viewed as an attitude of those who may be immature, but the Scriptures say that if the "little one" (immature one) is offended, it may be advisable to remove the hindrance.

[40] Since the time of societal ferment in the late 1960s, an approximate point when post-modern times began, the role of women in the life of the denomination has been changing. In 1964 the General Conference established a precedent by seating the first woman delegate. By 1976 it seated several dozen women, and in the 1970s, women gained representation on its major boards. C. O. Wittlinger, "Who Are the Brethren in Christ? An Interpretative Essay," *Brethren in Christ History and Life, I, 1* (June 1978), p. 14.

[41] The apostle Paul addressed his letter "to the saints and faithful brethren in Christ" (Col. 1:2). It is interesting that the saints were not included in the Brethren in Christ name as in the case of the Church of Jesus Christ and Latter Day Saints. Perhaps the saints were overlooked because the "Brethren," a modest and humble group, were not prepared to self-designate themselves as "saints."

[42] The Mennonite Brethren, of European origin, were also much affected by Pietism.

[43] Other *New Testament* references to being "in Christ" include 2 Cor. 5:17, "if anyone be in Christ he is a new creature . . ." and Romans Chapter 8 gives a grand view of what the Holy Spirit does for the believer once they are in Christ Jesus.

In fact, displayed on the wall of a building at the Niagara Christian Collegiate campus (April, 2007), Fort Erie, Ontario, Canada, (an educational institution of the Brethren in Christ) was the following prominently placed rendering, headed by the title, **WHO AM I, IN CHRIST?** The heading was followed by the following list: (Rom. 8:16) A child of God; (Eph. 2:8) Saved by grace through faith; (1 Jn. 5:11,12) An heir of eternal life; (Eph. 1:7) Forgiven; (Rom. 8:14) Led by the Spirit of God; (2 Cor. 5:17) A new creature; (Gal. 3: 13) Redeemed from the curse of the law; (Is. 46:4) Kept in safety wherever I go; (Eph. 6:10) Strong in the Lord and in His mighty power; (2 Cor. 5:7) Living by faith and not by sight; (Col. 1:13) Rescued from the dominion of darkness; (Rom. 5:1) An heir of God and co-heir with Christ (Rom. 8:17); (Eph. 1:3) Blessed with every spiritual blessing; (Rev. 12:11) Overcome by the blood of the Lamb; (Mt. 5:14) The light of the world; (Eph. 5:1) An imitator of God; (1 Peter 2:24) Healed by His wounds; (Rom. 12:2) Being transformed by the renewing of my mind; (Gal. 3:14) Heir to the blessings of Abraham.

[44] There are widespread misconceptions about the true meaning of the church. The church in the New Testament never refers to a building or structure. The Greek word translated "church" is *ekklesia* and means a gathering of people, but more than this, the Pietists saw the church as a "new community."

[45] While clearly not intended, some may read a title that uses a masculine term only as portraying women to be adjuncts, or tending toward subjugation of them.

[46] A frequent practice, especially for new church plantings, is to identify their body and place of worship with a special congregational moniker (with the name Brethren in Christ projected less obtrusively), which may say something about the value placed on the denomination's name—as to either the attractiveness of its message, or the ease in conveying an understanding of its full meaning. A lesser prominent use of the name by congregations is borne out in the official "Annual Directory of the Brethren in Christ, 2007-08" where about seventy-five of some two hundred congregations presently use a moniker that has no trace of Brethren in Christ in either their official name or the address they offer to identify themselves. These seventy-five are largely made up of more newly established congregations.

[47] The Christian faith proclaims that both male and female are made in the image of God (Gen. 1:27), and that sinful enmity (according to gender, nation, or race) has been overcome by the death and resurrection of Jesus (Gal. 3:28).

Chapter XI

Beyond the Present

For more than two centuries Brethren in Christ have gathered to worship the triune God and joined for ministry and service. Despite the church body experiencing significant changes during this period, including dramatic "about faces" (largely on issues related to their degree of engagement with the world) they have remained true to their founding identity. The denomination has always reflected a mix between Pietism and Anabaptism—with Pietism being the most determinative at their beginning.

Looking more closely at the question of where the Brethren in Christ are today regarding the early Pietist-Anabaptist dialectic—there appear to be three key factors (independent considerations) that give credence to the view that the church today continues to view Pietism as its continuing primary theological tradition. They are: (1) In a study made by Yeatts and Burwell toward the close of the twentieth century rank and file Brethren in Christ members clearly designated the term *evangelical* as the best one-word descriptor of the Brethren in Christ; (2) numerous historians have found that Pietism (German in origin) was the direct antecedent to Evangelicalism (British);[1] and (3) there is substantial evidence that Pietism and Evangelicalism are highly congruent in their theological emphases.[2]

Throughout the previous chapters of this work an effort was made to clarify the unique identity of the denomination. As a people who have been first and foremost followers of the Bible, rather than tradition *per se*, one should be hesitant to predict interpretive turns the body might take. We reside in ever-changing times and have come to serve increasingly diverse peoples—both of which have influenced prior turnings (that were largely of a cultural nature). The church's identity is also shaped and maintained by the emphasized principles and by the order of priorities that command its attention. For example, one area that seems to call for increasing care and attention in the future is matters related to or involving "the Christian mind."

The Christian church has recently been confronted by a spate of best-selling anti-God books from a group of prominent writers and first-rate minds, including Richard Dawkins, Sam Harris, Daniel Dennett, and Christopher

Hitchens. These men portray deep hostility to religion in general and Christianity in particular. They are also formidable debaters. The Christian church has some writers who are responding to such challenges. Dinesh D'Souza, a Christian born in India and educated in America, has given an answer to them. He goes the distance with atheists in his recently published book, *What's So Great About Christianity* (Regenery, 2007). It is a systematic response to the main arguments put forth by contemporary atheists and the historical figures on whom they rely.[3] Another current scholar who responds in a comprehensive and impressive fashion is Francis S. Collins, head of the Human Genome Project. He reconciles his Christian faith with scientific theory, including evolution, in *The Language of God: A Scientist Presents Evidence for Belief* (Free Press, 2006).

Because of increasing challenges that confront our society from a secular worldview perspective it would be wise for the Christian church, and for denominations in general, to see that their educational arms[4] are not only thoroughly committed to Christian goals, but are also prepared to diligently set forth a comprehensive Christian worldview.[5]

Looking beyond specific ministry areas that appear to be timely—such as speaking to Christian mind issues—perhaps an even more pertinent consideration for the Brethren in Christ body would be to answer the question: How do we maximize our ministry? Surely it would involve attending to certain corporately-held biblical convictions that God has given to the Brethren in Christ.

Since effectiveness is yearned for the church ahead of us, and we dare not merely rely on the church behind us to discern the way through new terrain, an additional question should be asked. What are the Christian principles, insights, and understandings that can be gained from other Christians or groups that may shed particular light on potent ministry opportunities for these changing times? In this search for greater effectiveness and outreach, however, it seems clear that it would not be highly fruitful to seek guidance from mainline Protestant groups. Religious sociologists have long noted a steady membership decline in these groups.[6] Sociologists have also noted their waning understanding of distinctive beliefs, and a seeming abatement of spiritual vitality. It seems more appropriate to compare a projection of where the Brethren in Christ may presently stand alongside a current Christian movement or group that seems to be garnering insights, showing evidence of advancing ministry, and exhibiting spiritual verve. What might come next theologically, beyond the standard systematic theologies formed in the modern world (Protestant systems largely came from around 1500 to 1950)?

On being on the cutting edge and exhibiting a sense of dynamism and traction—especially by significant writings attributed to the movement—the "Emergent Church Movement" may be an appropriate group to review. It is essential to unpack the basic beliefs, understandings, and emphases set forth by the movement so as to be informed on key matters where it may contrast with the Brethren in Christ today. Perhaps as important, we must understand areas where the Movement may correspond with where the Brethren in Christ appear to be presently positioned. One additional reason for choosing the Emergent Church Movement is their special sense of being called of God during this era to serve the rapidly changing times and varied cultures of the post-modern period.

A Description of the Emergent Church

Those who claim an emergent-church connection are generally considered part of a new world of alternative evangelical Christianity, better known as the emerging church. As a phenomenon, the movement is several decades old, but it particularly portends to be suited to the complexity, ambiguity, and decentralized authority of today's postmodern times—a period already spanning nearly three decades. There is a growing discussion about the emerging movement in that it seems to eschew both hierarchy and dogma. In fairness to it, even though it acknowledges being focused on current times and the future church, and less on the church behind us, the movement seems grounded in the belief that the church, even though faltering at times, has contributed to all eras—early, medieval, modern, and post-modern.[7]

According to some estimates, several hundred emerging-church congregations, or "communities" have sprung up around the country. Perhaps its most defining group currently is the gathering of authors who identify with emergent principles and emphases. Emergent-type beginnings can be traced to the Vineyard churches in the latter decades of the twentieth century, but the author who gave the movement its greatest visibility has been Brian D. McLaren. In view of his voluminous writings, McLaren has been viewed as something of a spokesperson for the movement.[8] Beyond McLaren as the presumptive leader, others who have contributed to exploring the emergent church idea are Dan Kimball, author of *The Emerging Church* (Zondervan); Ray S. Anderson, author of *An Emergent Theology for Emerging Churches* (IVP Press); and Tony Jones, national coordinator, Emergent-US, and author of *The Sacred Way.*

Views that the Brethren in Christ and the Emergent Church Appear to Hold in Common—and Some Diverging Points

After consulting the writings of a number of Emergent Church authors as cited above, and others, the following assessments are offered regarding the theological understandings that seem to be particularly suited to the post-modern times of today—some have perhaps also been of influence on Brethren in Christ life and worship:

One. Both groups, the Emergent Church and the Brethren in Christ, profess to be doctrinally evangelical. Each of them believes in the authority of Scripture, seeks to spread the Gospel, and stresses a personal relationship with Jesus Christ. One possible distinctive, though difficult to measure, is that the emergent identity may be more closely associated with conservative Christianity theologically than in being conservative in cultural-related issues. ("Emergents" at times are characterized, by either themselves or others, as being "Progressive Evangelicals"). In the progressive tradition, "Emergents," tend not to be far-right in their political goals, or to occupy themselves with "culture-war" type issues.

In contrast many Brethren in Christ tend to draw back from political issues, even though during the late twentieth century they were found to be strongly Republican in party preference. In contrast, as well, the corporate church body has essentially removed itself from the political-realm, except for issues regarding the taking of human life. Brethren in Christ tend to reserve culturally-related questions and political stands largely to the discretion of its individual members.

Two. The book, *Emergent Theology*, is outlined in author Ray Anderson's table of contents and prefaced by this statement: "What Has Antioch to do with Jerusalem?" He offers the following theological outline, which appears to be highly attuned to post-modern type conceptualizations, but nevertheless communicates messages that, it seems, would be both perceived and endorsed by Brethren in Christ:

A. It's about theology, not geography.
B. It's about Christ, not Christology.
C. It's about the spirit, not just spirituality.
D. It's about the right Gospel, not just the right polity.
E. It's about kingdom living, not kingdom building.
F. It's about the work of God, not just about the Word of God.
G. It's about the law of love, not the letter of the law.
H. It's about the community of the spirit, not just the gifts of the spirit.

Three. The first major book written by Brian D. McLaren, entitled *Reinventing Your Church,* and a later work of his, *Everything Must Change,* considered together, present many of the varied commitments or inclinations of the Emergent Church. These two works offer clear prescriptions for change that set forth significant differences, with traditional church expressions, on behalf of individual members and the corporate church body. McLaren's contention is that we live in a time when "not merely things are changing. Change itself has changed, thereby changing the rules we live by."[9]

These two book titles, verbatim, in a significant sense, transpired in the life of the Brethren in Christ church in the middle of the twentieth century before post-modernity began and well before these respective ideas were elucidated and recorded as bold Emergent principles. Even though vastly different in context at that time, profuse change and restructuring of the Brethren in Christ, in both intensity and magnitude, came to the denomination around 1950. By its own measure and leadings from God, the denomination, it seems, was preparing to better meet the times—an enhanced future ministry—including a coming post-modern era. The denomination "abandoned structures that had become outgrown."[10] "Outgrown" is a key Emergent principle. Becoming "outgrown" for the Brethren in Christ, was not merely a size factor, but the calling of God to an enlarged mandate. As a result, the denomination gained new light and emerged with new life in the mid-twentieth century. The reinventing and changing of everything for the Brethren in Christ started well before these Emergent concepts entered the scene. McLaren quotes Francis Schaeffer as follows: "One of the greatest injustices we do to our young people is to ask them to be conservative. Christianity is not conservative, but revolutionary."[11]

Looking back, the changes enacted within the Brethren in Christ at that time were not only revolutionary in preparing them to serve both modern and post-modern times—they accomplished important church goals by living out emergent-type principles, later to emerge in the broader church.

Four. *An Emergent Theology for Emergent Churches,* Ray Anderson gives special emphasis to the importance of one "Being in Christ, not just believing in Christ." Anderson points out that according to Emergent theology "those who are children of God, (are those) whose lives are personally drawn into the very life and being of Christ."[12] Just as the apostle Paul experienced the reality of Christ (in every letter he wrote there is an underlying theme of union with Christ), and for Emergent followers it begins with being baptized into Christ by the Spirit (1 Cor. 12:13), just so the Brethren in Christ are reminded by the church in Colosse of their experience in Christ, not just their faith in Christ—a reality so intimate and personal it defies explanation in rational terms: "Christ in you the hope of glory" (Col. 1:27). "Examine yourselves," Paul exhorts. "Do you not realize that Christ is in you?" (2 Cor. 13:5). As cited in the name, Brethren in Christ, there are clear connections here with the Emergent Church who also profess to be "in Christ."[13]

Five. Emergent churches do not claim to be the one true church, and the Brethren in Christ have never made such a claim—they both demonstrate that the church of Christ extends beyond denominational or religious-tradition boundaries. Brian D. McLaren in his book, *A Generous Orthodoxy,* finds genuine ways to embrace the good in many traditions and historic streams of the

Christian faith. He integrates them into considerations that are fresh, relational, and uplifting. His "generous orthodoxy" theme opens the door for him to examine positive aspects within Catholicism, Pentecostalism, Fundamentalism, Calvinism, and other varied traditions. His careful probing of liberal/conservative, charismatic/contemplative, mystical/poetic and additional dialectics also enriched the broadened view that seemed to permeate his study. Brethren in Christ were recognized historically as being highly relational with other Christians[14] and open to serious exchange with non-believers thus signifying a positive attribute that they hold in common with Emergents.

Six. In the work, *Reinventing Your Church,* McLaren seems to be directive in spots. One of the places this shows through is in the chapter "Design a New Apologetic." Among insights he shares with potential Emergents are these four: (1) We don't just offer answers; we offer mysteries. (2) We don't debate minutiae; we focus on essentials. (3) We don't push credibility alone; we also stress plausibility. (4) We don't condemn our competitors; we see them as colleagues of sorts and reason with them with winsome gentleness and respect.[15] These points, consistent with the invisible church idea, are also foundational to understandings the Brethren in Christ gained from their Pietist forbears—which they have reflected and continue to be exemplary of as witnessed by their sense of openness to others.

Seven. In McLaren's book, *Everything Must Change*, chapter 19, under the title "Joining the Peace Insurgency," he proposes "we might also call the transforming story of God's divine peace insurgency, God's un-terror movement," and continues, "God's new global love economy, or God's sacred ecosystem." In another chapter of the book (p. 171), "The Suicidal Logic of the War Business" he critically looks at issues connected with weapons preparations, the vast global arms exports, and their futility. When one adds his quote from *A Generous Orthodoxy,* (p. 184) that "the 'fundamentals of the faith' boil down to those given by Jesus: *to love God and to love our neighbors*"—basic principles of forbearance and reconciliation—McLaren seems to flirt with, if not align to, the Brethren in Christ church's historic peace position. While it is difficult to know how far and deep McLaren's war-and-peace expressions extend to other emergents, Brethren in Christ would surely consider Chapter 19 of this work to be integral to its peace position.

Eight. In the book, *Reinventing Your Church,* under the chapter, "Enter the Post-modern World"—Part B: "Engage It," Brian McLaren offers a number of aids to facilitate the church and its members in becoming more effectively engaged in our post-modern world. Key guidance points made by McLaren, along with responses from a Brethren in Christ perspective are cited as follows: (1) "We need to be more experiential." As a denomination faithful to its historic theological roots, including Pietism—manifested in a divine relationship and transforming love for Jesus—the Brethren in Christ have been and are experiential on faith matters. (2) "We must rely more than ever on art, music, literature, and drama to communicate our message." Recognizing that just as the ideal peace-and-war positions cited above, compares well with nonresistant churches, it may be that numerous emergent congregations could be suspected of falling far short of this ideal. This proposed model, setting forth a more pronounced music and arts ministry for some emergent congregations, may be more urbane than their accomplishment. In contrast, the Brethren in Christ have demonstrated a long and strong tradition in sacred music. Their development in drama and other arts (including the Taize movement) is more recent, but nevertheless real in parts of the church. (3) "We must believe that the Holy Spirit is out there at work already." Again, the strong Pietist connection and ideals of the denominations related to the holy life, and sanctification, including entire sanctification, are indications of Holy Spirit dependency. (4) "We must become Seekers again." The long-standing commitment of the denomination to seeking a living faith for believers seems to be maintained by the Brethren in Christ. (5) "We must reassert the value of community and rekindle the spirit of it." The Anabaptist background and commitments of the Brethren in Christ continue to be borne out in a sense of community.

In light of this short, general review of places where the Brethren in Christ and certain leaders of the Emergent movement seem to portray common cause, an overriding conclusion can be expressed. The Brethren in Christ possess or identify with a goodly number of the basics presumed to be required for optimal Christian ministry to the current culture and into the future.

Being the Church in Our Post-Modern World

As one studies the post-modern *zeitgeist* and the works of Emergent writers one is clearly led to the conclusion that we live in highly pivotal times. It is clear that many things are changing. This is an era when many individuals question whether there is any truth, but at the same time they often appear to be hungering for authenticity and verity. Many post-moderns in our society appear to be hunting certainty (a typical modern-type goal).

In closing, one surely needs to expect continuing societal change that may mean additional modifications or adjustments on the part of the church. Such considerations will confront us with church-nature questions. Two alternatives are: (1) Do we look at the church anxiously and sentimentally as a body that ideally should not change? (2) Or do we look with wonder, awe, and expectation at the church as a living, breathing, changing, and marvelously unpredictable body? Over the course of more than two centuries the Brethren in Christ have experi-

232   The Soul of the Brethren in Christ

enced the latter of these two alternatives. Even alongside numerous changes, the church's view of the centrality of Christ, and the importance that the body placed upon a united vision—since both factors appear to have remained quite constant—the denomination can testify to being within the will of God.

For individual Christians who make up the church, clearly the answer during unforeseen times will need to continue to rest on the promise that all who find Christ can possess the confidence of "being in Christ"—a seeming imperative for those who claim the name "Brethren in Christ."

---

[1] See chapter 2 and its defining of both Pietism and Evangelicalism.

[2] See chapter 10 of this work for an accounting of such evidence.

[3] D'Souza sets out to demonstrate seven things: First, Christianity is the main foundation of Western civilization and the root of our most cherished values. Second, the latest discoveries of modern science support the claim that a divine being created the universe. Third, Darwin's theory of evolution strengthens, not undermines, evidence for supernatural design. Fourth, nothing in science makes miracles impossible. Fifth, it is reasonable to have faith. Sixth, atheism, not religion, is responsible for the mass murders of history. And seventh, atheism is motivated not by reason but a kind of cowardly "moral escapism."

[4] Brian D. McLaren in his book, *Reinventing the Church*, (p. 128) points out that the world is becoming more educated, but that "Christians have fared better in evangelizing the less educated than the more educated people of the world for the last several hundred years. As Europe became more intellectual, the missionary frontier moved to America; then as America grew more educated, the frontier moved to Africa, South America, and Asia. But where do we go as the countries on these continents catch up to us?" In response, to McLaren's question, it should mean that an increasing number of Christians, prepared with a Christian worldview, should consider a call to higher learning and seek to penetrate the citadels of learning armed with a more holistic scholarship than is typically presented from a secular perspective. Being Christian and intellectual are not mutually exclusive. Faith withers because of a lack of dependence upon God—not because one's intellectual quotient rises.

[5] A recent (2008) Pew Research Center survey of 35,556 respondents (a very large study) produced data for a report entitled "The Changing Faiths of America," which said that 44% of American adults have left the faith in which they were raised (this includes Protestants who have switched to other Protestant faiths) and 16% of them say they are unaffiliated with any religion (including atheists, agnostics, and nothing in particular). This study concluded that religions that demand the most of people are growing the fastest. The findings also stressed the importance of the church becoming increasingly serious regarding Christian mind issues.

[6] See report of mainline church membership data in notes of chapter 1.

[7] This does not mean that all their scholars agree that a church with a broad mission was continually being perpetuated—especially in times when it was dominated by a sterile and unbiblical "Christendom mode." Yet during such times some monasteries continued to maintain a spiritual dynamism that became extended to the church at large.

[8] His initial work entitled, *Reinventing Your Church*, (Zondervan, 1998) was followed by *The Church on the Other Side* (Zondervan). He also authored *Finding Faith* (Zondervan), *A New Kind of Christian* (Jossey-Bass), *More Ready Than You Realize* (Zondervan), *The Story We*

Find Ourselves In (Jossey-Bass), *Generous Orthodoxy* (Zondervan), and other titles.

[9] A quote from William Easum (p. 19) who was stressing that the future belongs to those willing to let go, stop trying to minimize the change we face, but rather maximize the importance of discontinuity.

[10] "Abandon Structures as They Are Outgrown" is the title of one of the strategy chapters offered by McLaren in his original work, *Reinventing Your Church*.

[11] Quoted from *The Church at the End of the Twentieth Century*, InterVarsity Press, 1970, pp. 81, 82.

[12] A quote from Ray Anderson's *An Emergent Theology for Emergent Churches*, p. 213.

[13] For further consideration of the "in Christ" theme for the Brethren in Christ see chapter 10.

[14] For further consideration of the openness and relational dimension of the Brethren in Christ see chapter 8.

[15] Quoted from pp. 77-81 of *Reinventing Your Church*.

Chapter XII

The Soul of the Brethren in Christ: "A Living Faith"

This book seeks to portray the identity of the Brethren in Christ church. It began by responding to a key question for these changing times—Why should a denomination's identity be reviewed? This was followed by defining the theological streams that have been of greatest impact on the Brethren in Christ, and assessing the comparative impact of the respective streams on the body. The general thesis contends that the identity of a religious body consists of more than simply recognizing the denomination's primary beliefs and assigning them to respective theological traditions. It further contends that the Brethren in Christ interpretation of faith, in its most complete sense, is more than a religious culture consisting of doctrines, values, actions, and behaviors. Identity analyses should include discernments regarding the denomination's priorities and a review of unique qualities that may be evidenced by the body. Since a distinct denominational identity is dependent on following a clear vision it seems necessary to reach even more deeply in order to examine the exact nature of its vision. The vision of a body of authentic Christian believers ideally emanates from its soul. Stated another way, the true identity of a denomination cannot be contrived or forced by words or facades—it springs from the very soul of the body.

Some forty years ago it was the author's task to interpret the soul of Messiah College.[1] That was during the 1960s, a time of turbulence in society and ferment within colleges and universities. It was a period when the general culture ate soul food, listened to soul music, and spoke of people as lacking or having soul, but at the same time there was doubt about the existence of a soul. At the very moment that trappings regarding the soul were freely being alluded to, the culture was crying out—God is dead!!!

What is a soul anyway? Does it really exist? Our secular society often seems to say that the world is made up of purely material elements. One can quite easily and successfully slice a person in search of a kidney or rib, but can one dissect a person and find a soul? And yet, though not verifiable by sensory experience, the soul does exist.

Plato separated the soul, or psyche, from the material body and argued that this reasoning part of our body is immortal. Aristotle defined soul as the primary principle by which we live, move, and understand. The Old Testament rejects a dualism of body and spirit and stresses the soul as being a whole response of the person to God. The New Testament emphasis relates more to the soul as a living thing and the source of life's activities. The body may die, Christians believe, but the soul lives on into eternity. Deepak Chopra, in his work, *How to Know God,* suggests, "The soul is the carrier that takes us to beyond; it is the essence connecting us to God." He continues, "It holds reality together. . . . I can think, talk, work, love, and dream, all because of the soul."[2] Dallas Willard in "Grey Matter and the Soul," likens the soul to "a computer system that runs an entire operation."[3]

In ordinary present day usage the term soul, when used alone, refers to the human soul. It is the foundation of consciousness and will. Your soul is what you are. The soul is the unitary essence of being and is inseparably linked to the spirit and the body of mankind, and it continues to live on even after the death of the body. The soul is where God works and lives within us. God can possess our soul—but only we can lose our soul.

Just as mankind has a soul, so a church has a seat of life that reaches out to the world and to God.[4] The soul is in the hands of God. Man has no control over it. It is an inner thing that is nourished by prayer and fasting. For a denomination, its plans can be amended and its image can be designed or even manipulated, but its true vision and identity spring from its soul. The soul is invisible and it evolves but it is the most distinguishing quality of a denomination. The soul is exhibited in the church's convictional responses and its deepest yearnings. In fact, the identity and vision of a church body may be modern words for "soul."

David Weaver-Zercher in defining a mindset theory for the Brethren in Christ saw it as "a heightened sense of God's activity in the lives of believers."[5] His theory seems very compelling. The theory is clearly evidenced in the reason the denomination began ("new birth" emphasis). It is manifested in the church's one significant doctrinal supplement ("entire" sanctification) It is borne out in the denomination's major shift regarding God's whole truth, a change in worldview (evangelization is furthered). A denominational bend in the direction of spiritual idealism is surely apparent in its history. The mindset described by Weaver-Zercher seems to say that the group demonstrates a habitual interest to become "perfect," "entire," "whole," in Christ. The history of the denomination shows a tension between the actual and the ideal. The Brethren in Christ are not satisfied with the spiritual status quo. The tension coincides with that of St. Paul who (pressing toward the mark) manifested in his soul a classic description of spiritual idealism. The same mindset was evident in St. Augustine, who lived with a tension so keenly expressed in his *Confessions*.

The Weaver-Zercher mindset interpretation, "a heightened sense of God's activity in the lives of believers" can also be viewed as one of the church's primary convictional yearnings, and in this sense be considered part of the Brethren in Christ soul. "A yearning for God and for godliness" demonstrates a great deal of concern about righteousness. Within that concern the Brethren in Christ clearly acknowledge that man is not righteous by his own best efforts, it is a righteousness imputed (by grace) and imparted (through the Holy Spirit) to the believer. The thirst (spiritual desire) for God and godliness, for Brethren in Christ, is out of a sense of who God is, rather than out of who they are as a Christian tradition.[6] This thirst is viewed as being satisfied only through Christ. Jesus said, "Whoever drinks water will get thirsty again; but whoever drinks the water I give will never thirst again . . . it will become in him a spring of living water. . . " (John 4:13-14).

A continued longing for God's activity in their lives and a thirst for increased godliness should be viewed as part of a larger concept of the soul demonstrated in the life of the Brethren in Christ. A more encompassing picture of the Brethren in Christ soul appears on the seventh line of the church's original *Confession*. The statement described the faith of the early group as being "a living faith."[7] These three confessional words encapsulated the chief principle of life at their founding, and its truth has endured. "A living faith" has remained at the crux of the denomination's vision and a key to its identity. It is proposed here that "a living faith" is the soul of the Brethren in Christ.

To facilitate examination of the Brethren in Christ soul a short piece that appeared in the very first issue of the *Evangelical Visitor* is cited as follows:

> The Scriptures give four names to Christians, taken from the four cardinal graces: Believers, for their faith; saints, for their holiness; brethren, for their love; and disciples, for their knowledge.

The following four scriptural appellations for Christians, and their associated graces, are offered to outline several dimensions of the Christian soul and to account for it being descriptive of the Brethren in Christ soul: Believers—faith. "A living faith" is demonstrated through a new birth experience of the divine witness to the world according to a new life in Christ, which in turn is maintained via prayer and fellowship with the living God. Saints—holiness. "A living faith" is portrayed as fully yielded Christians surrender to Jesus as Lord, receive a life-empowering anointing from the Spirit, and as holy ones manifest gifts to be used for His purposes. Brethren—love. "A living faith" evokes a response to God and others that is evidenced as Christians transformed by God live in obedience to Him, seek to follow the example of Jesus in spreading love and light, and recognize that faith and works, while not saving *per se*, will yield the fruits of good works—all through God's enabling presence. Disciples—knowledge. Just as Christ's disciples gained first-hand knowledge about faith and life through an intimate relationship with Him, so His current followers have access to a personal knowledge and to imparted insights that reach beyond propositional knowledge. These are all gained through communion with God and His people. As learners, Christians cultivate the spiritual disciplines that yield discipleship.

The four Christian appellations with their contributing graces, in sum, epitomize both theological wholeness and ecclesial balance, but more than this they encapsulate "a living faith." While the Brethren in Christ have not remained static in either doctrine or practice, it appears that its soul—"a living faith"—has been constant. Indeed, as members of the Brethren in Christ body witness to and observe these graces the soul of the body, both individually and collectively, will continue to be alive and well. Ideally, "a living faith" becomes a way of life whether for the believer, the saint, the brother and sister, or the disciple—a faith centered on experiencing a relationship with the Divine and receiving His ultimate power.

As the Brethren in Christ move forward, they should exult in the treasures exhibited by the heritage begotten to them. Their deep thirst, a yearning for God and for godliness, has been the seat of their vision and of their unfolding identity. Also, as the essence of the body continues, the Brethren in Christ can move from a position of faith not fear, practice rather than theory, and be at the center of ministry rather than at the periphery. Their satisfaction as the people of God will be to delight in the Lord and do His will. As this happens they will portray "a living faith."

---

[1] For a description of the soul of Messiah College see the 1971 President's Report of the College where the soul is outlined as being five institutional convictions.

[2] Deepak Chopra, *How to Know God*, Harmony Books, New York, 2000, pp. 274 and 278.

[3] Quoted from the November 18, 2002 issue of *Christianity Today*, p. 74.

[4] In a letter to Diognetus around 150 A.D., an unknown author, like the Gospel-writer Luke, wrote to explain the Christian faith to a serious enquirer: "To put it simply—the soul is to the body as Christians are to the world. The soul is in the body but is not of the body. Christians are in the world but not of the world."

[5] *Brethren in Christ History and Life*, Vol. XIX, No. 1, April, 1996, p. 174.

[6] While recognizing that Brethren in Christ church traditions were founded on a biblical base, Doneen Dourte, in a presentation at the 1995 Study Conference on Identity of the Brethren in Christ, called for the church to renew its search for "biblical based peculiarities" rather than tradition for its own sake. (The crux of traditionalism is that it tends to weaken the gospel of grace.) *Brethren in Christ History and Life,* Vol. XIX, No. 1, April 1996, p. 214.

[7] See page one, line seven, of the Church's original confession as cited in the appendix on page 241.

Appendix

Confession of Faith of the
Early Brethren in Christ (Circa 1780)

As translated by Bishop Charles Baker[1]

We believe in and acknowledge one triune and Ever-existing and Almighty being, and that this one Ever-existing Almighty God always existed and ever will exist, and has foreseen for us an Ever-existing Savior before the foundation of the world. To learn to know this Savior, or to find him, we must pass through true repentance unto forgiveness of sins and become reconciled with God, wrought by God, through the blood of Christ. And through this reconciliation receive we the living faith in Christ. So therefore must this faith be laid for a foundation upon the Word, and the Truth, for upon the Truth rests the whole Godhead and Majesty. And while this faith is a sure confidence, yet— since we have not this faith according to nature, it is therefore first necessary to consider where this faith takes its beginning; while Adam and all his seed lost the Godly likeness, that is, faith, love, and confidence, and instead awake fear, unrest and doubt, which we have inherited from generation to generation. But since God in the beginning had promised the serpent Treader, the Messiah, the Savior, from the loss which man sustained, who in fulfillment of time came into the world, laying aside his glory and honor, and gave himself, both body and blood, as a ransom from this loss, and thereby has reconciled us again unto the Father. All this, however, is all of grace, and not of works. But to know or experience this in our heart, the grace of God hath appeared, to convince and to teach us that we according to nature have wandered from God with a wayward and sinful heart. If we learn this and acknowledge it, it will work in us true repentance and sorrowfulness of heart. In short, the Light reveals unto us the fall wherein Adam and we have fallen, and this causes within us longings, praying, weeping, and calling upon God through the promised Redeemer, who, bleeding, died for such poor sinners, and in such a poor sinner's opened heart the Lord Jesus will enter and sup with him and he with Him. This is consolation, love, peace and trust bestowed. Then is our sinful record as the guilt of

Adam erased. That is consolation, forgiveness of sins and receiving of ever-lasting life and that feels and experiences every poor sinner that comes to God through Christ. Here will his name be written in the book of life, and here has the living faith its beginning, wherein the poor sinner is saved, then offers and fully submits himself to the Lord Jesus to live and to be true to him who has adopted him into the family of God. And this acknowledge we to be the new birth, renewing of the mind and the Holy Ghost.

Now has the Lord Jesus become our Savior, so shall he also be our exam-ple. And since children now love Him, who begot them, so they also shall now love them that are begotten of Him. And this acknowledge we to be a believing body of Christian believers, united through the unity of the Spirit, which is the first requisite necessary for personal reception into Christian fellowship. Where this is lacking there always will remain a lack, and water cannot give or make good that which is wanting. And while we said the Lord Jesus has become our example, so we believe and acknowledge from the example given in the writ-ten Word, and through the leading of the good Spirit, that the Lord Jesus Christ gave for an outward bond-token for such new-born children, the outward water baptism, having observed it Himself and His apostles, and that likewise the early churches observed the same, after denying the devil, the world and all sinful life, and were baptized by a three-fold baptism under water, in the name of the Father, and of the Son, and of the Holy Ghost, as a token of the burial.

We believe and acknowledge as a foundation that all true penitent, believing and forgiven souls that have upon their faith in Jesus been baptized, have entered into Zion, and all of this spiritual body, as God's children, are born, as new men, as the dew of the morning glow. We also believe that the Lord Jesus instituted the Lord's supper and observed it with his disciples, with bread and wine in the last night of his suffering when he was betrayed, that they, after his departure, when partaking of the same, should remember his broken body and shed blood for them, wherein also his disciples and followers were steadfast in the Apostles' doctrine and fellowship, and in breaking of bread and in prayer, did eat their meat with gladness and singleness of heart, praising him with a joyful heart.

We further believe and acknowledge that the Lord Jesus Christ at the time he instituted the Lord's supper, also washed his disciples' feet, instituted it, ob-served and commanded it to be observed as a token of free humility and hum-bleness, in obedience, out of love to Jesus, our example. Here we stand by God in grace separated from the children of this world, yea, branches of the true vine, members of the body of Christ. We also acknowledge a growth in grace according to the Holy Scriptures, cleansed, sanctified, and saved by the wash-ing of regeneration and renewing of the Holy Ghost. To accomplish this, it is necessary to have public gatherings where the Word is preached and the people are exhorted to repent. To this end there are also private gatherings necessary and helpful, where the penitent souls can confess and relate their experiences in a childlike manner one to the other, by so doing the love of God in their heart will increase and their faith and their confidence will be strengthened. And inasmuch as such childlike confessions one to the other at such gatherings will have a tendency to uncover the craftiness of the enemy, and that good advice can be given to those present, so that the body of Christ can be built up. And since such children are yet in the flesh, there is therefore a Christian order necessary in the household of God according to Matthew 18. And furthermore, while such children are in duty bound, out of love, to watch over one another, we therefore deem it necessary that no one undertake anything of importance without asking brotherly advice in such matters as might endanger the peace and progress of the brotherhood; such as change of residence, buying of property and other important matters.

We also acknowledge an order in separation of disorderly members, yet with the difference, as above stated from Matthew 18, "If thy brother shall trespass against thee," etc. This, of course, can have its beginning in small matters. If the offender shall have a submissive spirit and accepts the brotherly admonition in childlike love, does not defend or justify himself, neither is strong or domineering, it is all right, but if he will not acknowledge his fault, nor mend his ways, then take with thee one or two more, and at last tell it to the church. If the offender, however, is not submissive to the church, then let him to be unto thee as an heathen man and a publican. But one who is called a brother, or according to the German, "one who allows himself to be called a brother," 1 Cor. 5:11, but remains in sin, then there is no official investigation necessary, but only to give them into the hands of God for judgment. Notice the expression of Paul: "Now we command you, brethren, in the name of the Lord Jesus Christ, that you withdraw yourselves from every brother that walketh disorderly, 2 Thess. 3:6 & 14; and have no company with him, that he may be ashamed." 1 Cor. 5-11, "But now I have written unto you not to keep company" or to eat with such, who are so ungodly, and have fallen into such grievous sins and to utterly withdraw yourselves from greeting them with the right hand of fellowship, and with the holy kiss and in eating and drinking, until they are truly enlightened and in penitence and humbleness again obtain pardon for their transgression, in Jesus' blood, then will also the other members, having become acquainted with their penitence and humbleness of mind, feel the unity of the Spirit, and thus can such again be received into church membership, to comfort and strengthen them so that they may not in over much sorrow sink into despair.

What, however, belongs to other fundamentals, such as the baptism of infants and the unconverted, we leave it with them who are satisfied therewith.

Where the teachings of our Lord Jesus and that of the disciples are silent, there we will be silent also. Then also we believe and acknowledge if two believing persons living apparently as man and wife, who before God have solemnly agreed between themselves to live together in righteousness, that if one or the other should come to the new life, or become reconciled and yet not baptized, but is not opposed thereto, such a person has the privilege of being baptized after being united in marriage, for if souls are accepted by God, so are we also willing to accept them (to church membership). Then also obedient brethren's children, who are obedient whilst they are under their parents, and the parents are under the church and the church under Jesus Christ, and everything else is in order and right, so can the marriage of such children take place with members in the church, with advice, and not be set out to the world. Yet, after all it is the wish of our heart and prayer to the God the All Highest, that everyone and all did first unite themselves in the spiritual marriage with Jesus the bridegroom of the soul, and afterward the outward or natural marriage. And inasmuch as oaths are altogether forbidden in the teachings of our Lord Jesus, they are therefore forbidden to be used by us. Matt. 5:34. The sword, revenge and self-defense are also entirely forbidden, verses 39 and 40.

Out of the teachings of our Lord Jesus and his apostles we also understand that no member or follower of Jesus Christ is allowed to serve in worldly governmental offices, therefore it ought also be forbidden to us. But we ought not withstand the worldly governments, but be subject to them in all that is good, and earnestly pray for them that God may give them light and wisdom, so that they may be able to perform their duties truly. We are also exhorted to pay tribute, or protection money unto the governments, because Paul calls them God's ministers, Romans 13, and since God rules the whole universe, so God has ordained that man should rule natural men, of the world, and that is also for the good of God's children, otherwise it would still be worse to live in this world. Therefore, Paul commands us to pray for them, as above stated, so that they may be able to perform their duties truly, so that the children of God under their protection may be able to live a quiet and God-fearing life, and that they do not use the children of God as a power or force in order to quell disturbances or to oppress or to bring others into subjection to the government under whose protection we live. Further we wish from God the All Highest, that he may build and plant and keep his church in healthy growth, and that we also may be green branches on the true vine, and remain so in all the length of eternity, through Jesus Christ. Amen. (The *Confession* was signed in the name of the congregation by Johannes Meyer, Johannes Funk, Samuel Bentzner, Jacob Engel, Stofel Hollinger, Philip Stern, Johannes Greider, and Benjamin Beyer.)

[1] Bishop Baker of Nottowa, Ontario, Canada, was born in Germany and retained an active use of the German language. He translated the "Confession" a little over a century after it was written. Baker was familiar with the religious language and the traditions of the early Brethren in Christ. He was a well-read individual who biographer E. Morris Sider, in *Nine Portraits* called "the best Brethren in Christ leader in the tradition of the church during his time." Bishop Baker had the assistance of a German teacher from Chambersburg, Pennsylvania in this translation. In addition to his own capabilities in the German language, Baker had a son, Albert, who spent a career as a German language professor at the University of Manitoba at Winnipeg. This translation seems to be more complete than other translations.